THE
COURTAULD
CÉZANNES

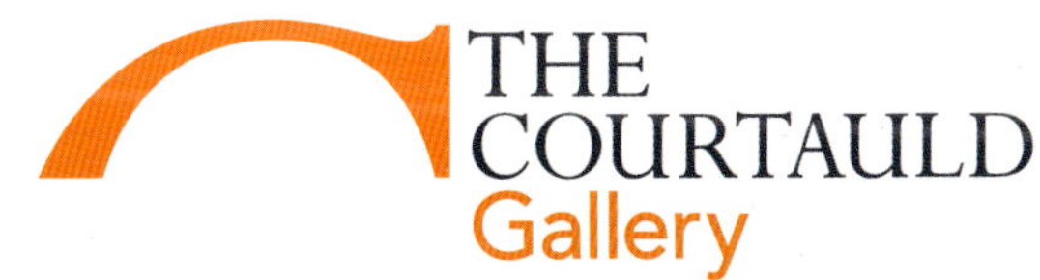

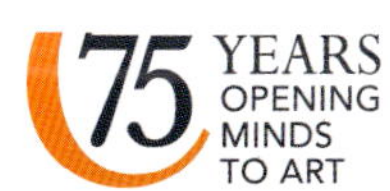

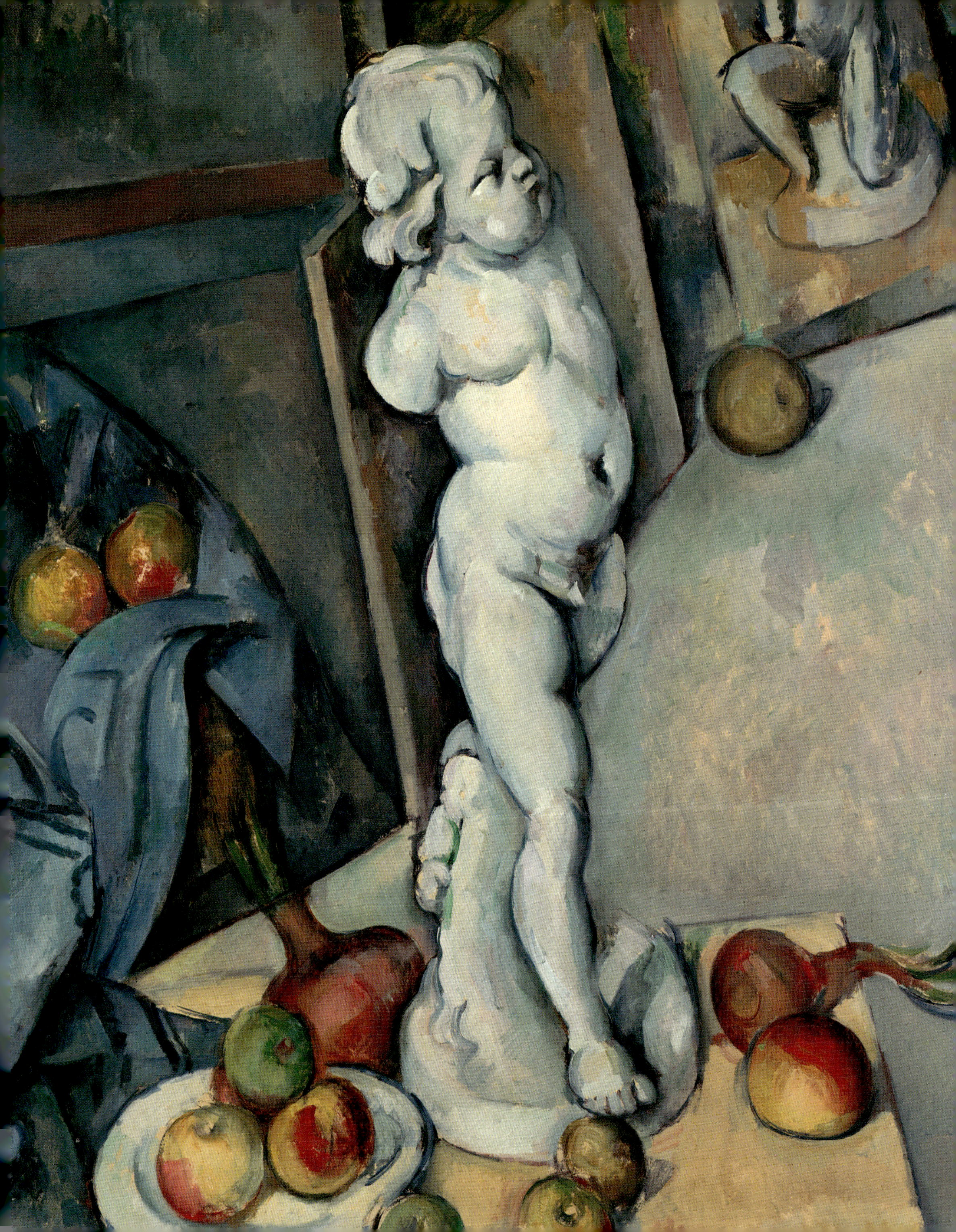

THE COURTAULD CÉZANNES

Edited by
STEPHANIE BUCK, JOHN HOUSE,
ERNST VEGELIN VAN CLAERBERGEN
AND BARNABY WRIGHT

ESSAYS BY
John House, Elisabeth Reissner
and Barnaby Wright

CATALOGUE BY
Stephanie Buck, John House
and Joanna Selborne

THE COURTAULD GALLERY
IN ASSOCIATION WITH
PAUL HOLBERTON PUBLISHING
LONDON

First published to accompany the exhibition

THE COURTAULD CÉZANNES

at The Courtauld Gallery
Somerset House, London
26 June – 5 October 2008

The Courtauld Gallery is supported
with funds from the Arts and Humanities
Research Council (AHRC)

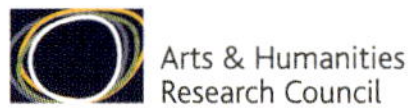

ISBN 9781903470848

British Library Cataloguing in Publication Data

A catalogue record for this book is
available from the British Library

Produced by Paul Holberton publishing
89 Borough High Street, London SE1 1NL
www.paul-holberton.net

Designed by Philip Lewis

Origination and printing by
e-graphic, Verona, Italy

FRONT COVER: Detail, *La Montagne Sainte-Victoire*, cat. 4
BACK COVER: *Apples, Bottle and Chairback*, cat. 17
FRONTISPIECE: Detail, *Still Life with Plaster Cupid*, cat. 8
PAGES 10–11: Detail, *Apples, Bottle and Chairback*, cat. 17

CONTENTS

FOREWORD

The Courtauld's collection of works by Paul Cézanne is the largest and arguably the finest in Britain. It is a particular strength of the collection that it includes not just celebrated oil paintings but also drawings, watercolours, prints and letters, thus giving a particularly rich account of Cézanne's achievement across a variety of media. *The Courtauld Cézannes* is the first time that the complete collection has been shown together. As the final exhibition of The Courtauld Institute's 75th anniversary year, it is highly appropriate that it celebrates the artist who was at the heart of the collection formed by our founder, Samuel Courtauld, as well as the legacy of scholarship which Courtauld's gift of his collection initiated.

At the same time as Courtauld was assembling his private collection he was also acquiring works for the nation through the Courtauld Fund, assuming a central role in the formation of the national collection of modern French paintings. Similarly, Courtauld always intended that his private collection should enter the public domain. His generosity in leaving these works for the benefit of The Courtauld Institute was echoed in further bequests in subsequent decades, including, perhaps most gloriously, that of Count Antoine Seilern, whose 1978 bequest included several important works by Cézanne. In addition to making their works available to the public through The Courtauld Gallery, their generous gifts may also be understood in the context of a rich tradition of intellectual engagement with the work of Cézanne at the Institute. At its best this has drawn from across The Courtauld's community, including the curatorial staff of the Gallery, the academic faculty, post-graduate students, the libraries and the Department of Conservation and Technology.

The present exhibition and its catalogue are the latest expressions of this collaborative approach, and I would like to thank all my colleagues who have contributed variously to the realisation of this project. They include, amongst others: Stephanie Buck, Aviva Burnstock, Mary Ellen Cetra, Kerstin Glasow, John House, Elisabeth Reissner, Joanna Selborne, Ernst Vegelin van Claerbergen and Barnaby Wright. Elisabeth Reissner's major technical research project on The Courtauld's Cézanne holdings was undertaken as Caroline Villers Research Fellow in the Department of Conservation and Technology.

In presenting its successful and distinctive programme of focused exhibitions, The Courtauld relies heavily on a generous and loyal group of friends and supporters. Specifically, *The Courtauld Cézannes* would not have been possible without the support and enthusiasm of Mr and Mrs Gilbert Lloyd, Nassau, Bahamas; The Doris Pacey Charitable Foundation; Apax Partners; Klein Solicitors; and Toray Industries Inc. We are profoundly grateful to them for enabling us to present this internationally important collection of works by Paul Cézanne together for the first time.

DEBORAH SWALLOW
MÄRIT RAUSING DIRECTOR
THE COURTAULD INSTITUTE OF ART

Bob Ratcliffe was born and brought up in Derbyshire. After taking a degree in Fine Arts at Reading and the post-graduate Diploma at The Courtauld, he was employed at The Courtauld until his retirement in 1990, briefly in the Technology Department and then as a lecturer, specialising in French painting of the later nineteenth and early twentieth centuries, and especially the art of Cézanne.

On paper, his legacy is sadly thin: some brief but impeccable notes in the catalogue of the exhibition of Cézanne drawings and watercolours organised by Lawrence Gowing in 1973, and his pioneering but sadly unpublished PhD on Cézanne. That PhD thesis, completed in 1960, is a formidable piece of work; still, nearly half a century later, it is a necessary port of call for any serious researcher on the artist, with its combination of scrupulous documentation and deep insight into the making of Cézanne's pictures. It is no exaggeration to say that Bob's intense scrutiny of the material evidence offered by the paintings was unique in the Impressionist field in the 1950s.

It was, though, through his teaching, and especially through his series of lectures on Cézanne, that Bob wielded a profound influence on successive generations of art historians; that influence is his most significant legacy. Illustrated by a remarkable sequence of slides, made by Bob himself from the pictures under discussion and from the landscapes around Aix-en-Provence, the lectures offered an astonishingly vivid entry into Cézanne's creative process, as the surfaces of the canvases were scrutinised, in image and word, to reveal the ways in which they were made. Many people whose only encounter with Bob's teaching was these lectures have told me what a profound impact they had on them. I heard the series at least six times, and learned new things on every occasion.

Those whom he taught in small groups encountered another dimension of his teaching. In some senses he was not a teacher at all. He did not engage in the sort of Socratic dialogue by which one tries to draw logical thought or coherent argument out of a reluctant student. Rather, he taught by example, and the arena in which this was most effective was in front of the works themselves, in The Courtauld Gallery in its old home in Woburn Square, and in the National Gallery.

His insistence on the problems posed by viewing conditions was revelatory. You can recognise a former Ratcliffe student when (as I did recently) you see someone viewing a picture through a rectangle formed by their hands or, better still, cut out in cardboard – devices that Bob demonstrated as means of minimising the effects of invasive picture frames, inappropriately coloured walls or unsympathetic lighting. And woe betide the student who (as one did when I was a student) came to a gallery wearing tinted spectacles!

But most important was the example that he set through the close scrutiny of the pictures themselves. It was this that he sought to replicate in his slides, but the lesson was of course still more vivid in front of the original canvases. Encountering this was a crucial moment in my own education. I had just 'discovered' Monet when I arrived at The Courtauld, but I did not have the training or visual skills to analyse what I was seeing in his art; Bob's example was precisely what I needed at that point. His insistence that the scrupulous analysis of the appearance and physical make-up of a painting was the necessary starting-point for our subject has remained with me ever since. Rereading his thesis, in preparation for the present exhibition project, has reminded me how much my viewing of paintings owes to his example, though he should in no way be held responsible for my conclusions.

Bob's teaching career was interrupted by illness, and many students passed through his classes without being able to take full advantage of what he offered. But, for those who could, the impact of his teaching has had a lifelong effect, though none of us can match the exacting standards that he set himself – standards that played so great a part in preventing him from feeling able to publish his work.

JOHN HOUSE

SAMUEL COURTAULD SOCIETY

The Courtauld is grateful for the significant annual support that
it receives from the members of the Samuel Courtauld Society.

DIRECTOR'S CIRCLE

Andrew and Maya Adcock
Apax Partners
Christie's
Nicholas and Jane Ferguson
Sir Nicholas and Lady Goodison
Paul and Jill Ruddock
Sotheby's
The Worshipful Company of Mercers

PATRONS' CIRCLE

Anonymous
Agnew's
Lord and Lady Aldington
Jean-Luc Baroni Ltd
Philip and Casie Bassett
Sabine Blümel
Mrs Elke von Brentano
Charles and Rosamond Brown
The Lord Browne of Madingley
Mr Damon Buffini
David and Jane Butter
Julian and Jenny Cazalet
Mr Colin Clark
Eric Coutts
Nick Coutts
Mr Mark Cunningham
Mrs Samantha Darell
David Dutton
Mr Gary Eaborn
Mr and Mrs Thomas J. Edelman
Mr Roger J. H. Emery
Ms Veronica Eng
Mr Sam Fogg
The Lady Goodhart
Lucía V. Halpern and John Davies

Elaine Hansen
David Haysey
Hazlitt, Gooden & Fox
Mr and Mrs Schuyler Henderson
Philip Hudson
Nicholas Jones
Ms Jill Kastner
Daniel Katz Ltd
James Kelly
Norman A. Kurland and Deborah A. David
Helen Lee and David Warren
Gerard and Anne Lloyd
Stuart Lochhead and Sophie Richard
Mr Jay Massey
Clare Maurice
The Honourable Christopher McLaren
Cornelia S. Edelman Moss and James Moss
John and Jenny Murray
Mr Morton Neal CBE
Mrs Carmen Oguz
Mr Michael Palin
Lord and Lady Phillimore
Mr Richard Philp
Leslie Powell
Mr and Mrs Armins Rusis
Pam Scholes
Mr Richard Shoylekov
William Slee and Dr Heidi Bürklin-Slee
Colin Stewart and Sarah Kell
Sir Angus Stirling
Johnny Van Haeften
Erik and Kimie Vynckier
The Rt Hon. Nicholas and Lavinia Wallop
Susan and Jeffrey Weingarten
Jacqui and John White
Matthew and Molly Zola

ASSOCIATES

Anonymous
Mrs Kate Agius
Lord Jeffrey Archer
Rupert and Alexandra Asquith
Dr Charles Avery FSA
Simon and Caroline Barnes
Bonhams 1793 Limited
Mr Oliver Colman
Emma Davidson
Simon C. Dickinson Ltd
Mr Andrew P. Duffy
Margaret L. Ford
Mrs Judy Freshwater
The Rev. Robin Griffith-Jones
Jill Kastner
Timothy and Megan Kirley
Dr Chris Mallinson
Philip Mould Ltd
Mary Oury
Jilly Parsons
Paul Stimson
Mr Robert Stoppenbach
Dr Deborah Swallow
Yvonne Tan Bunzl
The Ulrich Family
Nicholas Wrigley

EXHIBITION SUPPORTERS

This exhibition has been generously supported by:

Mr and Mrs Gilbert Lloyd, Nassau, Bahamas
The Doris Pacey Charitable Foundation
Apax Partners
Klein Solicitors
Toray Industries Inc.

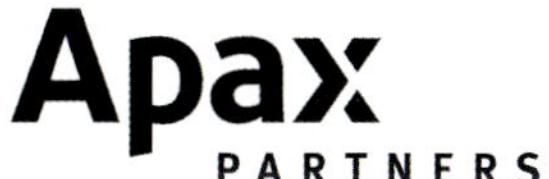 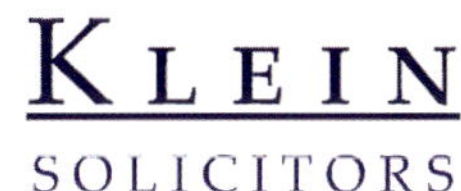 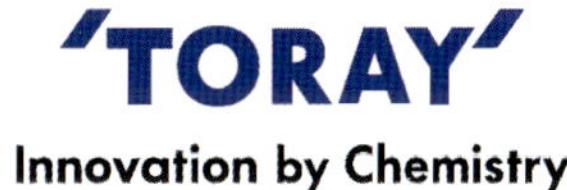

ACKNOWLEDGEMENTS

This exhibition would not have been possible without the contributions
of many colleagues at the Courtauld Institute of Art and we would like
to thank especially Graeme Barraclough, Julia Blanks, Helen Braham,
Aviva Burnstock, Caroline Campbell, Mary Ellen Cetra, William Clarke,
Ron Cobb, Alexandra Gerstein, Kerstin Glasow, Antony Hopkins and
Natalia Owdziej.

We would also like to acknowledge the help and advice of other
supportive colleagues and friends, in particular Pamela Barr,
Ruth Butler, Inken Freudenberg, Anita Haldenmann, Hilary Hamer,
Friederike Kitschen, Bernard Lecomte, Christopher McLaren,
Gregory P. J. Most, Daphne Ratcliffe, Anne Robbins, Marie-Pierre Salé,
Jutta Schütt, Margret Stuffmann and William Weston.

The curators would like to thank especially Rachel Billinge of the
National Gallery, London, for producing the digital infrared
reflectograms used in this catalogue.

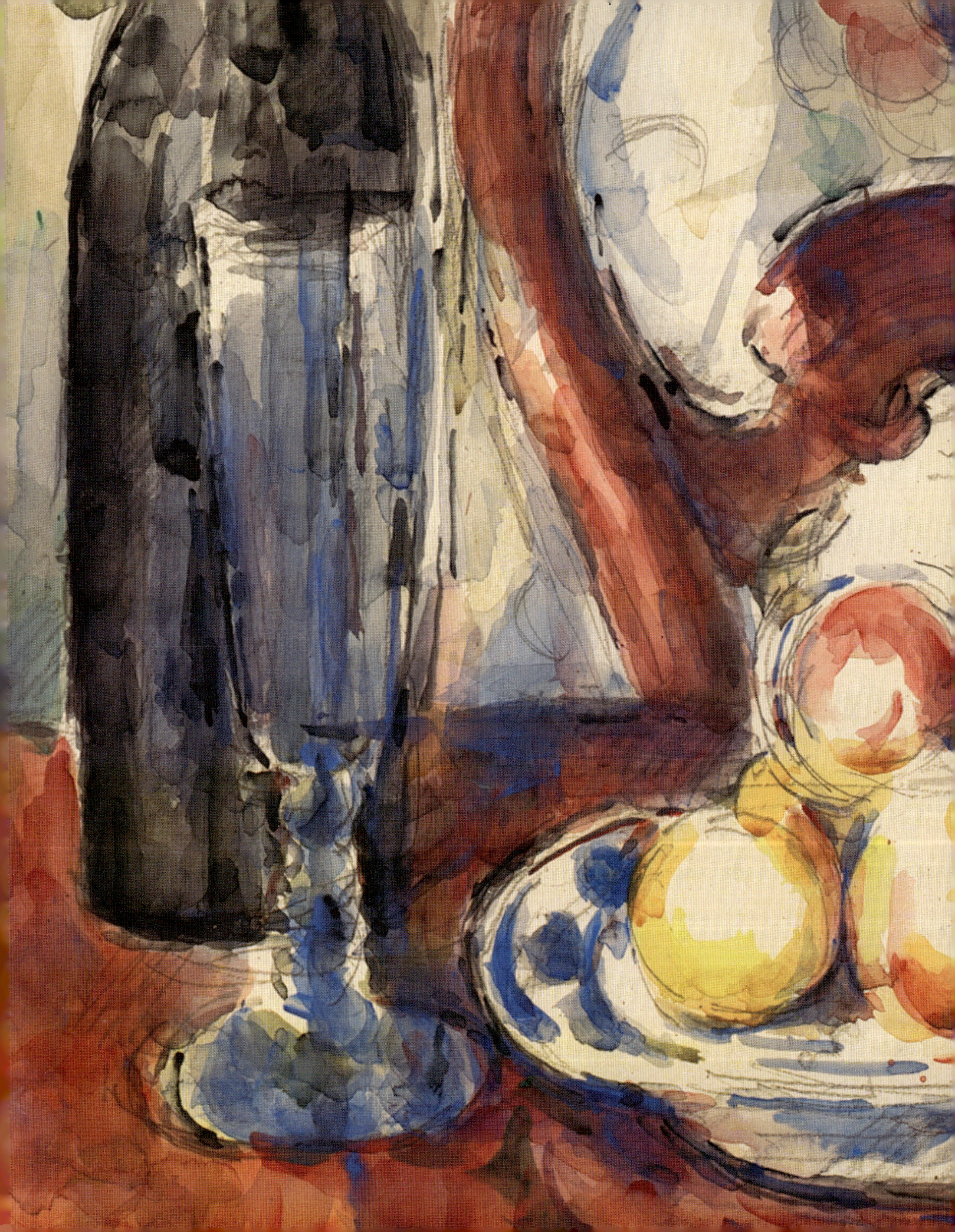

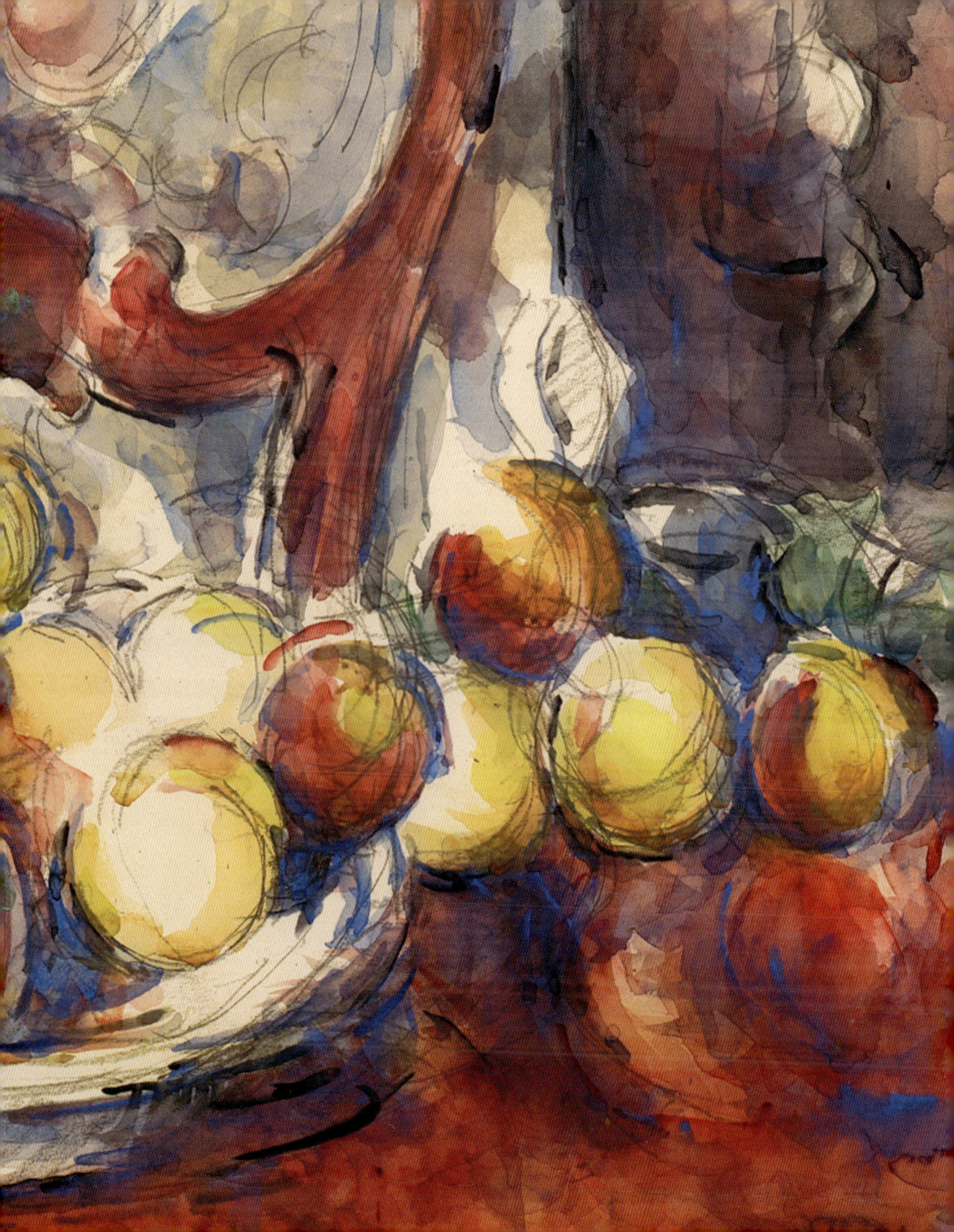

The Courtauld Cézannes

BARNABY WRIGHT

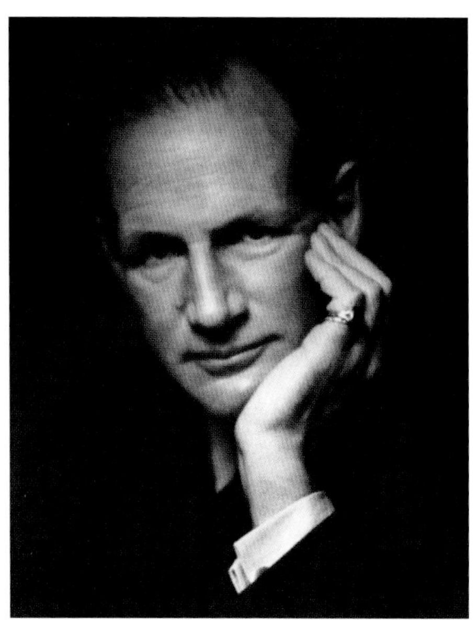

Samuel Courtauld (1876–1947)

The Courtauld Gallery's holdings of work by Paul Cézanne are the most extensive in Britain. Its exceptional quality across a range of material, including paintings, watercolours and drawings makes it the pre-eminent Cézanne collection in this country. The majority of the works were assembled by the wealthy textile manufacturer and philanthropist Samuel Courtauld (1876–1947) during the 1920s and 1930s (fig. 1). They formed the core of the private collection of French Impressionist and Post-Impressionist art which became part of his founding gift that established The Courtauld Institute of Art in 1932. This rich collection of Cézannes was supplemented in 1978 when a small group of further works by the artist was bequeathed to The Courtauld by Count Antoine Seilern (1901–1978) as part of his collection of primarily Old Master paintings and drawings. Concentrating principally upon Samuel Courtauld's Cézannes, the present essay explores the formation of this remarkable collection, which was largely assembled at a time when the artist's status was being hotly debated in Britain and his artistic achievements viewed with deep scepticism by certain influential members of the country's art establishment. Courtauld's passionate commitment to the art of Cézanne played a vital role in establishing the artist's reputation in Britain. Through his gifts and bequests to The Courtauld Gallery and by his separate establishment of a fund to acquire modern French paintings for the nation, Courtauld took a pioneering role in ensuring that important examples of Cézanne's work were secured for public benefit in Britain.[1]

In 1922 Samuel Courtauld saw a painting by Cézanne which changed his life. The work, *Mountains in Provence* (RP391; fig.2), had been rejected the previous year as a loan to the National Gallery, Millbank (the Tate Gallery). Its owner, the pioneering Welsh collector Gwendoline Davies, instead lent it to the Burlington Fine Arts Club's exhibition of nineteenth-century French art,[2] where its exceptional vibrancy and energy had a profound effect upon Courtauld. He later recalled the experience of his first encounter with the picture:

"A young friend who was a painter of conventional portraits, and had been serving in the R.F.C., led me up to Cézanne's *Provençal Landscape* .... Though genuinely moved he was not very lucid, and finished by saying, in typical airman's language, 'It makes you go this way, and that way, and then off the deep-end altogether!' At that moment I felt the magic, and I have felt it in Cézanne's work ever since."[3]

Courtauld was not alone in feeling the painting's magic. One of its first owners, Paul Gauguin, counted the picture among his most treasured possessions, and Roger Fry, the foremost champion of Cézanne in Britain in the early twentieth century, thought it one of the artist's finest landscapes. In 1921 he publicly attacked the Tate Gallery's rejection of the work and their exclusion of Cézanne from national display, claiming that "A Gallery of Modern Foreign Art without Cézanne is like a gallery of Florentine art without Giotto".[4] For Courtauld, seeing *Mountains in Provence* was not only revelatory of Cézanne's powers as an artist but also symbolic of the British art establishment's entrenched conservatism with regard to modern developments in French painting over the previous fifty years and more, with the result that at the beginning of the 1920s the work of the Impressionists and Post-Impressionists was very poorly represented in the national collections.[5]

Courtauld's encounter with Cézanne's art in 1922 moved him to act decisively and that year he took his first steps in assembling what would quickly become the finest private collection of French Impressionist and Post-Impressionist paintings in Britain. Whilst such work was not widely appreciated in Britain, Courtauld was buying at a time when Impressionist and Post-Impressionist masterpieces were attracting increasingly high prices on the international art market. Remarkably, less than three years after Courtauld began buying, Osbert Sitwell could confidently claim in an *Apollo* article dedicated to the collection that the quality and comprehensiveness of Courtauld's pictures ably demonstrated that "the latter half of the French nineteenth century was one of the supreme moments of world-painting".[6] Over the following five years Courtauld more than doubled the size of the collection to include exceptional works by most of the major modern artists of the period, ranging from Manet, Monet and Renoir to Cézanne, Van Gogh and Gauguin. In only a little over ten years after making his first acquisitions, Courtauld presented much of this extraordinary collection, together with his London residence, Home House, in which it was displayed, to establish the Courtauld Institute of Art (fig. 3). The Institute opened in 1932 as the first institution in Britain dedicated to the study and dissemination of art history. Courtauld gave the first tranche of pictures in that year to endow the Home House Society (now reconstituted as the Samuel Courtauld Trust) which holds the collection in trust for the benefit of the Courtauld Institute and its Gallery. Further gifts of work came in 1934 and 1938. Courtauld retained a selected part of the collection for his new residence at 12 North Audley St, including several Cézannes (fig. 4). He bequeathed them, along with most of his other pictures, to the Home House Society upon his death in 1947.

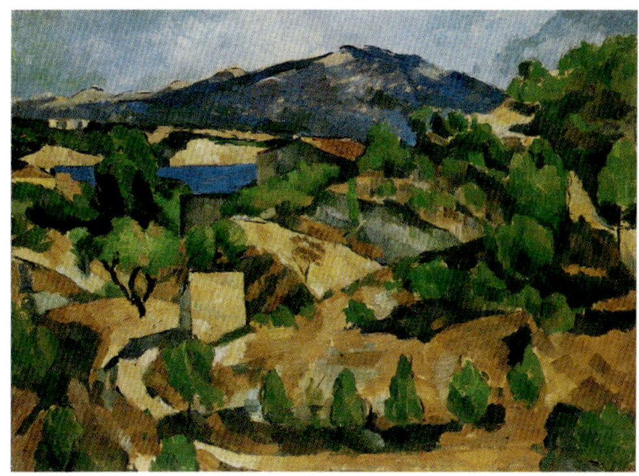

FIG. 2
Paul Cézanne, *Mountains in Provence*, c. 1879
Oil on canvas, 54.2 × 74.2 cm
National Museum of Wales, Cardiff

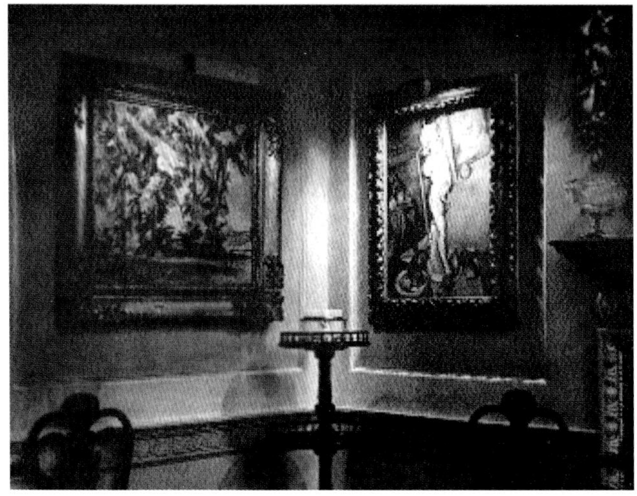

From the outset, Cézanne was at the very heart of Courtauld's collection. In total he bought some eleven major canvases and several watercolours – significantly more works than by any other single artist in the collection. Courtauld purchased his first Cézanne, *Still Life with Plaster Cupid* (cat. 8), in May 1923 from the celebrated Glasgow-based modern art dealer Alexander Reid. Reid included the work that year in one of his last major commercial exhibitions, 'Masterpieces of French Art', held at Agnew's in London's Old Bond Street.[7] The painting is one of the artist's most complex late still lifes and it was an ambitious first purchase for Courtauld, suggesting that his taste for Cézanne was already sophisticated and well-informed. Just over a month later he bought his second Cézanne, also from the Reid-Agnew exhibition, *L'Etang des Sœurs, Osny* (cat. 1) - this time a landscape from a pivotal period in the artist's early development, when he was working in the orbit of the Impressionists. Throughout the rest of the decade Courtauld bought at least one work by Cézanne each year, and typically more, developing the scope of the collection with figure subjects and primarily landscapes, mainly from the artist's mature period of the 1880s and 1890s. Two of his most important purchases during these years came in 1925 and 1929 respectively when he acquired *La Montagne Saint-Victoire* (cat. 4) and *The Card Players* (cat. 6), which alongside *Still Life with Plaster Cupid* became the cornerstones of his Cézanne collection. Although his acquisitions slowed after 1929, Courtauld continued to buy important works by Cézanne until his collecting activities effectively ceased in 1937. That year he not only bought *Farm in Normandy* (cat. 2) but also purchased one of the artist's most magnificent late watercolours, *Apples, Bottle and Chairback* (cat. 17).[8]

A small number of Courtauld's Cézanne purchases came through the agency of Percy Moore Turner of the Independent Gallery in London's Grafton Street. Courtauld entrusted Turner as his principal advisor, dealer

THE COURTAULD CÉZANNES

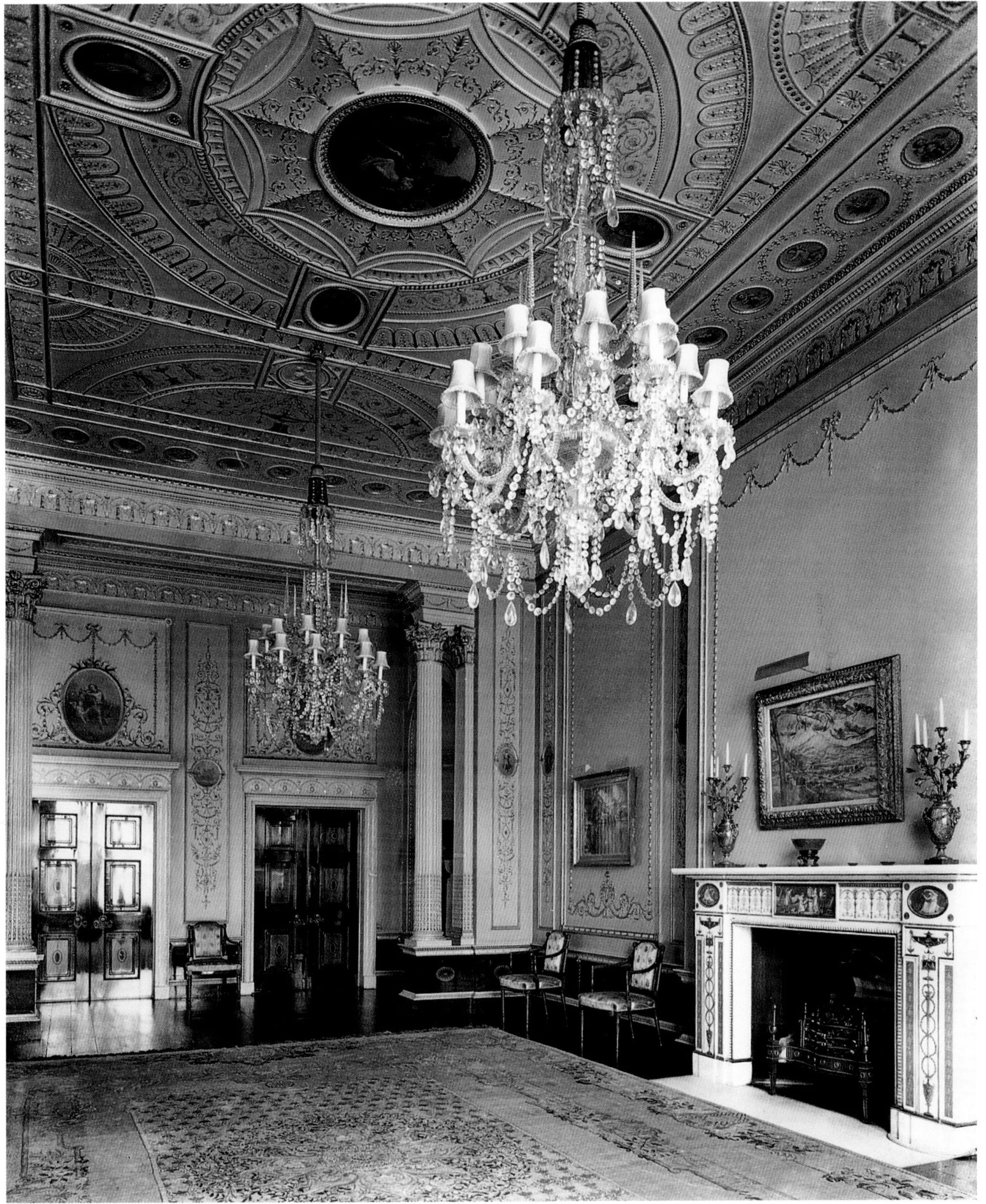

and intermediary during the formation of his collection of French paintings, which Turner fully catalogued with Paul Jamot, resulting in a luxurious privately printed volume in 1934.[9] Having run a gallery in Paris before the First World War, Turner was well connected in the French art world and was ideally placed to source works and negotiate purchases; services which earned him commissions from Courtauld for transactions including the acquisitions of Renoir's *La Loge* (1874), in 1925, and Manet's *A Bar at the Folies-Bergère* (1881–82) the following year (both Courtauld Gallery, London). But Courtauld also quickly established his own connections with major international dealers, from whom he would often buy directly, as was the case with the majority of his Cézanne purchases. As a shrewd and experienced businessman (he took up the chairmanship of his family's highly successful textile firm, Courtaulds Ltd, in 1921) Courtauld was not averse to negotiating on price and would on occasion offer dealers existing works in his collection in part-exchange for new acquisitions. His 1929 purchase of *The Card Players* from a private collector represented by the Berlin dealer Alfred Gold is a case in point. Courtauld pressed Gold on the asking price, which the dealer eventually set at £13,000. This sum was close to Courtauld's most expensive Cézanne purchase, which a recently discovered document has revealed to be *La Montagne Sainte-Victoire*, acquired in 1925 for £14,250.[10] According to Gold's account, Courtauld suggested the dealer take either one of his other Cézannes, *Le Lac d'Annecy* (cat. 9) or *Madame Cézanne* (RP 685; fig. 5), or his Gauguin, *Bathing Women, Tahiti*, 1897 (Barber Institute, Birmingham), in part-exchange for *The Card Players*.[11] However, Gold promptly informed him that the owner would only accept a cash settlement. In a last ditch attempt to see the deal concluded, Gold wrote to Courtauld on March 17 1929 informing him that he was struggling to keep several other interested parties at bay including, "the director of an important Museum and a Swiss private collector". The ploy worked but Courtauld could not resist negotiating the price down further and four days later telegrammed an offer of £12,500 which Gold accepted immediately.[12]

Personally selecting and negotiating purchases went with Courtauld's wider approach to collecting and appreciating art, which he strongly believed should be based upon an individual's personal emotional response rather than being directed by convention or professional 'expert' opinion. It was, he maintained, vital to remain an "unadulterated amateur" and that unless one's "initial impulse is spontaneous, or at any rate comes to him naturally if inspired by others, perhaps he had better leave pictures alone".[13] Equally, he was quite prepared to revisit his earlier judgements on pictures in his collection and to sell works which no longer captivated him in order to fund new acquisitions, as is apparent from his dealings with Gold and others. We know, for example, that he bought an unidentified Cézanne still life watercolour from Turner's Independent Gallery in 1926 which he kept for only one year before selling it back to Turner for the same price, £850, as a small part-exchange in a £14,500 deal to buy Van Gogh's *The Crau at Arles: Peach Trees in Flower* (1889; The Courtauld Gallery, London) and Renoir's *Spring, Chatou* (*c.* 1873; private collection).[14] Courtauld's most significant sale of a Cézanne was the painting of the artist's wife, *Madame Cézanne* (mentioned above), which he bought in 1926 from Pierre Rosenberg for £4,500. He subsequently sold the canvas back to the same dealer at a profit in 1929 for £8,000, as part of negotiations for Gaugain's *Te Rerioa*, 1897 (for which Courtauld paid £13,600).[15] We can only speculate as to possible reasons for the sale of this significant Cézanne portrait, beyond a purely financial motivation. John House has suggested that Courtauld may have found the artist's austere treatment unsettling for such an intimate subject as the artist's wife.[16] Madame Cezanne's melancholic expression may also have proved uncomfortable for Courtauld at this time with the onset of the illness of his own wife, Elizabeth, which would lead to her death in 1931. More broadly, the painting might be considered something of an anomaly in the context of Courtauld's taste for Cézanne's landscapes and for his detached and monumentalising figure subjects of rural peasants, strongly represented in the collection by *The Card Players* and *Man with a Pipe* (cat. 7). It has previously been believed that Courtauld owned and subsequently sold a second, more major, Cézanne portrait of his wife, *Madame Cézanne in a Striped Skirt*, *c.* 1876 (RP 324; Museum of Fine Arts, Boston). This painting is illustrated as belonging to Courtauld in a 1929 article by Dormoy, dedicated to his collection in the French journal *L'Amour de l'Art*. However, the recent discovery of a copy of the article annotated with Courtauld's pencil notes reveals that he never owned this painting. Next to the illustration of the portrait he writes emphatically "Not mine (ever) SC" and crosses out the accompanying text which discusses the painting as being owned by him, writing "No never" in the margin.[17]

So far as one can tell from surviving correspondence and other writings, Courtauld's collecting was not directed to any great extent by the opinions of art world professionals, even those he clearly respected, such as Fry and Turner.[18] Rather, Courtauld's belief in his own 'spontaneous impulse' remained the guiding principle of his collecting. In 1929, for example, Fry wrote to Courtauld at length extolling the virtues of Cézanne's *Gardanne*, 1885–86, which was for sale at Pierre Rosenberg's gallery in Paris, and encouraged him to consider buying it, describing the canvas as "a most magnificent thing" which "stands almost in a class by itself". Despite such a glowing recommendation, Courtauld decided against the picture and his decision seems to have compelled Fry to reconsider his earlier opinion; looking again at the painting Fry conceded to Courtauld that it was in fact "not one of his supreme *travailles*" after all. Fry, the great Cézanne expert and theorist, clearly respected Courtauld's judgment on the artist: "A collection like yours",

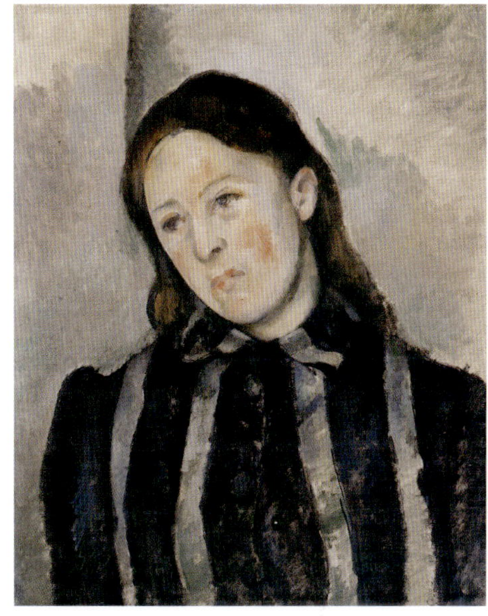

FIG. 5
Paul Cézanne, *Madame Cézanne, c.* 1890–92
Oil on canvas, 61.9 × 51.1 cm
Philadelphia Museum of Art

he wrote, "must aim at having anything of the finest possible quality and indeed in Cézanne you are already well on to that end."[19]

Fry's assessment of the collection chimes with Courtauld's approach as a collector. With Cézanne, Courtauld did not aim at assembling a representative account of the artist's development, nor did he seek, in a systematic way, to reunite related canvases or drawings. Clearly he appreciated connections between works, for example when he bought *The Card Players* he must have undoubtedly regarded it as having a close relationship with *Man with a Pipe*, already in his collection. Likewise, his acquisition of the watercolour, *La Montagne Saint-Victoire* (cat. 14), in 1924, anticipated his purchase, the following year, of his major *Montagne Saint-Victoire* canvas from the same period. However, Courtauld principally selected his Cézannes according to a personal instinct for images which he considered to be examples of the artist's most powerful work, judged by his own emotional response in front of each picture. His particular preference was for Cézanne's landscapes, which comprised more than half his collection. According to Anthony Blunt's recollections of conversations with Courtauld, he appreciated above all the sustained and penetrating manner in which the artist observed nature.[20] This accorded with Courtauld's own love of the countryside, which was a profound source of inspiration to him, as is revealed in his unpublished essay, 'The Origin of Beauty'. His meditation on beauty begins with an evocative description of a walk through barley fields, which he describes in terms which could equally well describe a Cézanne landscape: "I let the beauty sink in, and constantly changing my angle of view, I got the utmost value out of every swell and hollow in the ground, every rich-hued tree trunk, grey and pink and brown, and every luminous grassy hedgerow."[21] Indeed, Blunt remembers Courtauld specifically telling him that his appreciation of *Le Lac d'Annecy* (cat. 9) was informed by his own observations of nature which accorded completely with the artist's treatment of the complex distorting effects of reflections on water.[22]

For Courtauld, Cézanne's work was particularly open to a personal emotional response that drew upon one's own visual experience rather than upon knowledge of art history or mastery of aesthetic theory. And it was this 'personal' rather than 'professional' approach to art that underpinned Courtauld's humanist belief in the importance of art to society (discussed below). It was an approach that resonated strongly with the writings of Fry and others in his circle, particularly Clive Bell, who both drew from Cézanne qualities that spoke to profoundly personal aesthetic emotions and thus had the radical potential to challenge the strictures and conventions of the professional art establishment.[23]

As we shall see, during the 1920s Courtauld did more than anyone in Britain to confront head on the elitism and conservatism of the country's art institutions by championing the cause of Cézanne in particular and modern French art in general.

The ambitious and pioneering character of Courtauld's commitment to collecting Cézanne in Britain is thrown into relief when one considers the British artistic climate within which he was collecting during the 1920s and 1930s.[24] During this period the artist's reputation was far from being established in this country and several leading figures questioned even the proficiency, let alone the historical importance, of Cézanne's art. This was at a time when other, once controversial, modern French artists, especially Gauguin, were being actively sought for the nation as part of a concerted effort to develop holdings of nineteenth-century French art. The Tate's rejection of Gwendoline Davies's offer of the loan of her *Mountains in Provence*, together with a second Cézanne, *Provençal Landscape (c. 1888;* RP 613; National Museums of Wales, Cardiff) in 1921, prompted considerable debate. D.S. MacColl (then Keeper of the Wallace Collection and previously Keeper of the Tate) in a piece for the *Saturday Review* entitled, 'The Nonsense about Cézanne', argued that the artist was of decidedly minor interest. He claimed Cézanne was "very imperfectly qualified" as a painter, with little control over his technique and "nervously impotent" in front of his subject-matter. Whilst MacColl could find certain successes in the artist's oeuvre, he rounded upon Fry and those who agreed with his championing of the painter as 'the father of modern art', claiming that they "elevate the impotence and the disabilities into virtues, and found an esoteric system upon the accidents that the master himself would have gnashed his teeth about".[25] In other writings, C.J. Holmes (Director of the National Gallery) and Charles Aitken (Director of the Tate) both demonstrated their coolness towards Cézanne's work.[26] Holmes had previously passed up the opportunity to buy an example of Cézanne's work for the National Gallery on a Treasury funded buying trip to the Degas estate sale in Paris in 1918 with John Maynard Keynes (then an advisor to the Treasury). Holmes bought several important modern French paintings for the Gallery, including a Gauguin and a Manet. However, despite Keynes' encouragement, Holmes refused to buy anything by Cézanne and stood aside whilst Keynes bought the artist's exquisite small *Still Life, Apples (c. 1879;* RP 346; King's College, Cambridge, on loan to the Fitzwilliam Museum, Cambridge) for his private collection.

On the other side of the Cézanne debate, Fry had been arguing the case for the artist with increasing sophistication since first displaying his work in strength in this country at his seminal *Manet and the Post-Impressionists* exhibition at London's Grafton Galleries in 1910. Against stiff opposition, by the early 1920s, he had helped to achieve significant support for Cézanne, not only among his immediate circle of artists and writers within the so-called 'Bloomsbury Group', but also more widely. For example, important critics such as Arthur Clutton-Brock, of *The Times*, and Frank Rutter, of *The Sunday Times*, both found much to admire in Cézanne's work and came out in condemnation of the Tate's decision

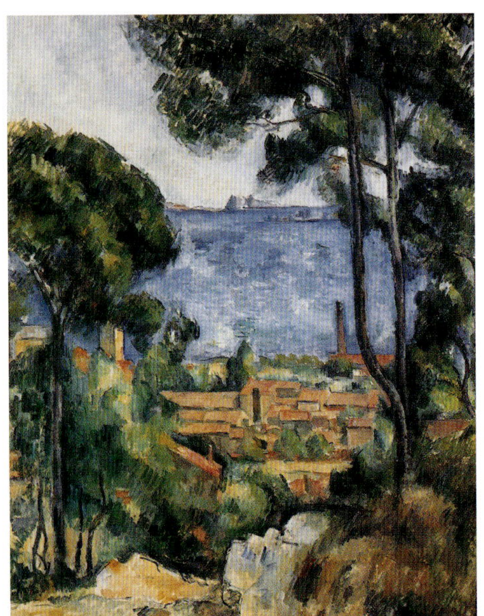

to exclude him from national display.[27] The pressure was such that the Tate reconsidered its earlier decision after the two Davies Cézannes had been shown at the Burlington Fine Arts Club in 1922 and accepted them on loan later that year. It was the first time work by Cézanne had hung on the walls of a national collection in Britain. Despite this break-through for supporters of Cézanne, opportunities to see the artist's work over the next few years were mainly limited to his inclusion in commercial group exhibitions. Cézanne's first ever monographic exhibition in this country did not come until 1925 when the pioneering London dealership, The Leicester Galleries, held a show of thirty paintings and watercolours by the artist, to which Courtauld lent his newly acquired *Tall Trees at the Jas de Bouffan* (cat. 3) and his *Montagne Sainte-Victoire* water-colour. It may have been here that he first saw the richly coloured landscape, *View over L'Estaque* (RP 531; fig. 6), which he eventually bought in 1936, and was one of two Cézannes in his collection which he left to those close to him. However, this exhibition came late in the day considering that there had been regular monographic commercial shows of Cézanne's work in France since 1895 and he had been posthumously honoured with a major retrospective at Paris's Grand Palais in 1907. Among others, there had also been solo exhibitions of his work in Berlin (1907), New York (1911), Venice (1920) and Basel (1921).

Given the paucity of works by Cézanne in Britain during this period and the artist's equivocal status here, Courtauld's commitment to assembling a collection which aimed to represent some of the artist's finest achievements is particularly significant. Whilst there were a few notable Cézanne works in earlier British private collections, such as those of Davies, Keynes and Michael Sadler, Courtauld was the first and only collector in Britain with the resources and the determination to put together a collection of the artist's work which could begin to compare in quality (although certainly not in quantity) with contemporary major international private collections of Cézanne, such as those of Auguste Pellerin in France and Dr Albert C. Barnes in the United States. But for Courtauld the cause of Cézanne in particular and modern French painting in general went well beyond the amassing of his private collection (however 'public' he made that collection through loans, publications and its eventual gift to The Courtauld Gallery). He believed that the spiritual and cultural life of contemporary society had been degraded by excessive materialism brought about under the conditions of industrial capitalism. Rather than feeling compromised by his own position as a leading industrialist, Courtauld argued that certain types of art could play a vital role in restoring the spiritual qualities of modern life. As he put it in his presidential address to the Association of Art Institutions in 1943: "I see art as the most uniformly civilizing influence which man has ever known."[28] Like Fry, who argued a broadly comparable case for the role of art in society, Courtauld identified modern French art as the most forceful recent manifestation of those spiritually restorative qualities.[29] This fuelled Courtauld's desire to see examples of such work secured for the nation.

To this end, at the same time as he was beginning to assemble his private collection, Courtauld made a bold move to address the lack of modern French painting in the national collections by establishing The Courtauld Fund in 1923 with a gift to the nation of £50,000 for the purpose of acquiring examples of such work. Courtauld was the dominant member of the Fund's Board of Trustees, which included Holmes and Aitkin among others. Courtauld expressed his belief that the focus of their collecting should be artists whom he described as the "central men of the movement". He listed them as "Manet, Renoir, Degas, Cézanne, Monet, Gauguin and Van Gogh".[30] After an energetic campaign of collecting between 1923 and 1926, the Trustees had exhausted the Fund and added to the national collections some of the country's finest Impressionist and Post-Impressionist works, including Manet's *The Waitress*, *c*. 1878/79, Van Gogh's *Sunflowers*, 1888, and Seurat's *Une Baignade*, 1883–84 (all National Gallery, London). Despite such exemplary purchases by the Trustees, there remained lingering scepticism on the part of Aitkin and Holmes towards Cézanne and Courtauld had to work hard to ensure that the Fund was able to acquire two examples of the artist's work. The first came in 1925 with the purchase of Cézanne's *Self-portrait* (RP 482; fig. 7) which was the first ever painting by the artist to enter the national collections. The second, *Hillside in Provence*, *c*. 1890–92 (National Gallery, London, RP 718), was bought the following year but only at Courtauld's personal insistence and with additional funds provided by him especially for this acquisition. Fry in particular was delighted with these Cézanne purchases, writing in the *Nation* in 1926: "It is a matter for the greatest satisfaction that we should possess two first-rate Cézannes".[31] And in an act of personal homage to Cézanne and the cause of his work, Fry painted a copy of the *Self-portrait* in 1925, the year that it entered the national collections, which he later bequeathed to The Courtauld Gallery.

As John House has convincingly argued, by the beginning of the 1930s the Courtauld Fund's purchases had "effectively crushed the opposition in England to the French 'modern movement' of the later nineteenth century".[32] And within this group of artists Cézanne was now widely acknowledged to be a principal figure. This was demonstrated most powerfully in the Royal Academy's major 1932 winter exhibition, 'French Art 1200–1900', for which both Courtauld and Fry were on the Executive Committee. Cézanne was represented by fifteen major works, four of them from Courtauld's private collection, including *The Card Players* and *La Montagne Sainte-Victoire*. In his review of the exhibition for the *Studio*, Tancred Borenius recognised that an important battle for Cézanne had been won in Britain: "May one hope that the promotion of Cézanne to rank uncontestedly among the great and permanent glories of French art will serve as a forcible reminder of that necessity of an unprejudiced vision, without which no art can thrive and flourish at any period."[33]

Two years later the newly appointed Director of the National Gallery, Kenneth Clark, wrote to Courtauld gratefully accepting his offer of the loan of Cézanne's *La Montagne Sainte-Victoire*, together with Manet's *A Bar at the Folies-Bergère*. Clark informed him that even Sir William Llewellyn (President of the Royal Academy and member of the National Gallery Board of Trustees) had been enthusiastic about having the Cézanne, a response which Clark described as the "the collapse of this last stronghold of academic art".[34] Courtauld was surprised and delighted to discover Clark's enthusiasm for Cézanne (which stood in notable contrast to his predecessor, Holmes). He wrote, in typically modest tone, "For my part, I am pleased to help in getting official recognition for Cézanne in England."[35]

In fact Clark had greatly admired Cézanne's work since his teenage years, when he had seen the paintings owned by Gwendoline Davies hanging in the Victoria Art Gallery in Bath, sometime between 1918 and 1920. Clark's conversion to Cézanne came even earlier than Courtauld's but extraordinarily it seems to have been the very same painting, *Mountains in Provence*, which captivated both men. Clark described Cézanne as delivering him a "knock out blow" and the landscape in particular as giving him "the strongest aesthetic shock I have ever received from a picture".[36] During the 1930s Clark began acquiring numerous examples of the artist's work. On one famous occasion he bought a bundle of fifty drawings and watercolours from Paul Guillaume which had just been brought into the gallery for sale by Cézanne's son. Two Cézanne works that were bought from Clark's collection by Count Antoine Seilern in 1941 were bequeathed to The Courtauld Gallery by Seilern in 1978. They are the late unfinished landscape in oil, *Route Tournante* (cat. 10), and the watercolour *Statue under Trees* (cat. 16). He also bequeathed a further important watercolour, *Armchair* (cat. 15), and the magnificent drawing of the artist's wife *Portrait of Hortense Fiquet* (cat. 11). Although Seilern primarily collected Old Master paintings and drawings, he gathered a small but significant group of works by nineteenth-century artists. Writing about his collection in 1961, Seilern confessed to having lost the strength of his earlier interest in French nineteenth-century art with but one exception, Cézanne, whose work he held in the highest esteem. Whereas for Courtauld Cézanne's work manifested an artistic continuity with the civilising aesthetic qualities of the art of the past, for Seilern it was the intensity and sophistication of Cézanne's approach to specific questions of perspective and spatial organisation that had profound affinities with the approaches of the Old Masters. For example, Seilern suggested connections between Cézanne's landscapes and the landscape drawings of Rembrandt, examples of which were in his collection. In both artists' work he found innovative and exemplary

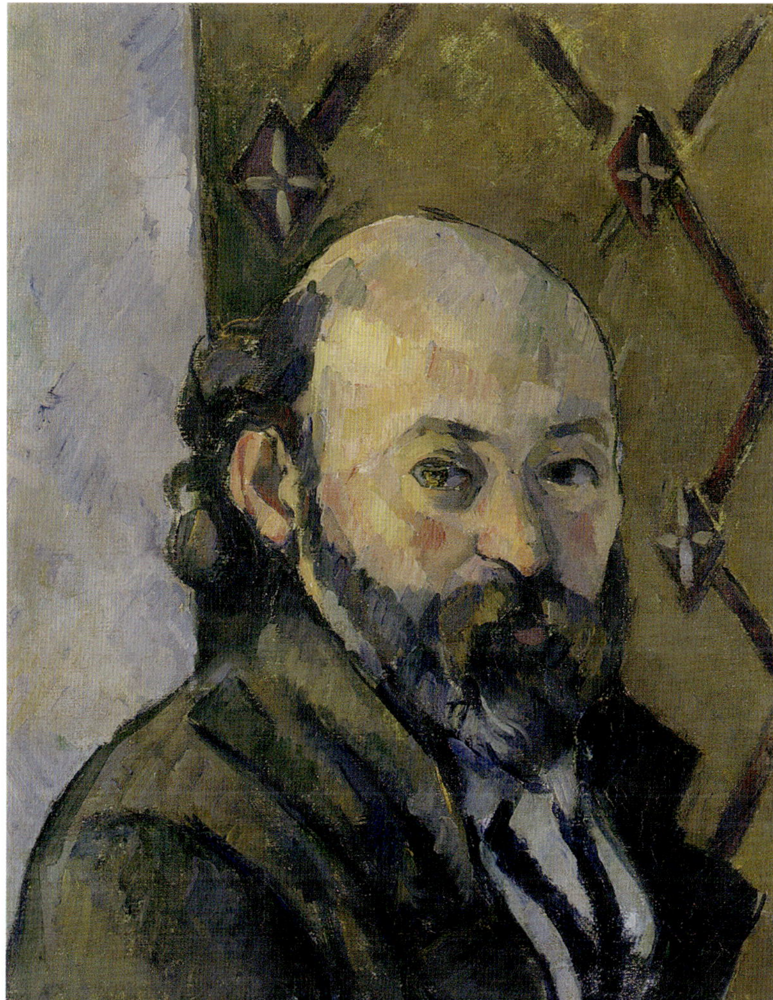

approaches to creating a sensation of perspective which combined spatial illusion and surface design. And of all nineteenth-century French artists it was, Seilern wrote, "only in the work of Cézanne [that] I still find the solution of these problems exciting".[37]

The addition of Seilern's four Cézannes to the larger holdings formed by Samuel Courtauld further enhanced what is now the richest collection of the artist's work in this country. It is testament to Courtauld's judgement as a collector that the works he assembled have remained central to our appreciation of Cézanne's achievement and feature extensively within the numerous publications and exhibitions which have variously interpreted and reinterpreted his art during the past century. The collection also attests to the strength of Courtauld's conviction of Cézanne's importance and to his pioneering efforts to secure the artist's status in Britain.

ACKNOWLEDGEMENTS

I am very grateful to Stephanie Buck,
John House, Christopher McLaren and
Ernst Vegelin for their help and expertise
in the preparation of this essay.

NOTES

1 The most comprehensive account of
Courtauld's activities as a collector is
Impressionism for England, London 1994.

2 Burlington Fine Arts Club, London,
*Pictures, Drawings and Sculpture of the French
School of the Last 100 Years*, 1922. Roger Fry
played a leading role in mounting the
exhibition and his influence can be
seen in the inclusion of eight works by
Cézanne, more works than by any other
artist in the exhibition, which contained
71 exhibits ranging from Corot and Ingres
to Rodin and Degas. Admission to the
exhibition was by invitation.

3 This passage comes from a series of essays
that Samuel Courtauld is said to have
written towards the end of his life and
perhaps intended to publish. They are
cited by Anthony Blunt in a 1954 essay
on Courtauld and were made available to
Blunt by Courtauld's daughter, Mrs R.A.
Butler. Unfortunately their present where-
abouts are unknown. This is frustrating
as the short passages quoted by Blunt
suggest that the essays contain much
important biographical information as
well as providing insights into Courtauld's
views on art. See Anthony Blunt, 'Samuel
Courtauld as Collector and Benefactor',
in Cooper 1954 (2), p. 4.

4 Roger Fry, 'Editorial', *The Burlington
Magazine*, May 1921, p. 209.

5 Pressure from various interest groups for
the national collections to acquire modern
French paintings gained momentum
from around 1905 onwards but with little
immediate success. It was not until 1917
with the exhibition of Hugh Lane's
collection at the National Gallery that
work by Manet, Monet, Renoir, Degas and
others was displayed as a group as part
of a national collection. It was this exhibition which initially inspired Courtauld's
interest in nineteenth-century French art
(see Cooper 1954 (2), p. 4). It was also from
this date that plans were being made to
establish an extension to the Tate Gallery
(endowed by Sir Joseph Duveen) for the
display of 'modern foreign' paintings,
Of all the various Impressionist and
Post-Impressionist artists considered for
inclusion in the new gallery, Cézanne
was particularly controversial. For further
accounts of the acquisition of modern
foreign art for the national collections
in Britain see *Impressionism for England*,
London 1994; and Brandon Taylor, *Art for
the Nation: Exhibitions and the London Public
1747–2001*, Manchester University Press, 1999.

6 Sitwell 1925, p. 63.

7 Most of Courtauld's original receipts for
his purchases of paintings and drawings
are held in The Courtauld Gallery archive.

8 A letter from Wildenstein & Co. to
Courtauld, 21 July 1937 (Courtauld Gallery
archive) reveals that Courtauld initially
wanted to buy a less highly finished
Cézanne watercolour in the collection
of the artist's son but as this was
unavailable the Wildenstein gallery
offered him *Apples, Bottle and Chairback*,
which he bought for £3,500 (over £1000
more than he paid for *Still Life with Plaster
Cupid* ten years earlier).

9 Jamot and Turner 1934.

10 This price is given in a handwritten Home
House collection catalogue note held in
the archive of The Courtauld Gallery.

11 Courtauld did in fact sell the Gauguin to
or through Gold as a separate transaction
sometime around 1930.

12 This correspondence is held in
The Courtauld Gallery archive.

13 Cooper 1954 (2), p. 6.

14 I am grateful to Stephanie Buck for
drawing this sale to my attention in the
receipts held by The Courtauld Gallery
archive.

15 These receipts are held in The Courtauld
Gallery archive.

16 John House, 'Modern French Art for the
Nation: Samuel Courtauld's Collection
and Patronage in Context', in *Impressionism
for England*, London 1994, p. 24.

17 Dormoy 1929. This annotated copy of
L'Amour de l'Art, belonging to Samuel
Courtauld, is held in the Special Collections
section of the Courtauld Institute of Art
Library. I am very grateful to Stephanie
Buck for helping me to source this
volume. The belief that Samuel Courtauld
owned *Madame Cézanne in a Striped Skirt*
(Museum of Fine Art, Boston) has always
been problematic as we only know of one
Courtauld receipt (Paul Rosenberg, 1926
[Courtauld Gallery Archive]) for a work
described as *Madame Cézanne en Bleu*, which
has previously been thought could refer
to either *Madame Cézanne in a Striped Skirt* or
Madame Cézanne (Philadelphia Museum of
Art) on the assumption that he owned
both works by 1929 when the article
published both paintings as being in his
collection. As we now know that he never
owned *Madame Cézanne in a Striped Skirt* we
can be confident that the receipt was in
fact for *Madame Cézanne* and that it was this
same painting which he sold back to
Paul Rosenberg in 1929. This is further
confirmed by Courtauld's pencil note
below the illustration of *Madame Cézanne*
in the article which reads "Sold 1928"
(Courtauld may have written these notes
some years after the article's publication
and therefore misremembered the precise
year he sold the picture). Further evidence

of the article's unreliability comes with the illustration of Renoir's *La Loge,* which is not an image of Renoir's primary version of the subject owned by Courtauld but of the small version of the picture (now in the collection of Diane B. Wilsey, San Francisco) which Courtauld never owned. By this illustration Courtauld has written "Study for my picture".

18 Courtauld described Fry as "an ideal art lecturer" and admired greatly his ability to communicate the "broad human emotions and the inner spiritual content of a work"; Samuel Courtauld, 'Art's True Evaluation' in his *Ideals and Industry: War-Time Papers*, 1949, Cambridge University Press (published posthumously).

19 This correspondence is held in The Courtauld Gallery archive.

20 Cooper 1954 (2), p. 8.

21 Samuel Courtauld, 'The Origin of Beauty', 27 June 1942, p. 1, unpublished typed manuscript held in The Courtauld Gallery archive.

22 Cooper 1954 (2), p. 8.

23 See especially Roger Fry, *Cézanne: A Study of His Development*, Hogarth Press, 1927; and Clive Bell, *Art*, Chatto and Windus, London, 1914.

24 For an account of the formation of British collections of Cézanne, see *Cézanne in Britain*, London 2006–07. For a very useful selection of British critical writings which feature Cézanne see *Impressionism for England*, London 1994, pp. 225–52.

25 D.S. MacColl, 'The Nonsense about Cézanne', *Saturday Review*, 19 November 1921, excerpted in *Impressionism for England*, London 1994, pp. 234–35.

26 See for example C.J. Holmes, 'Cézanne and the Nation' (letter to the editor), *The Burlington Magazine*, June 1921, pp. 313–14, and Charles Aitkin, 'Cézanne and the Nation' (letter to the editor), *Observer*, 10 April 1921, p. 15, excerpted in *Impressionism for England*, London 1994, pp. 232–34.

27 See for example Arthur Clutton-Brock, '"Anarchists" in Painting: French Classics of Last Century: Burlington Fine Arts Club', *The Times*, 23 May 1922, p. 13; and Frank Rutter, 'A Century of French Art', *The Sunday Times*, 28 May 1922, p. 7; both excerpted in *Impressionism for England*, London 1994, pp. 235–37.

28 Posthumously published in Samuel Courtauld, *Ideals and Industry: War-Time Papers*, Cambridge University Press, 1949, p. 45.

29 For an extended discussion of the connections between Courtauld and Fry and the Bloomsbury Group in relation to his ideas about art see Andrew Stephenson, 'An Anatomy of Taste': Samuel Courtauld and Debates about Art Patronage and Modernism in Britain in the Inter-War Years', in *Impressionism for England*, London 1994, pp. 35–47.

30 However, his ambitions for a French collection were much broader and encompassed earlier artists, including Chardin and Delacroix and contemporary artists, namely Picasso and Matisse, but he recognised this to be beyond the scope of the fund. See Madeline Korn, 'The Courtauld Gift – Missing Papers Traced', *The Burlington Magazine,* April 1996, p. 256.

31 Roger Fry, 'The Courtauld Fund', *Nation and Athenaeum*, 30 January 1926, pp. 613–14, in *Impressionism for England*, London 1994, p. 244.

32 John House, 'Modern French Art for the Nation: Samuel Courtauld's Collection and Patronage in Context', in *Impressionism for England*, London 1994, p. 20.

33 Tancred Borenius, 'French Art at Burlington House', *Studio*, February 1932, pp. 77–78; cited in *Impressionism for England*, London 1994, p. 21.

34 Letter from Clark to Courtauld, 19 February 1934 (National Gallery Archives), cited in *Impressionism for England*, London 1994, p. 21.

35 Letter from Courtauld to Clark, 15 February 1934 (National Gallery Archives), cited in *Impressionism for England*, London 1994, p. 21.

36 Kenneth Clark, *Another Part of the Wood: A Self Portrait*, London, 1974, p. 240.

37 Seilern 1961, 'Foreword', unpaginated.

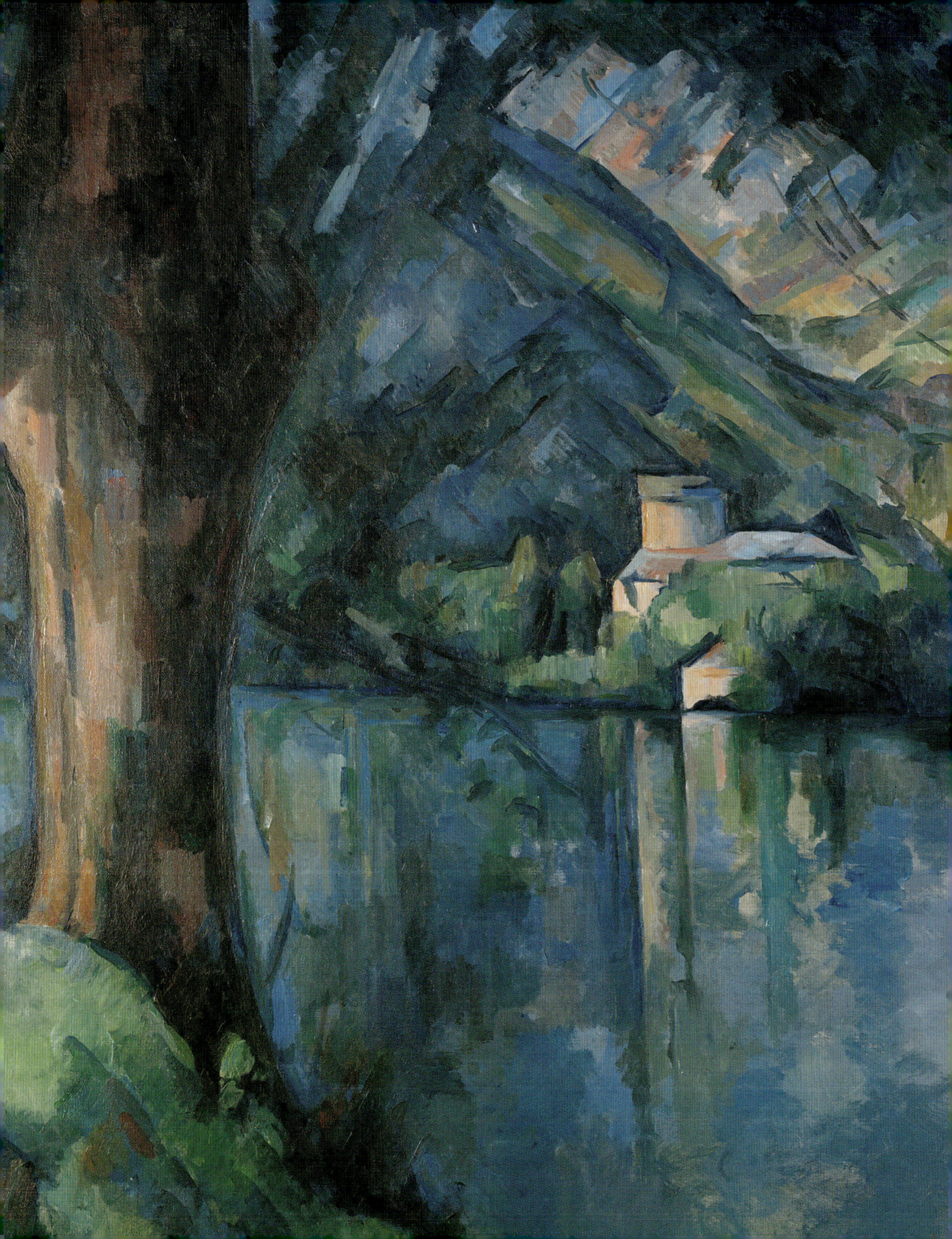

Cézanne's Project:
The "Harmony parallel to Nature"

JOHN HOUSE

It is difficult today to recapture the strangeness of Paul Cézanne's art as it was seen by its first viewers. In the wake of Cubism and its legacy, Cézanne's picture surfaces and his treatment of figures pose no great challenge. However, some sense of the strangeness of this art – its radical difference from the art of his contemporaries – emerged from the exhibition *1900: Art at the Crossroads*, presented at the Royal Academy of Arts in London in 1999; here, a small number of canvases by Cézanne in various genres – one portrait, one self-portrait, one bather subject, three landscapes, one still life – were juxtaposed with a vast array of canvases by his contemporaries. Viewed in this context, Cézanne's art stood out for his rejection of the dominant modes of the epoch – the attempt to give an illusion of physical presence to the figures depicted and a fluent, virtuoso handling of paint. By contrast, Cézanne's canvases seemed quiet and austere, withholding immediate visual gratification. This essay seeks to analyse what it was about his art that seemed so different, and to suggest how this might be described as the core of his artistic project.

From one point of view, Cézanne adhered to the established nineteenth-century frameworks of the art world, in his exploration of the various genres of subject-matter. Rather than specialising in one, as many of his contemporaries did, he continued throughout his career to paint canvases in all the major genres. The Bather subjects of his last years (e.g. RP 855; fig. 8) belong to the lineage of the classicising idyll, though wholly lacking any overt mythological or allegorical content; the Card Players of the 1890s (e.g. cat. 6) can be viewed in relation both to the low-life genre painting of the seventeenth century and to the French peasant paintings of the nineteenth century; he continued to paint portraits and self-portraits until his last years; landscape played a central role in his art from the early 1870s onwards; and still life became a theme of ever-increasing importance for him.[1]

In his determination to explore the potential of all the major genres, Cézanne had as models two immediate predecessors whose art offered him highly significant examples, and also a challenge, in his early career – Gustave Courbet and Edouard Manet, each of whom had refused to specialise in a single genre. However, in one crucial respect Cézanne did challenge the principles of classification by genre, by overturning

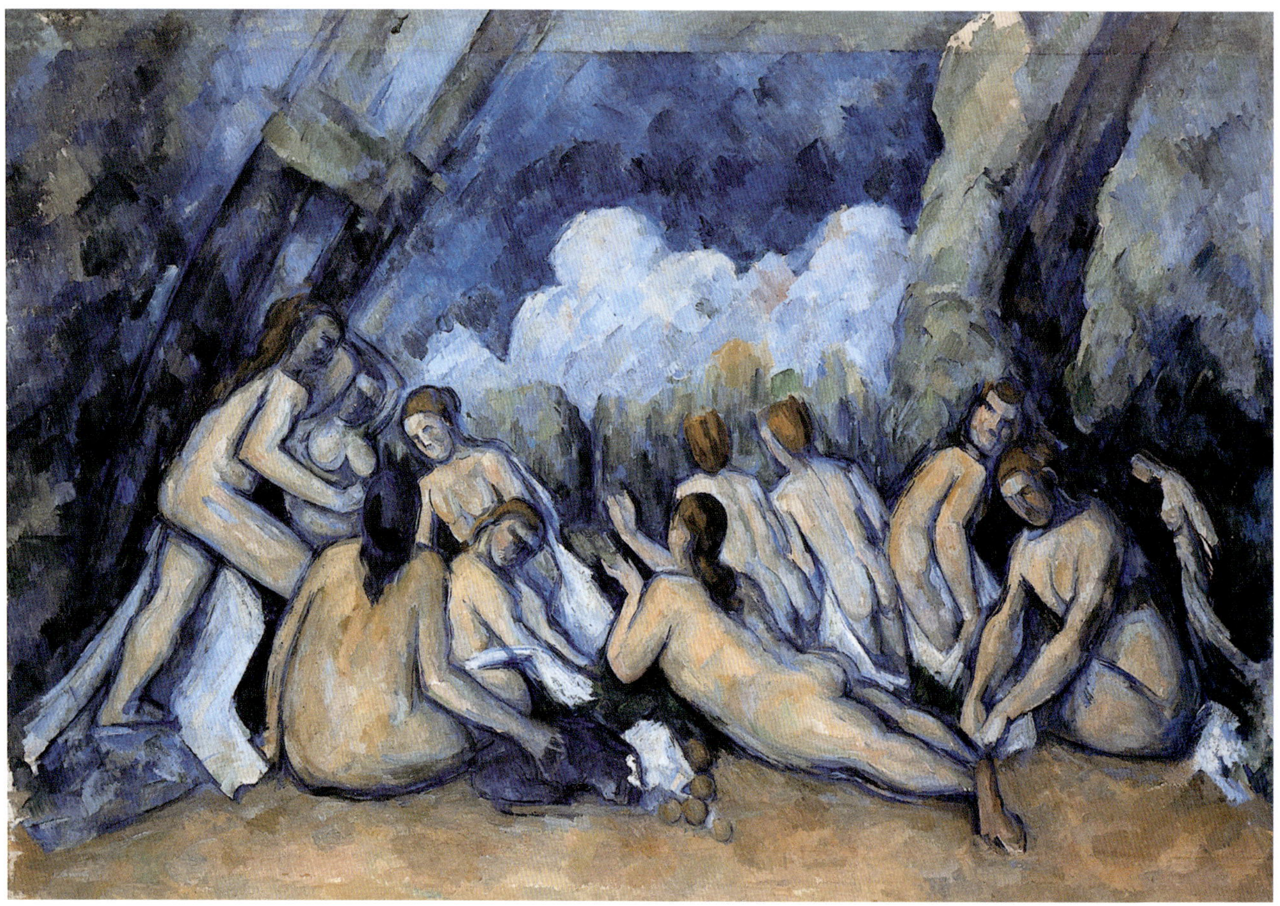

the hierarchy which had attributed supreme significance to major figure-subjects and considered landscape and especially still life as minor, subsidiary genres. In particular, the scale and ambition of his still lifes (see especially cat. 8) mark a rejection of this hierarchy and of the value systems for which that hierarchy stood, privileging significant human action over the study of inanimate objects. Cézanne's famous comment that he wanted to "astonish Paris with an apple" should perhaps be viewed in this context, rather than primarily as evidence of some special significance that apples held for him.[2]

Classification by genres allows us to see significant continuities through Cézanne's entire career; however, as is universally recognised, his specific choice of subjects and the ways in which he treated them changed dramatically, from the emotive content and bold facture of his early paintings to the inexpressive figures and taut structure of his late work. This change has conventionally been dated to the early 1870s and attributed to the effect that the experience of working alongside Camille

   CÉZANNE'S PROJECT: THE "HARMONY PARALLEL TO NATURE"

Pissarro in these years had on him. Certainly, as we shall see, his paint handling changed markedly and definitively at this date, but it has recently become clear that he continued to treat emotive and highly charged sexual themes such as *L'Eternel féminin* (RP 299; fig. 9) until the early 1880s,[3] thus proving that we cannot see the changes in technique and subject-matter as facets of a single catalytic moment.

The heightened emotional register and crude handling of the early paintings have conventionally been seen as unbridled expressions of Cézanne's personal feelings and his transformation in the 1870s as a process of disciplining himself, of "self-chastening",[4] of sublimating his desires into the process of painting.[5] However, André Dombrowski has recently argued most persuasively that Cézanne's manner in the 1860s should not be analysed in terms of self-revelation, but should, rather, be viewed as a calculated alternative to the disengagement of Manet's view of modern urban life, emphasising instead extremes of subjectivity, of human feeling and action, as the essence of modern experience.[6] In this, Cézanne's early works closely parallel the mood and tone of the early novels of his close friend Emile Zola, such as *Thérèse Raquin* of 1867, themselves such a contrast to the pseudo-scientific detachment of his later fiction.

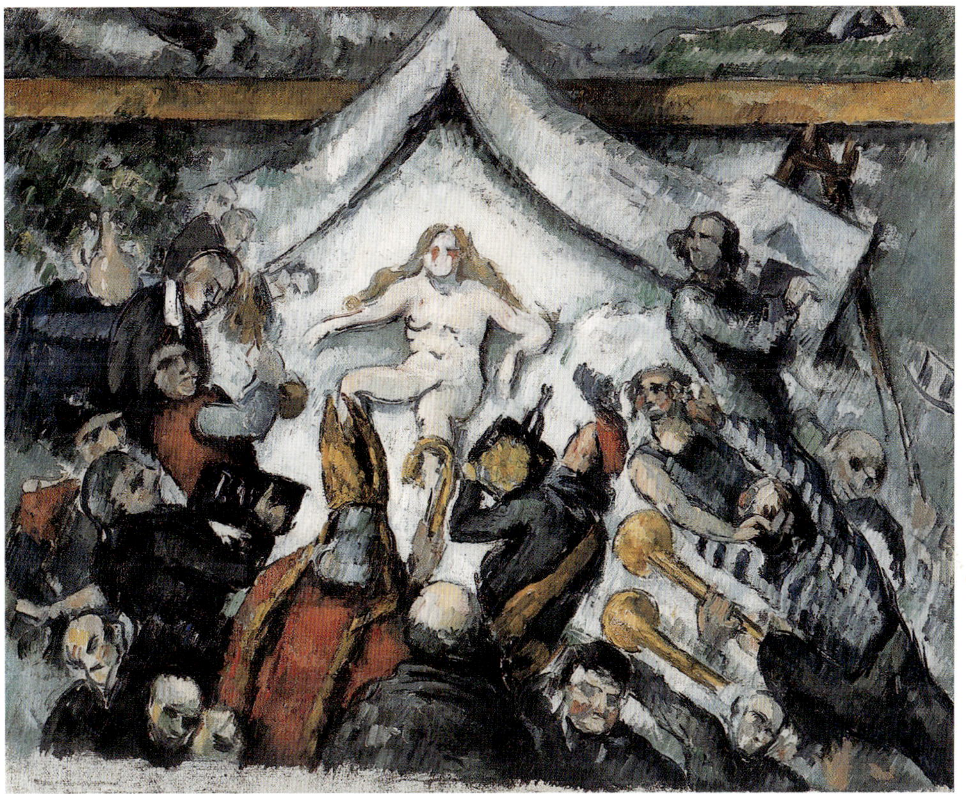

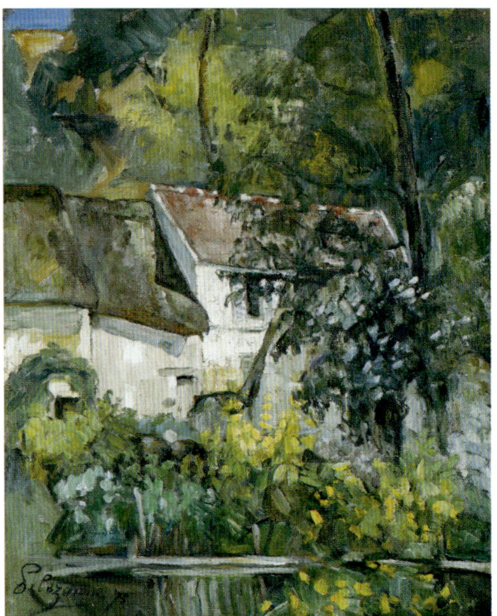

Viewed in this light, the changes in Cézanne's work through the 1870s should be seen as a deliberate change of pictorial mode in favour of a quite different notion of subjectivity, one that focused on the uniqueness of the individual's sensory experiences – his or her *sensations*.[7] This did not immediately preclude subjects that dealt with sexual desire as he explored the possibilities of figure painting, but by the mid 1880s he had come to focus on the theme of the male or female bather, treated in ways that eschewed any overt allegorical or narrative content.

In parenthesis, in the present context it should be noted that Samuel Courtauld's taste for Cézanne's art had its limitations. He bought none of the early work, and no Bather compositions. Most tellingly, he bought and resold a canvas by Cézanne depicting a subject that is not represented elsewhere in his collection – the artist's wife Hortense Fiquet (*Madame Cézanne*; R P 685; fig. 5). In the case of both the Bathers and the portrait, it seems possible that Courtauld was troubled by the austerity and detachment of Cézanne's depictions of the female body and his wife's face (such a far cry from Renoir's *La Loge*, one of Courtauld's favourite pictures), whilst responding enthusiastically to his treatment of the male peasant figure (see cat. 6 and 7), as well as landscape and still life.

Cézanne's mark-making

The key to the novelty of Cézanne's mature art in its original contexts lies in the relationship between his chosen subjects – all of them in broad terms conventional – and his mark-making on the canvas or the sheet of paper. The remainder of this essay will explore this, analysing his pictorial devices in relation to the precepts that he expressed in letters and conversation, and seeking to relate practice to theory. Virtually all of his pronouncements about his art date from the mid 1890s onwards, from the final decade of his life; we have very little verbal evidence from the artist from the years around 1880, when, as will be argued, the crucial developments in his practice took place. Indeed, his later comments are theory applied to practice, providing retrospective verbal formulations for already well-established visual developments in his art. Moreover, many of his comments, and particularly his letters to Emile Bernard of 1904–06, published in full below (pp. 146–65), were responses to younger artists and critics who sought to place theory before practice. Clearly Cézanne felt a need to articulate his ideas about his art in words; but, as the letters to Bernard make clear, these words were secondary to the practice that they sought to describe; they were verbal formulations of something ultimately non-verbal.

Cézanne's paint handling in the 1860s varied greatly, from the broad and free-flowing ribbons of paint in canvases such as *La Douleur* (*La Madeleine*) of about 1868 (R P 146; Musée d'Orsay, Paris) to the extrava-

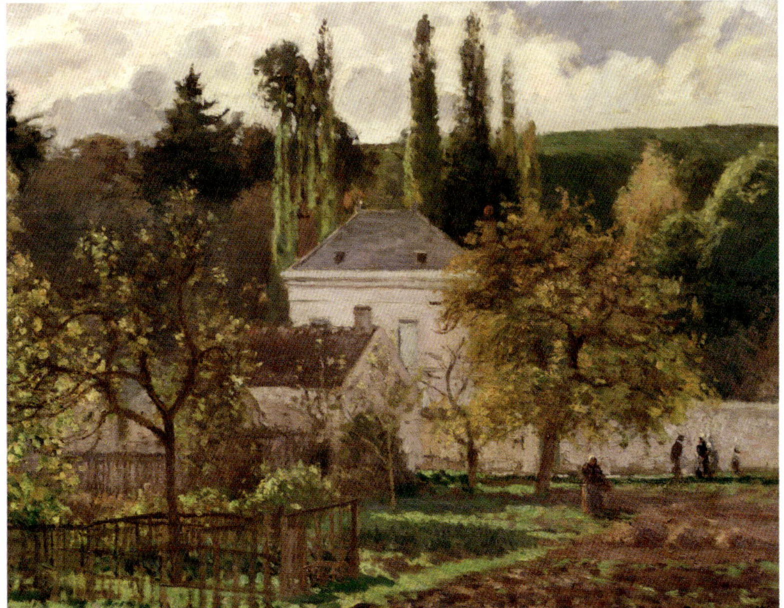

gantly encrusted palette-knife surfaces of his portraits of Uncle Dominic of *c*. 1866. These paint surfaces were an integral part of Cézanne's project, to create paintings that demonstrated the strength of his temperament and his *sensations*; it was this technique that Cézanne is reported, in later years, to have described as "*peinture bien couillarde*" – loosely translatable as ballsy or spunky painting.[8]

The contrast with Pissarro's technique, at the moment when Cézanne came to work with him around Pontoise and Auvers in 1872, could not be greater. By this date Pissarro, like Claude Monet in the same years, had evolved a delicate and flexible representational shorthand, which allowed him to deploy a very wide variety of paint-touches in response to the varied forms and textures that he saw in the scene before him. Around 1890, Monet put this procedure into words, in conversation with the American painter Lilla Cabot Perry: "When you go out to paint, try to forget what object you have before you .... Merely think, here is a little square of blue, here an oblong of pink, here a streak of yellow, and paint it just as it looks to you, the exact colour and shape, until it gives your own naïve impression of the scene before you."[9]

The lessons of this process, dependent on close visual scrutiny, never left Cézanne; to the last, he insisted that his visual *sensations*, based on the close study of nature, were the starting-point of his art (see e.g. Letter B9). But Cézanne's paintings of the early 1870s show that in practice he did not readily adapt to this approach to representation. For instance, in *The House of Père Lacroix* of 1873 (RP 201; fig. 10), a canvas that was probably exhibited in the first Impressionist group show in 1874 with the title *Etude: paysage à Auvers*, there is an awkwardness about the touch that suggests that he was finding it difficult to accommodate his mark-making to the task of notating the range of textures in the scene; comparison with the delicate, constantly varied touch in a canvas by Pissarro such as *Villa at L'Hermitage, Pontoise* (fig. 11), painted during the same summer, emphasises Cézanne's comparative lack of facility. Unlike Monet, Cézanne was never a fluent open-air sketcher in oil paint.

Cézanne's reversion to the use of the palette knife in the mid 1870s, shown in its most extreme form in *L'Etang des Sœurs* (cat. 1, detail fig. 44),

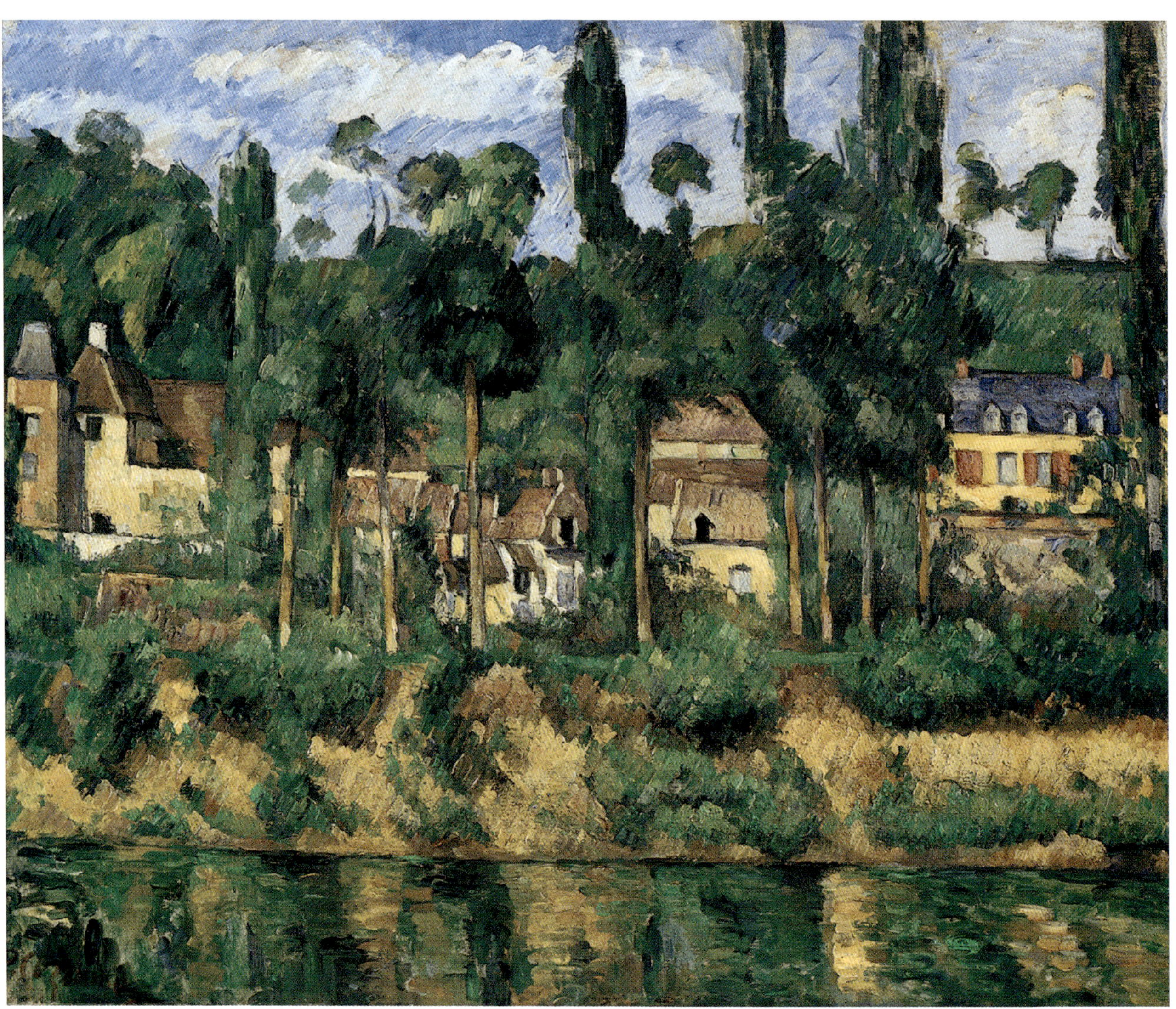

   CÉZANNE'S PROJECT: THE "HARMONY PARALLEL TO NATURE"

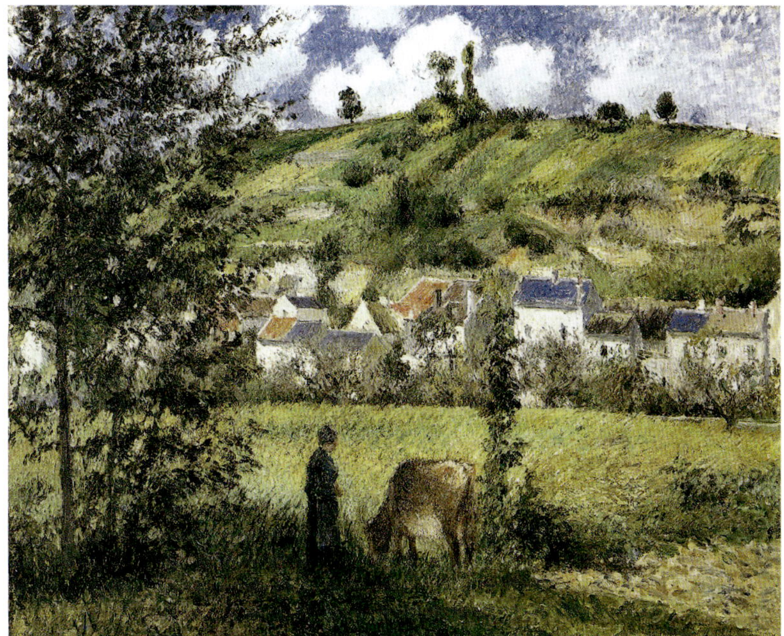

can be seen as an initial rejection of the informal, variegated touch so characteristic of Pissarro's, Monet's and Sisley's landscapes of *c.* 1872–74. Here, the movements of the knife give only the most approximate sense of the forms and textures of the trees; instead, sequences of loosely wedge-shaped colour planes suggest the two layers of foliage – the shadowed foreground tree silhouetted against the sunlit zones of leaves seen across the water. At just the same time, Pissarro, too, readopted the palette knife, creating surfaces with more closely integrated surface textures than his canvases of 1872–73;[10] comparison with his *Small Bridge, Pontoise* (fig. 43), very possibly executed side by side with *L'Etang des Sœurs*, shows a comparable interest in the surface effects that could be achieved with the knife, though Pissarro's strokes are smaller in scale and differentiate more delicately between the various forms and textures in the scene.

Cézanne seems not to have used the knife after 1875. In his landscapes of the next three years, he returned to the more broken textures of *Etude: paysage à Auvers*, but with one significant difference. Increasingly, in certain parts of the canvas, particularly in areas of foliage, groups of brushstrokes of roughly the same size and shape begin to run parallel to each other, so that whole zones of the picture take on a shared rhythm that ignores the varied directions of the foliage depicted.[11] By 1879–80, this effect became far more marked and far more systematic: in canvases such as *Le Château de Médan* of 1880 (RP 437; fig. 12) and *Houses in Provence* of around the same date (RP 438; fig. 16), much of the canvas is covered with evenly weighted parallel strokes – Cézanne's so-called 'constructive stroke'.[12] These run in extensive sequences and often from lower left to upper right, though other areas are less systematically worked; within these sequences of parallel strokes, nuances and variations of colour may be introduced without changes to the rhythm and scale of the strokes. In some areas of these canvases this can be seen as a mode of representing grass or foliage, though the systematically parallel strokes clearly do not record the actual textures that Cézanne saw; but elsewhere, for instance on the riverbank in *Le Château de Médan* and the rocky hillsides in *Houses in Provence*, the parallel strokes bear no visual relationship whatsoever to what is depicted. Seen from close to, they do not function representationally at all, and can only be seen as two-dimensional marks on the canvas; it is only when the image is seen as a whole that they fall into place and register as part of the fabric of the overall scene.

In the work of Pissarro and Monet in the same years, around 1880 (e.g. figs. 13, 14), we also find an increasing fragmentation of touch, so that the individual marks can less readily be seen as a shorthand for the separate elements within the scene represented. This, it may be argued, was a means by which they sought to give a sense of the extreme delicacy and finesse of their vision, translated into ever more complex sequences of coloured touches.[13] However, these marks never function in the same way as Cézanne's; they always convey some sense of the variety of the textures represented and continue to differentiate between distinct zones of the canvas.

Practice and theory

We must now stand back and ask what these developments in Cézanne's art signify. In his writing and his comments about his art, Cézanne made a distinction that the other members of the Impressionist group did not make, or at least did not make nearly so explicitly. He drew a categorical distinction between seeing and making – between, in his terminology, *sensation* and *réalisation*. The *sensation* was the uniquely personal sensory experience that formed the starting-point of a painting; by contrast, the *réalisation* was a question of artistic methods, procedures. In a letter to Bernard he insisted that these needed to be viewed separately: "I believe in the logical development of what we see and experience through the study of nature, even if that means concerning myself with technical questions afterwards" (Letter B9). Writing to Louis Aurenche in 1904 he made the same distinction: "If the strong sensation of nature – and for sure I have this – is the necessary basis for any conception of art . . . the knowledge of the means of expressing our emotion is no less essential, and can only be gained through long experience".[14] In relation to colour, he is on record as saying: "I wanted to copy nature, but did not

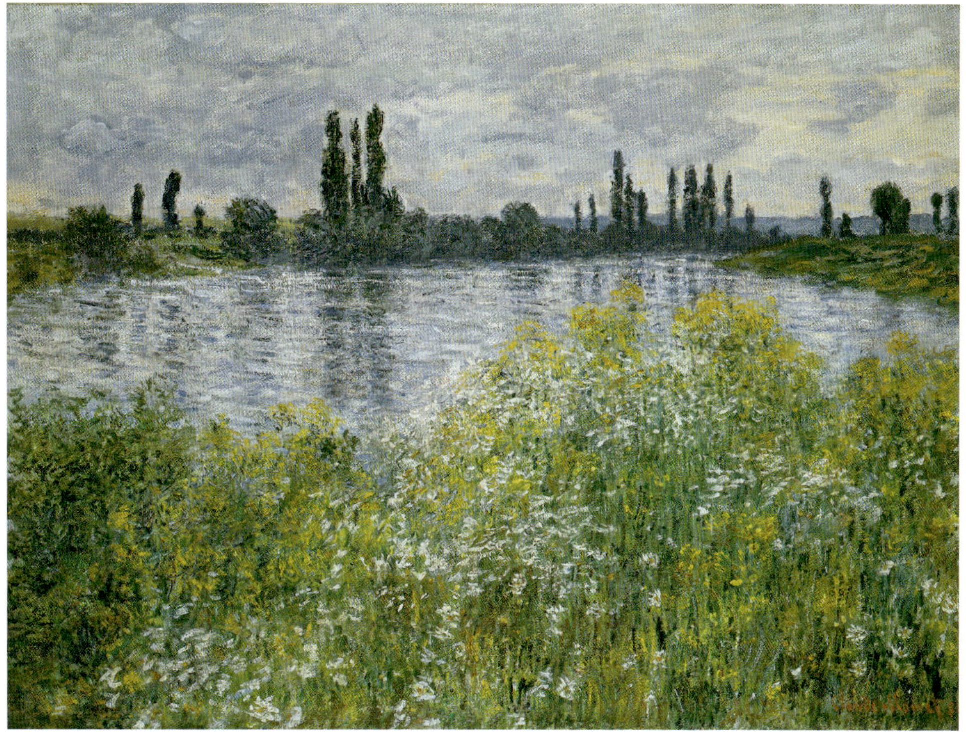

succeed. But I was pleased with myself when I discovered that sunlight
. . . could not be reproduced, but that it must be *represented* by something
else – by colour".[15] In 1897, he made the succinct formulation that art
was "a harmony parallel to nature", once again emphasising that it
was something categorically different from nature itself.[16]

This is the core of Cézanne's theory of art, but, as we have already
insisted, the crucial point about this theory is that it could never be
separated from practice. Cézanne did at times describe his views about
art as "theories", but everything that he said shows that theory for its
own sake was anathema to him, and he emphasised this in his letters
to Bernard, insisting that all Bernard's words were worth nothing if his
practice was not firmly grounded in the direct, sustained observation of
nature: "The painter should be wary of the literary spirit, which so often
diverts the painter from his true path, the concrete study of nature,
to lose himself for too long in intangible speculations" (see Letter B2).
"The painter must dedicate himself totally to the study of nature, and
seek to produce paintings that will be an education. Talking about art is
virtually useless. The *litterateur* expresses himself in abstractions while
the painter gives concrete expression to his sensory experiences, his
perceptions by means of drawing and colour" (see Letter B3).

The parallel stroke was Cézanne's first mode of establishing that the
work of art was categorically different from the experience of nature.

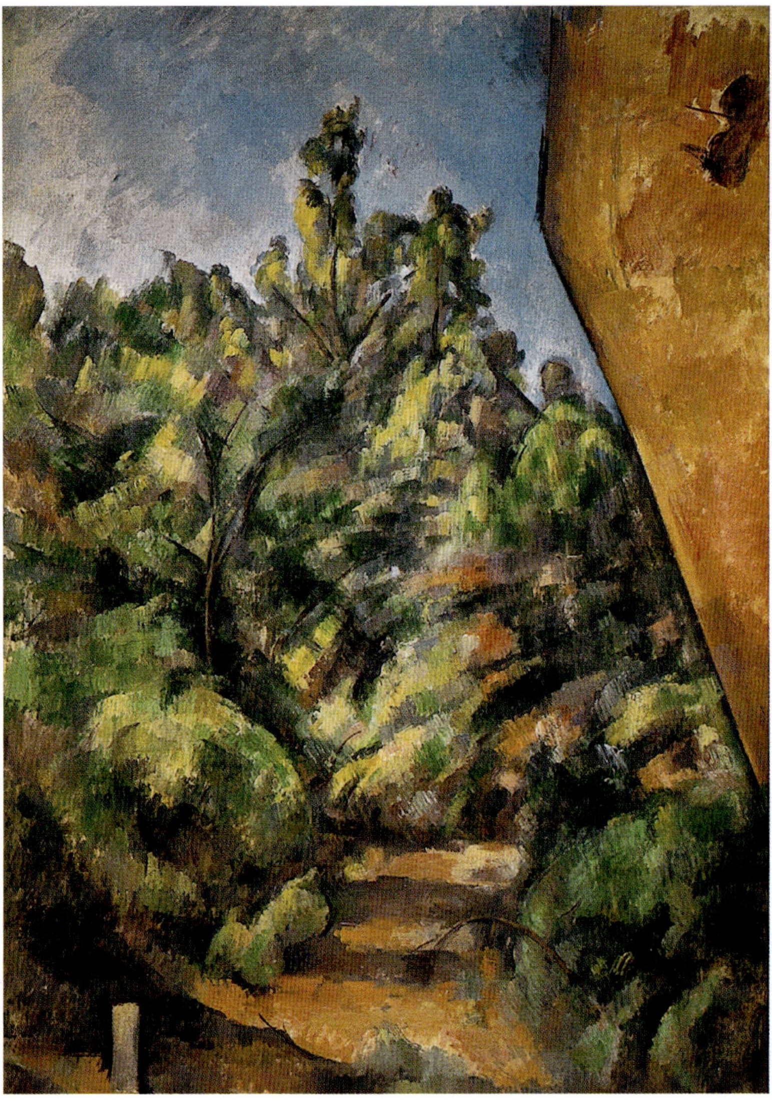

This was not a pursuit of flatness as such or a concern with the two-dimensionality of the picture plane as an end in itself, but rather a rejection of illusionism or trompe-l'oeil, insisting that the painter must seek the means most appropriate to his medium – colour on a flat surface – in his search to "realise" his *sensations*. The parallel stroke is assertively anti-illusionistic; it appears on the canvas as a thing in itself, a mark that cannot be seen in any sense as an attempt to create a transparent image of an underlying reality, out there in the external world.

Initially, around 1880, Cézanne seems to have needed to use this assertive brush-unit to ensure that his paintings were seen as just that, as paintings. However, he came gradually to realise that a whole range

CÉZANNE'S PROJECT: THE "HARMONY PARALLEL TO NATURE"

of touches could serve this purpose. The requirement was simple, but categorical; these strokes should expressly not function like the mark-making that Monet described to Lilla Perry: "... here is a little square of blue, here an oblong of pink, here a streak of yellow, and paint it just as it looks to you, the exact colour and shape". It was not only the parallel stroke that met the requirement. From the mid 1880s on, Cézanne's handling became more relaxed and far more varied; in *Le Lac d'Annecy* of 1896 (cat. 9), for instance, the marks on the background mountains are a variegated combination of smaller wedge-shaped strokes with flatter touches, whereas in *The Red Rock*, probably painted around 1895 (RP 799; fig. 15), he returned to a very soft parallel stroke in the foliage areas, but used it with such delicacy that it can never be seen as a direct representation of the textures of the pine trees.

In all of his later paintings, the shape of the individual coloured touches never resembles any one element in the scene depicted. Taken separately, these touches are not representational; they only gain their representational value as part of the whole. However, their role as an integral part of the ensemble was always crucial: Cézanne never gave the marks any value in their own right that was independent of the "harmony parallel to nature" that he sought to create on his canvas. A comparable role is played by his use of accents of closely related colour in different zones and different spatial planes of the canvas (see e.g. cat. 3, 4, 9); these ensure that the painting's "harmony" is viewed in terms of relationships within the fabric of the picture.

In this context, the Bather paintings (e.g. fig. 8) are an anomaly. Although this was clearly a subject to which he attributed great importance until the end of his life, the canvases were not based in any sense on the *sensation*, on his direct visual experience of the world around him. Though occasional figures were loosely related to poses from past art or from Cézanne's own youthful life studies, most of the figures and the overall compositions were the fruits of his imagination. Cézanne himself, speaking to Emile Bernard, attributed this to his age, saying that he could only ask a woman aged over fifty to pose naked for him, and that he would not be able to find such a model in his home town, Aix-en-Provence; in conversation with Francis Jourdain, he attributed this to the scrutiny to which he, as a Catholic, was subject from the Jesuits.[17] Bernard himself suspected that Cézanne did not trust himself in the presence of a young naked model – surely readily available in Paris, if not in Aix.

Personal anxieties may indeed have played a part in his decision not to work from the live model. However, the resulting qualities of his nude figures can also be viewed as wholly consistent with his treatment of other themes. Figures painted from the imagination ran no risk of appearing illusionistic; more precisely, they could never invoke imaginings of any sense except the visual. In 1907, Maurice Denis quoted his friend

Paul Sérusier's dictum about the "purity" of Cézanne's art: "About an apple painted by a vulgar painter, one says, I'd like to eat that. About one of Cézanne's apples, one says, it's beautiful! One wouldn't dare peel it, one would like to copy it."[18] Transposed to the representation of the nude, the comparison would be with Renoir's nude figures and the strong sense of tactility that they invoke; by contrast, one could never imagine reaching out to touch the flesh of a figure painted by Cézanne.

The later Bather compositions present images of a world of symbiotic harmony in an imagined, idyllic setting. In the paintings themselves, this harmony is transposed into the configurations of colour and form that make up the composition; the viewer never feels invited to enter those woodland glades. Rigorously – ruthlessly even, given the strange forms of some of his bather figures – he ensured that the only life that the viewer can imagine for his figures is their life within the visual field of the canvas. This disjunction between the world depicted within the picture and the effect evoked by the picture itself is still more vivid in *L'Eternel féminin* (fig. 9): here the subject itself is sexual voyeurism, as a motley assembly of figures, among them a bishop and a painter, crowd admiringly around a seemingly enthroned naked woman. Yet the picture itself is treated with insistent sequences of austere parallel strokes, characteristic of Cézanne's facture *c.* 1880,[19] and the figure is depicted so summarily, and her face with such apparent crudity, that the viewer of the picture is in no way invited to empathise with the sensual experiences of the men that the subject of the picture evokes.

A further way in which Cézanne emphasised the categorical distinction between the viewer's space and the world that he created within the painting was by placing barriers of various sorts across the foreground of his canvases, thus preventing any imaginative form of entry into the pictorial space. Sometimes this is achieved by a foreground that gives the viewer no foothold, as in *La Montagne Sainte-Victoire* (cat. 4), sometimes by a strongly horizontal band that blocks access into the space, as in the rocks and the band above them (a wall? or a path?) in *Houses in Provence* (fig. 16), sometimes by an area of open water, as in *Le Lac d'Annecy* (cat. 9), and sometimes by an open foreground that gives the scene no clear spatial articulation, as in *Tall Trees at the Jas de Bouffan* (cat. 3) and *Farm in Normandy* (cat. 2). Even where a receding road or path leads into the foreground, this is treated in a way that denies imaginative entry. Like-wise the Bather compositions are tautly staged within the rectangular format of the canvas, denying the possibility that the viewer might imagine observing the grouping of figures from any other angle, let alone joining them in their glade.

Taken together, the typical compositional formats and the execution of Cézanne's paintings ensure that the harmony they present is seen as categorically distinct from, as well as parallel to, the 'nature' they represent. Cézanne would have found welcome confirmation for this approach in Eugène Delacroix's unfinished *Dictionnaire des beaux-arts*, first published in 1895; here, Delacroix recognised this distinction overtly, insisting that the *touche* (the visible brushwork) was fundamental to the language of painting: "The *touche* is a means, like any other, that contributes to expressing thought in painting . . . . What can one say of the masters who drily emphasise contours while rejecting the *touche*? There are no more contours in nature than there are *touches*. One must always return to the means that best suit each art, that are the language of that art."[20]

In Cézanne's 'opinions' about his art, a set of maxims published by Emile Bernard in 1904, during the artist's lifetime, he defined what he was seeking in his art, thus demonstrating what he meant in practical terms by "*realisation*".

FIG. 16
Paul Cézanne, *Houses in Provence:*
The Riaux Valley near l'Estaque,
c. 1880
Oil on canvas, 65 × 81.3 cm
National Gallery of Art,
Washington
Collection of Mr. and Mrs.
Paul Mellon

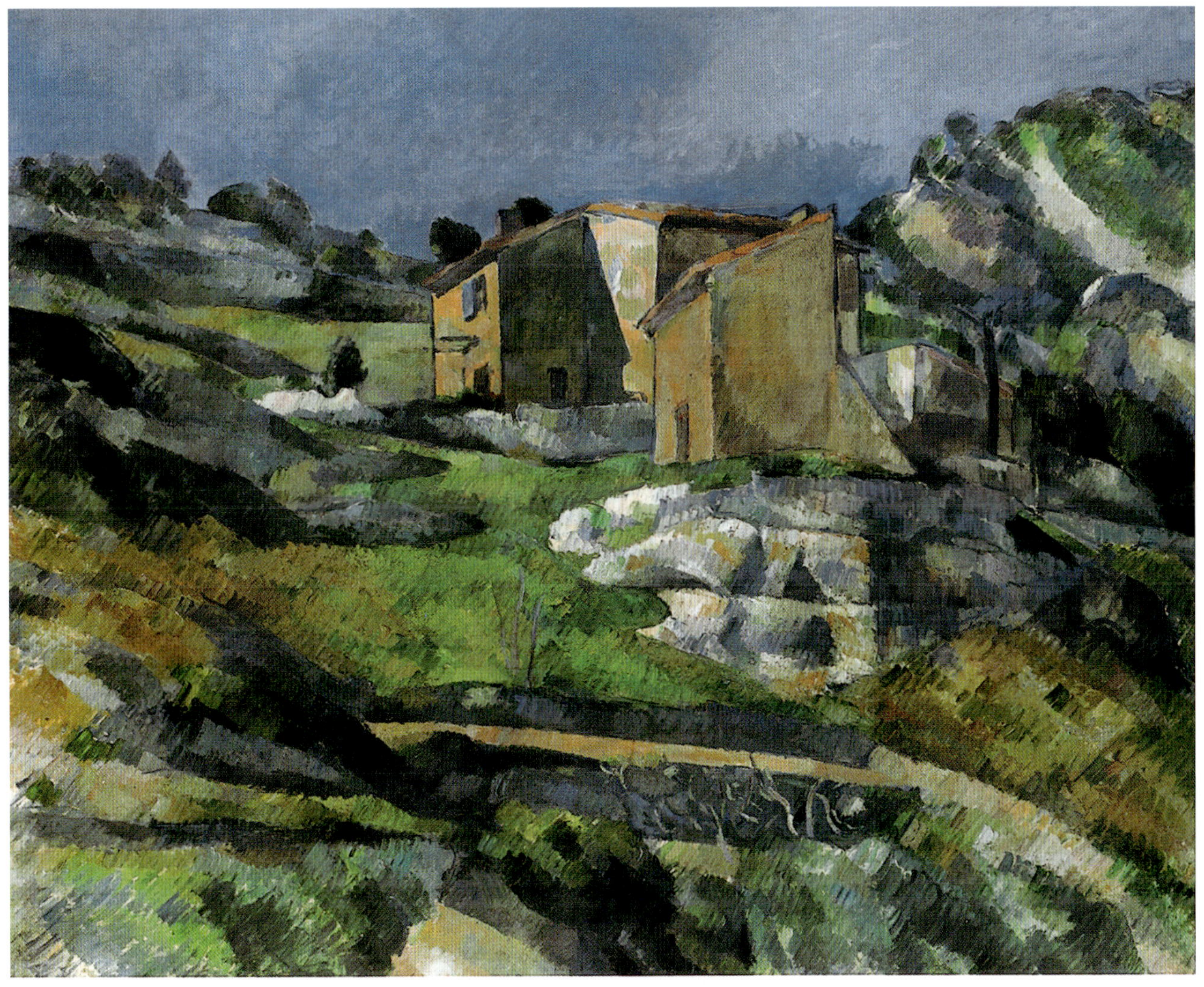

"To read nature is to see it through the veil of an interpretation in terms of coloured touches that follow each other according to a law of harmony. These principal colours are thus analysed through modulations. Painting is classifying one's coloured *sensations*."

"There is no line, there is no modelling, there are only contrasts. It is not black and white that create these contrasts, but the coloured *sensation*. Modelling results from the precise rapport of colours. When they are harmoniously juxtaposed and are all in place, the painting models itself."

"One should not say model, one should say modulate."

"Drawing and colour are in no way separate; as one paints, one draws; the more the colour harmonises, the more precise the drawing becomes. The form is at its fullest when the colour is at its richest. Contrasts and rapports of colours – that is the secret of drawing and modelling."[21]

Thus a fully realised painting for Cézanne was one in which form and space were conveyed by modulations and contrasts of colour alone. Line as an autonomous element played no part in this formulation. Viewed in these terms, a prime example of such realisation is the juxtaposition of orange and blue at the centre of *La Montagne Sainte-Victoire seen from Bibémus* of *c*. 1897 (RP 837; fig. 17), which so vividly evokes the miles of space between quarry and mountain by the contrast of colour-zones alone.

The question of finish

However, very many of Cézanne's canvases, whether landscapes or other subjects, do not function in this way. Areas are often left unpainted, and elsewhere dark lines, mainly though not always blue, remain visible on the canvas surface; and many forms seem unresolved or incomplete (see especially cat. 10). The lines and bare areas and the ambiguities of form force us to address the question of 'finish' in Cézanne's art – or rather, to ask how many of his canvases are fully "realised" in the terms in which he understood *réalisation*.

This issue played a central part in Robert Ratcliffe's doctoral dissertation of 1960,[22] and has again been much discussed in recent years. Writing in 1998, Yve-Alain Bois concluded: "This state of unfinish is of course not that...".[23] However, the exhibition *Cézanne Finished – Unfinished*, held in Vienna and Zurich in 2000, once again highlighted the issue, and revealed a Cézanne strikingly unlike the artist presented at the London–Paris–Philadelphia retrospective of 1995–96, concentrating as it did on canvases that were very unevenly worked, rather than the artist's most resolved paintings.[24]

Cézanne himself freely admitted that he had failed to achieve full *réalisation* in many of his canvases. A number of his recorded comments confirm that he was very well aware of this.[25] In 1906, he explained to

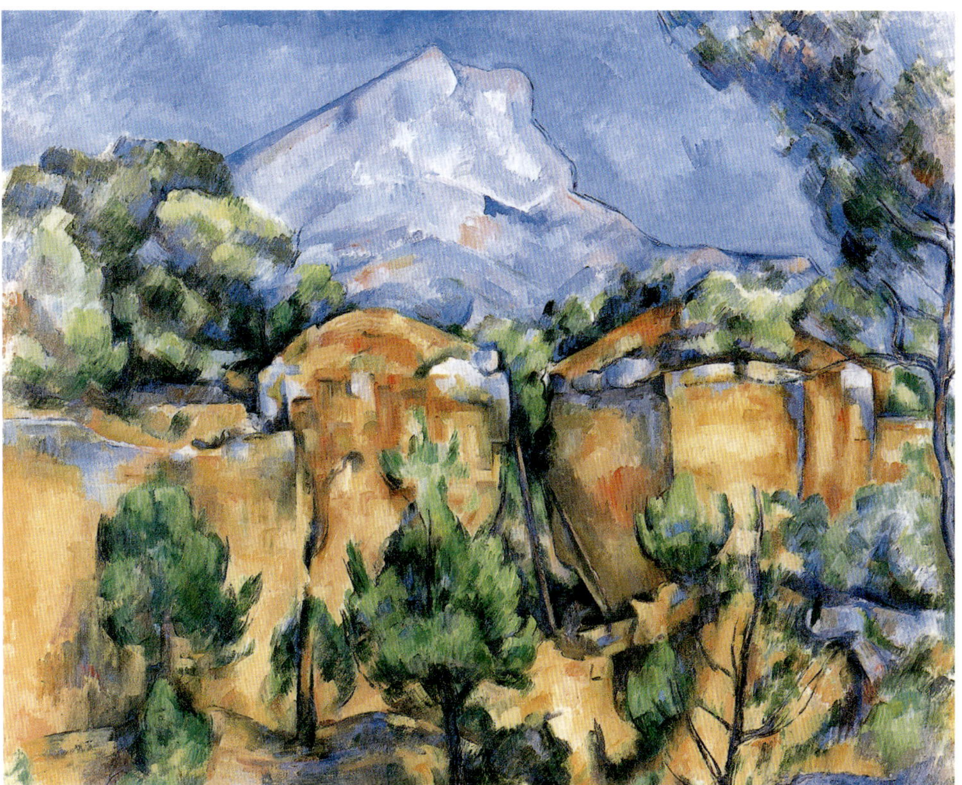

Karl Osthaus, founder of the Folkwang Museum at Hagen, the difficulties that he had in suggesting spatial depth by colour: "And saying this, his fingers followed the edges of various planes in his pictures. He showed exactly where he had succeeded in suggesting depth and where the solution had yet to be found; here the colour remained colour without becoming the expression of distance."[26] He explained to Bernard the reasons for these difficulties: "But being old, around seventy, the coloured sensory experiences that create light are the cause of abstractions that do not allow me to cover my canvas or to pursue the delimitation of objects when their points of contact are subtle and delicate; the result of this is that my image or picture is incomplete" (see Letter B8).

In the same letter, he vigorously criticised artists who surrounded their contours with a black line.[27] Yet dark lines, generally in deep blue, very frequently occur in his work. Sometimes these act as approximate contours to the forms depicted, as for instance around the mountain top in *La Montagne Sainte-Victoire* (cat. 4) and around much of the Cupid statuette in *Still Life with Plaster Cupid* (cat. 8); sometimes they are used to emphasise the direction of a particular form within a composition, without being tied to its contours, as in the foliage at upper centre of *Farm in Normandy* (cat. 2) and the branches at the upper right of *Le Lac d'Annecy* (cat. 9).

The clearest indication of the role and function of these lines in his paintings was recorded by R.P. Rivière and J.F. Schnerb after their visit to Cézanne's studio in 1905: "Cezanne did not seek to represent forms by a line. Contour only existed for him as the place where one form ended and another form began. If one looks at his unfinished canvases, the objects in the foreground plane are often left unpainted and their silhouette only indicated by the background against which they are profiled. No line in principle, a form exists only in relation to the neighbouring forms. The black lines that often run through his paintings were not for Cezanne an element that he intended to be added to colour, but merely a manner of restating more easily the ensemble of a form by contour before modelling it by colour."[28]

On this account, all of these contours must be seen as in some sense provisional, as markers to indicate points in the canvas that Cézanne intended to refine, or redefine, by coloured modelling. Since his financial security meant that he never had to complete works for them to meet the expectations of the market, many of his paintings were abandoned in this state, as he moved on to other canvases, other projects.[29]

However, we must ask whether his comments to Rivière and Schnerb, inflected with his customary modesty, tell the whole story, and whether the frailty of old age, invoked in his letter to Bernard, was the only explanation for the seeming non-resolution of so many parts of his canvases. These linear marks play such a central role in so many of his paintings, even those that he seems to have considered more fully realised, that we can only assume that Cézanne was willing to leave them visible on the canvas surface, even if, in principle, their presence indicated that he had failed to achieve total *réalisation*. They act simultaneously to lead the eye to particular elements within the scene and to reinforce the primary axes of the pictorial composition.

Beyond this, these lines provide another type of mark within the canvas that cannot be read illusionistically; for all their importance in articulating the forms and space in a scene, they remain categorically two-dimensional, complementing the effect of the non-illusionistic brushstrokes that we have discussed. Likewise, the areas of unpainted canvas that appear even in more highly worked pictures act as a further reminder of this; at times, they can be seen as playing a representational role when seen in relation to the coloured touches around them, as in the figures' hands in *The Card Players* (cat. 6), but, when viewed from close to, they reinforce the two-dimensionality of the picture and the artifice of its making.

A further indication that the linear marks were not merely marks of failure for Cézanne is their role in his watercolours. Here, the translucency of the paint-layers meant that the initial underdrawing necessarily remained visible, and close examination shows that Cézanne continued to add drawn lines, whether in pencil or watercolour, at later stages of the execution of many sheets (see e. g. cat. 15, 16, 17 and pp. 51–53).[30] Thus throughout the execution of a watercolour he was actively exploring the relationships between line and colour. The fact that he included watercolours in public exhibitions, both in the 1870s and at the end of his life, shows that he felt that they could effectively represent his pictorial project.[31]

Another recurrent feature in Cézanne's paintings may perhaps be viewed in the same terms – his apparent distortions of the objects in front of him. These take a number of different forms – sloping verticals (see cat. 6 and 8), discontinuous horizontals, misshapen or asymmetrical objects (see cat. 5), as well as shapes with incomplete or multiple edges (see cat. 8 and 10). Robert Ratcliffe demonstrated that these distortions emerged and became accentuated as Cézanne worked up a composition, focusing on local relationships of colour and form in the part of the canvas on which he was working, without being concerned with overall representational consistency.[32] A particularly visible example can be seen in the unfinished *Still Life with Water Jug* of *c*. 1892 (RP 738; fig. 18), where the horizontal line that indicates the back edge of the table to the left of the jug has been placed at three different levels; close examination suggests that the first was the lowest of the three, which coincides with the continuation of the edge to the right of the jug; then the highest

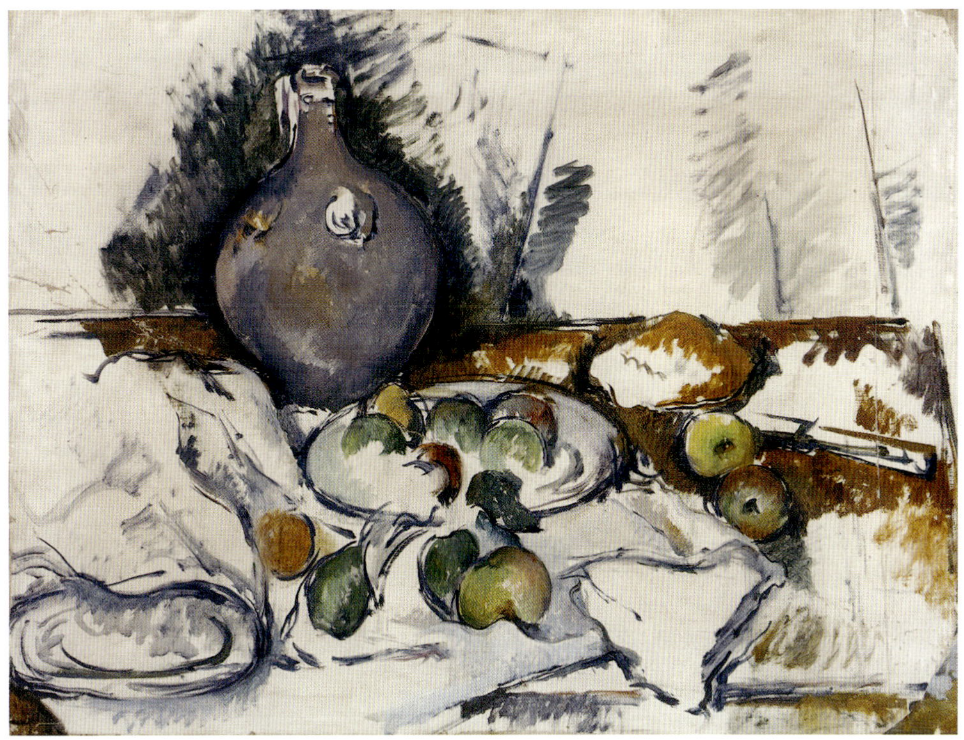

FIG. 18
Paul Cézanne, *Still Life with Water Jug*, c. 1893
Oil on canvas, 53 × 71.1 cm
Tate, London

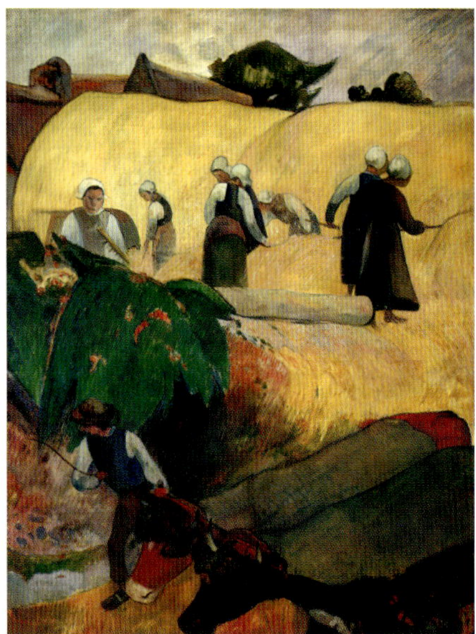

was inserted as an alternative, before he inserted a line between these two, and began to work up the colour planes to this third contour, without adjusting the contours to the right of the jar to match it. Similar manipulation of the edge of a table-top can be seen in *Pot of Primroses and Fruits* of *c*. 1888–90 (cat. 5).

As Rivière and Schnerb noted, Cézanne himself was typically, and perhaps ironically, modest about these distortions: "He did not seem to be unaware of the asymmetry of his bottles, the defective perspective of his bowls. Showing one of his watercolours, he corrected with his finger-nail a bottle that was not vertical, and said, as if excusing himself: 'I am a primitive, I have a lazy eye. I presented myself twice to the Ecole [des Beaux-Arts], but I couldn't get things in proportion: a head interests me, and I make it too big'."[33] However, we must ask whether, like the visible lines and unpainted zones of his paintings, these distortions were a further way in which Cézanne demonstrated the non-illusionism of his canvases. Without being expressly deliberate, they were something that he was happy to leave visible without correcting them, so as to ensure that the viewer's eye continued to explore the forms and colours on the canvas, rather than seeking to enter imaginatively into the physical world depicted.

Cézanne's project

The relative autonomy of Cézanne's brushwork, when described in these terms, invites comparison with the technical experiments of both Paul Gauguin and Georges Seurat during the same years. Gauguin had a complex relationship with Cézanne and formed a significant collection of his work in these years.[34] The two may have worked side by side in 1881, in company with Pissarro, and Gauguin's work of the early to mid 1880s shows an evident debt to Cézanne's use of parallel hatching strokes. However, Gauguin seems to have conceived this technique in rather different terms from Cézanne: in 1881 he wrote to Pissarro asking jokingly if Pissarro could administer a sleeping draught to Cézanne which would lead him to divulge his "exact formula . . . the recipe by which he can sum up the expression of all his sensations in a single, unique procedure";[35] his use of the phrases "exact formula" and "single, unique procedure" suggest that he saw Cézanne as having a systematic method that could be equally well applied to any subject or type of painting. It seems very possible that Pissarro told the ever-suspicious Cézanne something about this letter; whether he did or not, Cézanne in later years harboured deep resentment towards Gauguin, reportedly accusing him of having stolen his *petite sensation* and taken it away on the packet boats.[36] By the late 1880s, Gauguin had turned his back on painting from nature and was advocating a type of painting without emphatic, visible brushwork (*sans exécution*),[37] in which the forms were circumscribed by dark contours, though echoes of Cézanne's paint handling remain in the spare parallel touches in canvases like The Courtauld Gallery's *Haystacks* of 1889 (fig. 19). Speaking to Bernard, Cézanne emphasised his concern to give a clear sense of spatial planes in his paintings, and commented that this was something that Gauguin had never understood.[38] The paraded artifice of Gauguin's technique and the insistent flatness of his paintings creates a radical disjunction between art and nature, rather than seeking, as Cézanne did, to develop a flexible technique that would create a "harmony parallel to nature".

Though Seurat did continue to paint from nature in his landscapes, the pointillist execution that he evolved around 1886 was, like Gauguin's technique, a unitary method that he superimposed on to his entire canvas. It is perhaps no coincidence that it was in the years when Seurat and Gauguin first exhibited canvases displaying their systematic approach to painting that Cézanne began to adopt a more varied and flexible touch (see e.g. cat. 4), as if to demonstrate that his art could not be reduced to a "unique formula".

Working to a preconceived idea had no meaning for Cézanne; his methods were never systematic. Every canvas, throughout its execution, remained a sort of laboratory for him, and his method of painting was a process of constant improvisation, as each touch of paint had to be coordinated, harmonised with those already on the canvas, and in turn conditioned the touches that followed. Nor, as we have seen, did he have any defined notion of what constituted a finished painting; in principle, any canvas might be reworked in his pursuit of that most elusive quality, *réalisation*.

In one crucial respect, Cézanne retained his allegiance to Impressionist ideas until the end of his life, in his insistence on the centrality of his personal *sensations* of nature to his art. However, as we have argued, the relative autonomy of his mark-making differentiated his art from that of both Pissarro and Monet. The challenge that Cézanne faced is highlighted by his conversation with Osthaus, cited above, in which his demonstration of the working of the colour-planes in his pictures was preceded by the declaration that "the principal issue in a painting is to find the right distance. Colour needs to express all the breaks in space. It is there that one recognises a painter's talent."[39] Cézanne's project was to reconcile these two seemingly irreconcilable ambitions – to evoke the fullness of his experience of atmospheric space whilst retaining the autonomy of his personal painterly mark; it was thus that he sought to create a "harmony parallel to nature".

ACKNOWLEDGEMENTS

I am most grateful to Elisabeth Reissner for her helpful and constructive comments on this essay. Quotations from interviews and conversations with Cézanne are translated by the author from the texts published in Doran 1978, and Cézanne's letters, apart from those to Emile Bernard, from *Correspondance* 1978.

NOTES

1 For an illuminating analysis of Cézanne's career in terms of the genres, see Kear 1998.

2 Quoted by Gustave Geffroy in Gustave Geffroy, *Claude Monet: sa vie, son oeuvre*, Paris: Crès, 1924, II, p. 68: "*Avec une pomme je veux étonner Paris*". The seminal discussion of Cézanne's apple imagery is Meyer Schapiro's 1968 essay, 'The Apples of Cézanne. An Essay on the Meaning of Still-life', reprinted in Schapiro 1978, pp. 1–38. Although I am unconvinced by Schapiro's analysis of the implications of Cézanne's interest in painting apples, it does seem likely that his comment to Geffroy involved a *double entendre*, invoking echoes of the mythological subject of the Judgment of Paris – a subject Cézanne painted on at least two occasions (RP 92, 457).

3 See Benjamin Harvey, 'Cézanne and Zola: a reassessment of "L'Eternel féminin"', *Burlington Magazine*, May 1998, pp. 314–15, where *L'Eternel féminin* is plausibly redated to *c*. 1880/82; on similar stylistic grounds, *The Temptation of Saint Anthony* (RP 300; Musée d'Orsay, Paris), placed in 1875/77 by Harvey (p. 312) and *c*. 1877 by John Rewald, should also be redated to *c*. 1880.

4 Schapiro 1968, in Schapiro 1978, p. 33.

5 See e.g. *Cézanne: The Early Years 1859–1872*, exh. cat., Royal Academy of Arts, London, 1988, and articles by Theodore Reff such as 'Cézanne's Bather with Outstretched Arms', *Gazette des Beaux-Arts*, vol. 59, March 1962, pp. 173–90, as well as Schapiro's essay cited in note 2 above.

6 See Dombrowski 2006 and A. Dombrowski, 'The emperor's last clothes: Cézanne, fashion and "l'année terrible"', *Burlington Magazine*, CXLVIII, September 2006, pp. 586–94.

7 Dombrowski 2006, pp. 259–65.

8 Ambroise Vollard, *Paul Cézanne*, 1914, reprinted in Ambroise Vollard, *En écoutant Cézanne, Degas, Renoir*, Paris, 1938, p. 20; I owe this reference to André Dombrowski.

9 Lilla Cabot Perry, 'Reminiscences of Claude Monet from 1889 to 1909', *American Magazine of Art*, March 1927, p. 120.

10 It seems that all Pissarro's knife-worked canvases from the 1870s were executed in 1875; Cézanne must thus claim primacy in the use of the knife at this point, since there is knife-work in parts of the foreground of *The House of the Hanged Man* (RP 202; Musée d'Orsay, Paris), included in the first Impressionist group exhibition in spring 1874.

11 See House 2004, pp. 167–80.

12 This term was originated by Theodore Reff in 1962 (Reff 1962); on this, see below, note 19.

13 For further discussion, see House 2004, especially pp. 181–85.

14 Letter from Cézanne to Louis Aurenche, 25 January 1904, in *Correspondance* 1978, p. 298: "... *si la sensation forte de la nature – et certes, je l'ai vive – est la base nécessaire de toute conception d'art..., la connaissance des moyens d'exprimer notre émotion n'est pas moins essentiel, et ne s'acquiert que par une très longue expérience.*"

15 Maurice Denis , 'Cézanne', *L'Occident*, September 1907, reprinted in Doran 1978, p. 173: "*La nature, disait Cézanne, j'ai voulu la copier, je n'arrivai pas. Mais j'ai été content de moi lorsque j'ai découvert que le soleil ... ne se pouvait pas reproduire, mais qu'il fallait le représenter par autre chose ... par de la couleur.*"

16 Letter from Cézanne to Joachim Gasquet, 26 September 1897, in *Correspondance* 1978, p. 262: "*L'art est une harmonie parallèle à la nature*".

17 E. Bernard, 'Souvenirs sur Paul Cézanne et lettres inédites', *Mercure de France*, 1 October 1907, reprinted in Doran 1978, pp. 58–59; Francis Jourdain, *Cézanne*, Paris, 1950, reprinted in Doran 1978, p. 84; Cézanne did paint one oil and one watercolour from an ageing naked model in the late 1890s (RP 897; RWC 387).

18 Denis 1907, in Doran 1978, pp. 172–73: "*D'une pomme d'un peintre vulgaire on dit: j'en mangerais. D'une pomme de Cézanne on dit: c'est beau! On n'oserait pas la peler, on voudrait la copier.*"

19 See Harvey 1998; this dating counters Theodore Reff's argument (Reff 1962) that the parallel stroke evolved in paintings executed from the imagination several years before it appeared in his landscapes; on this, see also House 2004, pp. 171–80.

20 Eugène Delacroix, *Journal 1822–1863*, ed. A. Joubin, Paris, 1980, p. 612, journal entry for 13 January 1857: "*La touche est un moyen comme un autre de contribuer à rendre la pensée dans la peinture .... Que dira-t-on des maîtres qui prononcent sèchement les contours tout en s'abstenant de la touche? Il n'y a pas plus de contours qu'il n'y a de touches dans Il faut toujours en revenir à des moyens convenus dans chaque art, qui sont le langage de cet art.*"

21 E. Bernard, 'Paul Cézanne', *L'Occident*, July 1904, reprinted in Doran 1978, p. 36: "*Lire la nature, c'est la voir sous le voile de l'interprétation par taches colorées se succédant selon une loi d'harmonie. Ces grandes teintes s'analysent ainsi par les modulations. Peindre c'est enregistrer ses sensations colorées.*" "*Il n'y a pas de ligne, il n'y a pas de modelé, il n'y a que des contrastes. Ces contrastes, ce ne sont le noir et le blanc qui les*

22 *donnent, c'est la sensation colorée. Du rapport exact des tons résulte le modelé. Quand ils sont heureusement juxtaposés et qu'ils y sont tous, le tableau se modèle tout seul." "On ne devrait pas dire modeler, on devrait dire moduler." "Le dessin et la couleur ne sont point distincts; au fur et à mesure que l'on peint on dessine; plus la couleur s'harmonise, plus le dessin se précise. Quand la couleur est à sa richesse, la forme est à sa plénitude. Les contrastes et les rapports de tons voilà le secret du dessin et du modelé."*

22 Ratcliffe 1960, especially Chapter 4, 'Realization', pp. 216–308.

23 Bois 1998, p. 41.

24 *Cézanne*, Paris, London and Philadelphia 1996; *Cézanne Finished, Unfinished*, Vienna and Zurich 2000. For a thought-provoking discussion of the effect of Cézanne's paintings, see Shiff 1998.

25 See e.g. Vollard 1914, reprinted in Vollard 1938, p. 64.

26 Osthaus 1920–21, translated from the French version in Doran 1978, p. 97.

27 Although in this letter he named the manner of painting that he was criticising as 'Neo-Impressionism', it seems likely that he was in fact referring to painters such as Gauguin and Bernard himself, who had used such sharp contours, rather than to artists such as Paul Signac who were working in a 'pointillist' technique without such assertive outlines.

28 R.P. Rivière and J.F. Schnerb, 'L'Atelier de Cézanne', *La grande revue*, 25 December 1907, reprinted in Doran 1978, p. 87: "*Cézanne ne cherchait pas à représenter les formes par une ligne. Le contour n'existait pas pour lui qu'en tant que lieu où une forme finit et où une autre forme commence. Qu'on regarde ses toiles inachevées; les objets d'un plan antérieur sont souvent laisseés en blanc et leur silhouette n'est indiquée que par le fond sur lequel elles se profilent. Point de trait en principe, une forme n'existe que par les formes voisines. Les traits noirs qui cernent souvent ses peintures n'étaient pas pour Cézanne un élément destiné à s'ajouter à la couleur, mais simplement une manière de reprendre plus facilement l'ensemble d'une forme par le contour avant de la modeler par la couleur.*"

29 The importance of his financial security, definitively assured after his father's death in 1886, is stressed in Ratcliffe 1960, pp. 269ff, where it is noted that very many more canvases were abandoned in a lightly worked state after this date.

30 Matthew Simms's forthcoming study explores in detail the central role that the interplay of line and colour plays in Cézanne's watercolours.

31 He exhibited watercolours in both of the Impressionist group exhibitions in which he participated, in 1874 and 1877, and planned to mount a display of his watercolours at Ambroise Vollard's gallery in 1902 (see *Cézanne*, Paris, London and Philadelphia 1996, p. 560).

32 See Ratcliffe 1960, Chapter 3, pp. 113–215, for detailed examination of characteristic examples of Cézanne's 'distortions'.

33 Rivière and Schnerb 1907, in Doran 1978, p. 87: "*Cézanne ne faisait donc pas mine d'ignorer l'asymétrie de ses bouteilles, la perspective défectueuse de ses assiettes. Montrant une de ses aquarelles, il corrigeait de l'ongle une bouteille qui n'était pas verticale et il disait, comme en s'excusant: 'Je suis un primitif, j'ai l'oeil paresseux. Je me suis présenté deux fois à l'Ecole, mais je ne fais pas l'ensemble: une tête m'intéresse, je la fais trop grosse.'*"

34 See M. Bodelsen, 'Gauguin, the Collector', *Burlington Magazine*, CXII, September 1970, pp. 590–615.

35 Letter from Gauguin to Pissarro, July 1881, in Victor Merlhès (ed.), *Correspondance de Paul Gauguin*, I, Paris, 1984, p. 21: "*…la formule exacte …la recette pour comprimer l'expression outrée de toutes ses sensations dans un seul et unique procédé*".

36 Geffroy 1924, reprinted in Doran 1978, p. 4; Denis 1907, reprinted in Doran 1978, p. 180; Vollard 1914, reprinted in Vollard 1938, p. 49; the mention of packet boats refers to Gauguin's voyage to Tahiti.

37 Letter from Gauguin to Vincent van Gogh, 24/25 July 1888, in Merlhès 1984, p. 201.

38 Bernard 1907, reprinted in Doran 1978, p. 65.

39 Osthaus 1920–21, translated from the French version of Osthaus's German text in Doran 1978, p. 97.

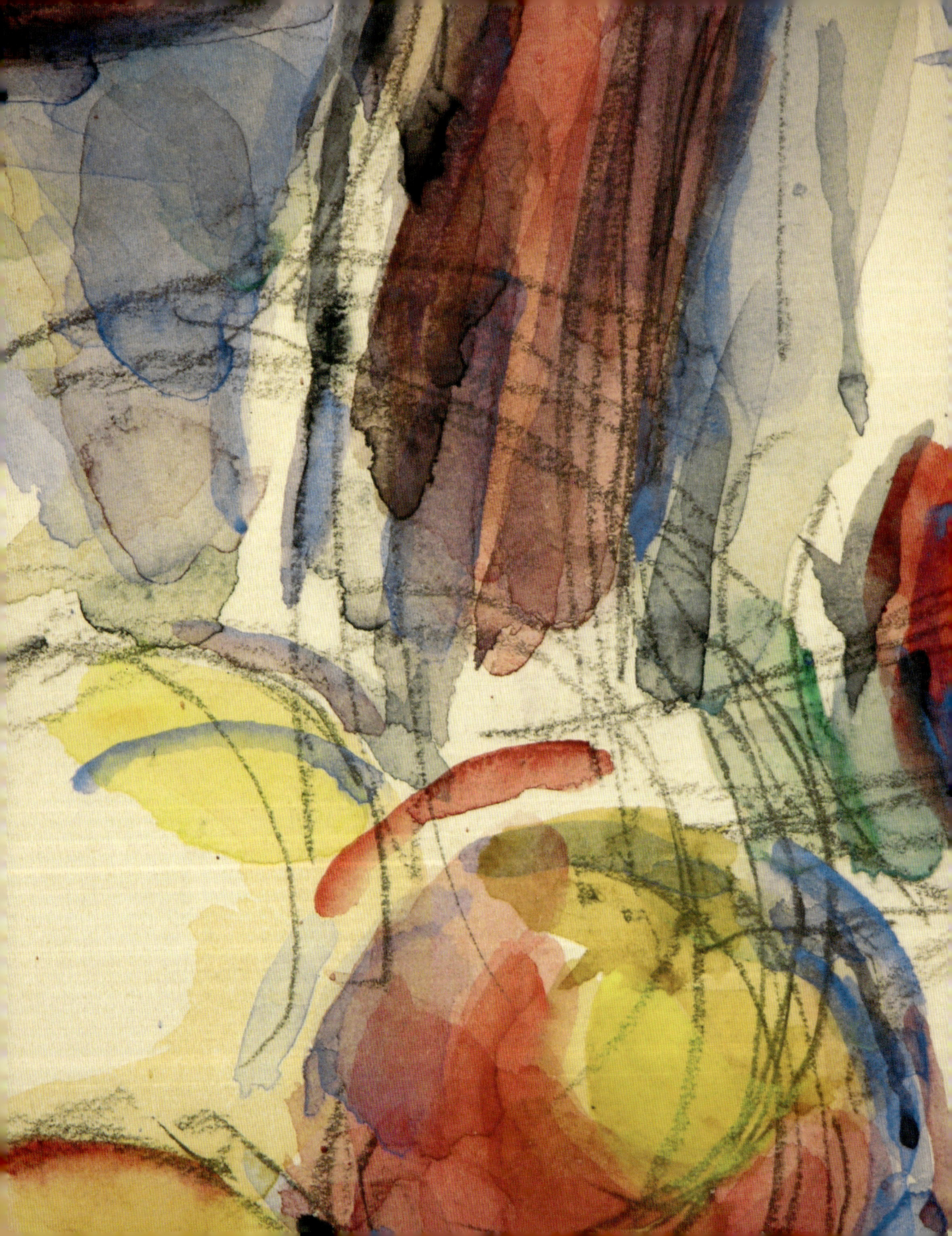

Transparency of Means:
'Drawing' and Colour in Cézanne's Watercolours and Oil Paintings in The Courtauld Gallery

ELISABETH REISSNER

Nineteenth-century French academic theory insisted on invisible execution and the dominance of line over colour.[1] Cézanne's painting practice and his theoretical statements engaged with contemporary debates within artistic circles around a supposed supremacy of either colour or *dessin*,[2] most recently played out by Ingres and Delacroix.[3] Accounts of Cézanne's oils and watercolours written in the late twentieth century have tended to perpetuate an opposition between line and colour. Lawrence Gowing suggested that Cézanne perceived that his mastery had to be "through colour and over colour"[4] and Götz Adriani wrote, "Finally, of course, the colour comes to triumph over the drawing".[5] Technical study of his oil paintings and watercolours in The Courtauld Gallery indicates that drawing for Cézanne might better be described as a form of visual thinking.[6] It involved a probing of the properties of colour and line and challenged an aesthetic that was bound up with hierarchies of medium and with the idea that reality could be represented by an artist following a clearly defined series of preparatory steps towards a finished painting. Cézanne's paintings evidence an extended experiential and experimental engagement with a notion of drawing that could encompass his use of colour.

To be avant-garde in the second half of the nineteenth century was in part to champion colour over line, but also to reject the tonal palette used in the academic *clair-obscur* method of painting. The period that Cézanne spent working along side Camille Pissarro in the 1870s points to his alignment with the avant-garde and was fundamental to the formation of his terms of engagement as an artist. Cézanne's adoption of Pissarro's prismatic or 'spectral' palette was a significant factor in the development of his painting practice. Camille's son Lucien reported that Cézanne copied a painting by Pissarro around 1872 in order to understand the new palette.[7] Technical analysis of the Courtauld oils and watercolours indicates that Cézanne's palette remained broadly the same until his death.[8] His innovation lay not in his pigment choice but rather in the ways in which he used his materials.

Cézanne's particular use of colour and line in both the oils and watercolours combined to challenge academic notions of drawing. Contact with Pissarro in this respect might also have been important.[9] Also significant was Cézanne's engagement with contemporary scientific and physiological ideas about vision and perception – where these could inform his practice. His exposure to such ideas can be surmised from the similarity between statements he made in letters and recorded conversations[10] and the writings of the scientist Hermann von Helmholtz and of the most popular exponent of Helmoltzian physiology, Hippolyte Taine.[11] They concern sensations of colour, the relationship between colour and light and the notion that painting based on observation is 'parallel to nature'.[12] In his *Optics and Painting* (1878) Helmholtz wrote: "What the artist must give us is not a simple copy of the object, but a translation of his impression into another scale of sensation".[13] According to the painter Emile Bernard, who visited Cézanne towards the end of his life, the artist stated: "To read nature is to see it through the veil of interpretation in terms of coloured touches that follow each other according to a law of harmony. These principal colours are thus analysed through modulations. Painting is classifying one's coloured *sensations*."[14] This appears related to Taine's belief that the artist could work simply by representing "patches of colour"[15] but must also be viewed in the context of an ongoing contemporary debate about the merits and disadvantages of a visible *touche* (brushwork).[16] It is in this context that Cézanne developed a way of painting which proposed that the relationships between carefully placed, discrete strokes or patches of colour might constitute drawing.

The theoretical statements that he made towards the end of his life and the painting practice that he developed in his oils and watercolours appear to acknowledge that when making a painting he was not copying or reproducing nature but, rather, representing, interpreting or finding material equivalents for his sensory experiences. One of the ways that he attempted to put this notion into words was his use of the term 'modulate' rather than 'model'.[17] 'Modulation' articulates an approach that rejects both tonal modelling to create form and classical paradigms of pictorial spatial organisation such as central perspective. In a letter to Bernard of 25 July 1904 Cézanne made it clear that the horizon with which he was concerned was located in the observer's eye and body rather than being an abstract construction: "The edges of objects recede towards a centre placed on our eye level".[18] 'Modulation' was also a way of describing how in both oils and watercolours Cézanne made visual and then physical journeys in paint, ranging across both the motif and the surface of the canvas, gradually building more and more complex colour relationships within groups of juxtaposed colours and between strokes of colour in very disparate parts of the canvas. This is perhaps what Cézanne was trying to convey when he described his painting process to Joachim Gasquet by first opening the fingers of his hands and then slowly locking them together.[19] It is an approach that encompasses the whole painting surface and is inclusive of strokes or areas of underlying colour, which remain visible to the viewer as a result either of paint's potential for transparency or simply by not being covered over.

In its purest form, Cézanne's practice of modulation was a process whereby the placement of patches of colour created form and spatial interval and enabled the finding of an edge without the use of line or contour. A number of statements attributed to Cézanne appear to refer to this new concept of drawing. According to Bernard, Cézanne stated, "There is no line, there is no modelling, there are only contrasts. It is not black and white that create these contrasts, but the coloured *sensation*. Modelling results from the precise rapport of colours. When they are harmoniously juxtaposed and are all in place, the painting models itself."[20] A similar apparent rejection of line was presented in the account of Cézanne's intentions by Rivière and Schnerb, after they visited him in 1905: "Cézanne did not seek to represent forms by a line. Contour only existed for him as the place where one form ended and another form began . . . . No line in principle, a form exists only in relation to the neighbouring forms. The black lines that often run through his paintings were not for Cézanne an element that he intended to be added to colour, but merely a manner of restating more easily the ensemble of a form by contour before modelling it by colour."[21] Such accounts have been used to support the idea that for Cézanne the *realisation* of a painting, or the ideal end point in his work, entailed the construction of colour relationships, which when successful would do away with the need for any line to remain visible on the surface. Line, in this interpretation, was only used or allowed to remain visible by Cézanne when he failed to control the form and build a painting with colour alone.[22]

A profusion of graphite lines appear in the Courtauld watercolours and coloured lines applied with brush both beneath and above the patches and strokes of colour are apparent both in his watercolours and in his oils. Thus Cézanne's statement, "Drawing and colour are in no way separate; as one paints, one draws; the more the colour harmonises, the more precise the drawing becomes. The form is at its fullest when the colour is at its richest. Contrasts and rapports of colour – that is the secret of drawing and modeling",[23] need not be interpreted as a description of drawing through the placement of patches of colour alone. Gowing acknowledged this when he included in his understanding of the term "precise drawing" repeated linear contours: "As the colour blossomed, successive contours narrowed down the zone of uncertainty round the forms in rhythms that made visible the force of the organizing logic".[24] Adriani also argued that Cézanne's statement referred to the co-existence of fine networks of lines and colour: "The drawing has continued to be a fully legitimate partner right up to the last application of colour. Even though many of its functions of outlining or indicating the relationships between surfaces have been wholly taken over by colour, this by no means nullifies the contribution of the drawing towards the solidification of the pictorial organism and the mapping of colour transitions."[25]

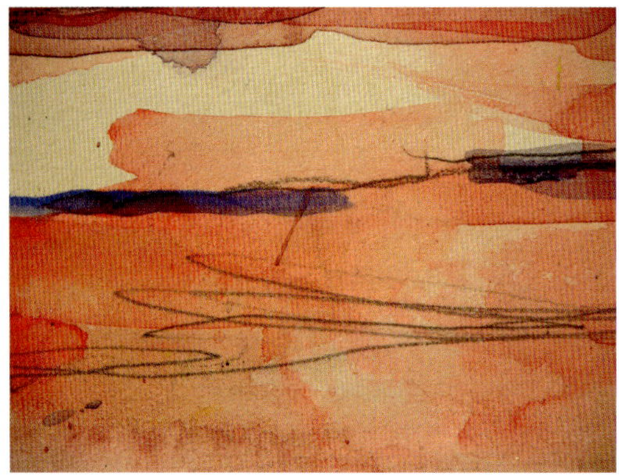

FIG. 20
Graphite lines clearly visible in the
foreground of *Apples, Bottle and Chairback*
(cat. 17)

Examination of the Courtauld oils and watercolours supports the notion that Cézanne's expanded conception of what drawing might be did not lead to an abandonment of linear components such as dry drawing using soft pencil or conté crayon. These are definitely present at the outset in *La Montagne Sainte-Victoire* (cat. 4), *Pot of Primroses and Pears* (cat. 5), *Still Life with Plaster Cupid* (cat. 8) and all of the watercolours (cat. 12, 14–18).[26] The present study has also revealed that in *Armchair* (cat. 15) Cézanne also applied dry graphite drawing after the application of watercolour paint. Hitherto it has been difficult to determine where in the layer structure of a watercolour the pencil lines lie. However, comparison of the image of the painting obtained when it was viewed in infrared light with an image in normal lighting conditions shows that Cézanne first sketched out the placement of the floor tiles with conté or graphite. He then applied watercolour, before finally redrawing the tiles on top of the watercolour, again with graphite or conté, this time in a slightly different position (see fig. 67). It is likely that the strong lines clearly visible in the foreground of *Apples, Bottle and Chairback* (cat. 17) were also applied on top of the colour, but even when the surface is viewed with a high powered microscope (fig. 20) it is impossible to be sure.

In the earlier watercolour *A Shed* (cat. 12) Cézanne's approach was more traditional and sequential in that the relationship between drawing and colour were additive – first a drawing in pencil, followed by a very partial filling-in with colour. Evidence that in *Armchair* he picked up his pencil during the painting process is significant, given the blurring of academic separation of drawing and painting that it reveals. Gone is the traditional linear process of making a painting which is underpinned by a clear distinction between line and colour and starts from an idea (about reality) which is first drawn (line) and is then executed (first tone, then colour), with the end point never in question.[27] This transgressive attitude is evident even when the graphite lines in the watercolours are not physically on top of the paint. Cézanne's use of watercolour means that the drawing often has the appearance of being on top of the colour even when it is not. Discussing the J. Paul Getty Museum *Still Life with Blue Pot* (RWC 572; *c.* 1900–06) Carol Armstrong writes that dark and free pencil marks "provide no certainty as to whether they were either final or later than the fainter marks located beneath areas of watercolour", suggesting "a threading of pencil through and through, and a reiterative, intricated, dialogic relation between graphite lines and watercolour veils".[28]

The infrared reflectogram of *Apples, Bottle and Chairback* (fig. 71) shows that beneath the watercolour there is a drawing which functions neither independently of the colour applied on top of it nor merely as a preliminary linear scaffolding.[29] It forms an integral part of the final painting's appearance. The graphite drawing and watercolour are intertwined visually and are in dialogue with each other. Sometimes the dialogue appears contradictory – for instance when no further paint is added to an area of hatched graphite (fig. 21); here the hatching suggests a dark colour or shadow but without paint it paradoxically becomes a highlight. Elsewhere in Cézanne's watercolours graphite hatching is reinforced with later paint but there are also instances when dark areas of paint have no hatching beneath. The amount of drawing and the degree to which the drawing is allowed to remain visible on the surface, as well as the number of underlying pencil lines in relation to later painted lines, vary within and between watercolours. Degrees of opacity and translucency vary even amongst watercolours executed at similar dates. Armstrong describes the dense build-up of layers in *Still Life with Blue Pot*, in which, unlike the Courtauld *Apples, Bottle and Chairback*, the underdrawing in graphite is largely obscured.[30]

With the exception of *Still Life with Plaster Cupid* (cat. 8) there is very little visible relationship between graphite drawing and colour in the oils. In *La Montagne Saint-Victoire* (fig. 22) the drawing is difficult to spot when viewing the painting in normal conditions. It is only clearly visible, outlining parts of the tree trunk and giving a very general indication of the fronds of foliage that pass across the sky on the right of the picture, when the painting is viewed with infrared light. In *Pot of Primroses and Fruit* (cat. 5) graphite is visible upon close inspection in the white flower and in the contour of the foremost pear on the plate in ordinary light,

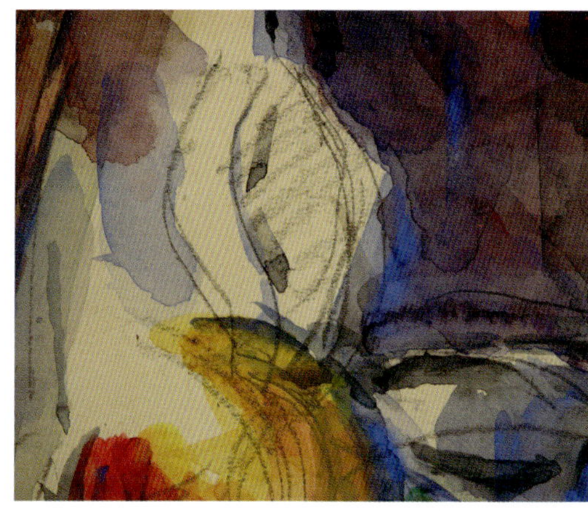

FIG. 21
Detail from *Apples, Bottle and Chairback* (cat. 17), where watercolour has not been added to an area of hatched graphite

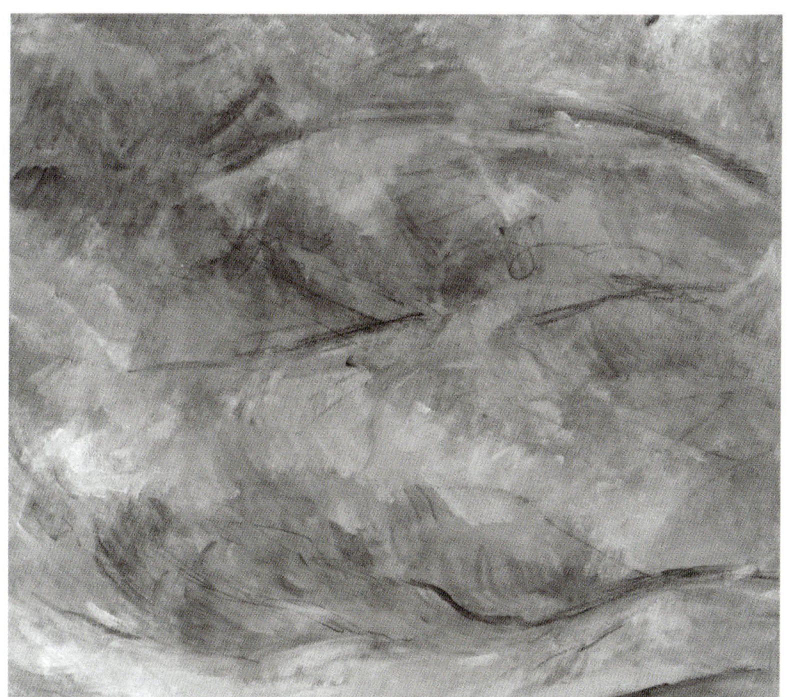

FIG. 22
Digital infrared reflectogram detail of *La Montagne Sainte-Victoire* (cat. 4) showing underdrawing in the foliage
© The National Gallery, London
All rights reserved

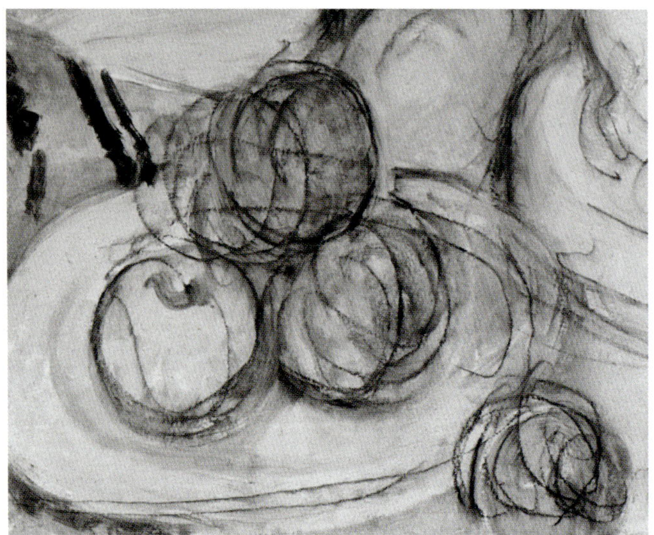

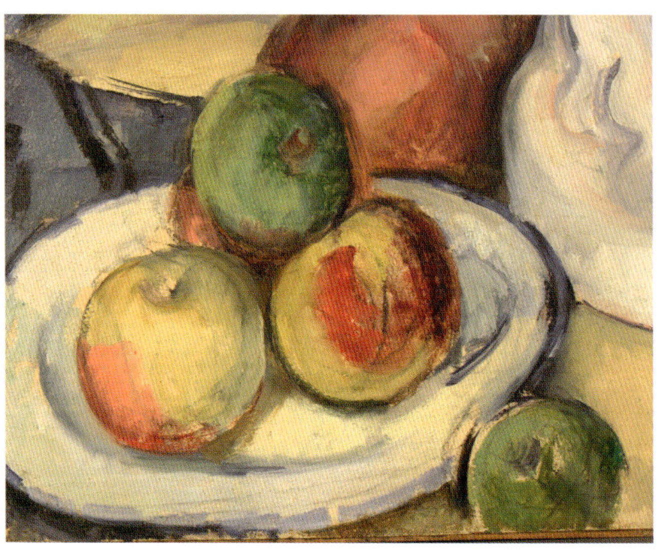

FIG. 24
Detail of the plate of fruit in *Still Life with
Plaster Cupid* (cat. 8) corresponding to the
infrared reflectogram (fig. 23)

but its presence scarcely contributes to the final aesthetic effect
of the painting. The looping lines of underdrawing in the plate of fruit
in *Still Life with Plaster Cupid* do, however, have a very strong presence
(figs. 23, 24). This work (executed in oil on primed paper) bears close
comparison with some of Cézanne's watercolours given the high
visibility of its underdrawing. As in the case in some of his watercolours, the infrared image (fig. 54) reveals more drawing than is
visible on the surface.

Visible in the Courtauld oils and watercolours are painted lines that
appear to interlace with the patches of colour and in some cases with
the graphite lines. In the watercolours it is very difficult to determine
whether these lines were applied before any of the colour patches; in
those oils, where there is less graphite drawing, they appear before,
during and after the application of thicker strokes or patches of colour.
In the oil paintings brushed lines, lying under the thicker paint, are
variously coloured greenish, grey, grey/blue, red/blue, purple, dark blue
and brown/black. The blue pigment is frequently ultramarine, although
in *Pot of Primroses and Pears* Prussian blue appears to have been used. They
are generally dilute, whilst later lines tend to have more body. The later
lines are more consistently dark blue (although red, green and blackish
lines are also visible) and in *La Montagne Sainte-Victoire* (cat. 4), *Le Lac d'Annecy*
(cat. 9) and *Route tournante* (cat. 10) some are cobalt blue. In the watercolours blue and purple lines are visible. In the case of *Apples, Bottle and
Chairback* they include cobalt blue and indigo. Cézanne's repeated use of
these coloured lines was another important way in which his practice

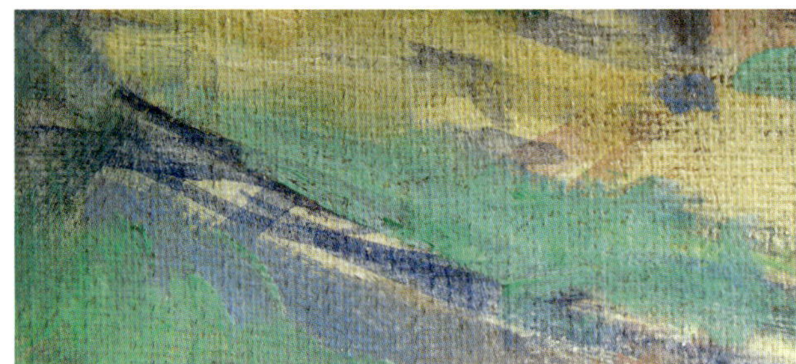

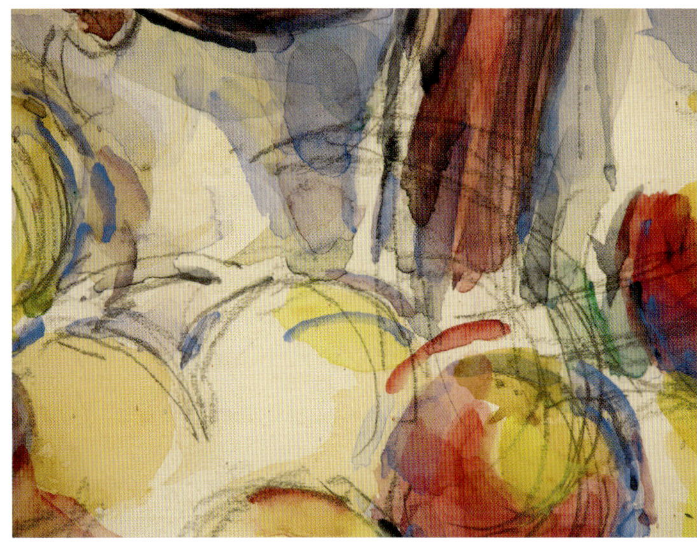

blurred distinctions between drawing and painting, colour and line, visually, functionally and in terms of hierarchy, since they function as both colour and line (fig. 25, 26). Armstrong, referring to blue and purple lines applied late in his watercolour painting process, writes that Cézanne "blurred the boundary between colour tache and draftsmanly line, laying them side by side and over one another so that the difference between one and the other is seen as a matter of thickness and thinness, translucency and opacity, the slightest distinction in emphasis between the faintest of light refraction (pigment) and the most basic graphism (line)".[31]

There is a tendency in Cézanne's paintings for the thickest paint to be found along contours. It is here that colour relationships, crucial to establishing form and space, are sought.[32] In the gap of a millimetre or so Cézanne often left between these more heavily worked areas to which he paid most attention, unpainted ground colour is allowed to remain visible. In the oil painting *La Montagne Sainte-Victoire* the pale ground is visible along the contour of the tree trunk (fig. 27), and bare paper can be seen along a number of contours in *Apples, Bottle and Chairback*. This practice has been described as painting the contours of objects 'in reserve'.[33] Cézanne was 'finding an edge' through the application of paint, rather than fixing a contour with line. Even in this part of his practice, however, actual line is not excluded. Underlying painted blue lines and occasionally graphite lines are visible in the space between colour patches (fig. 25). Coloured lines applied late in the painting process also occasionally run over and into the line created by the absence of paint.

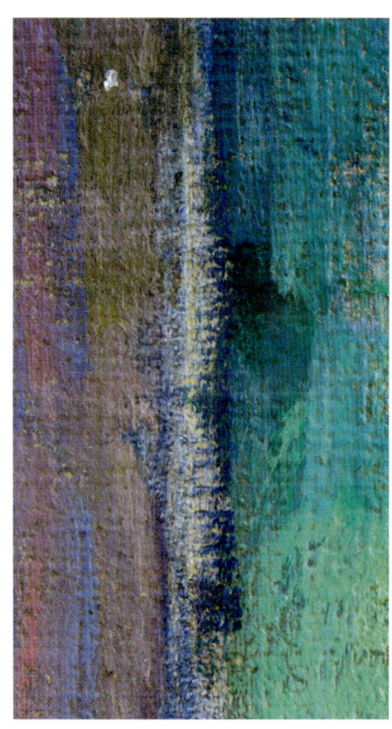

FIG. 27
Detail from *La Montagne Sainte-Victoire*
(cat. 4) showing the pale ground colour along
the contour of the tree trunk

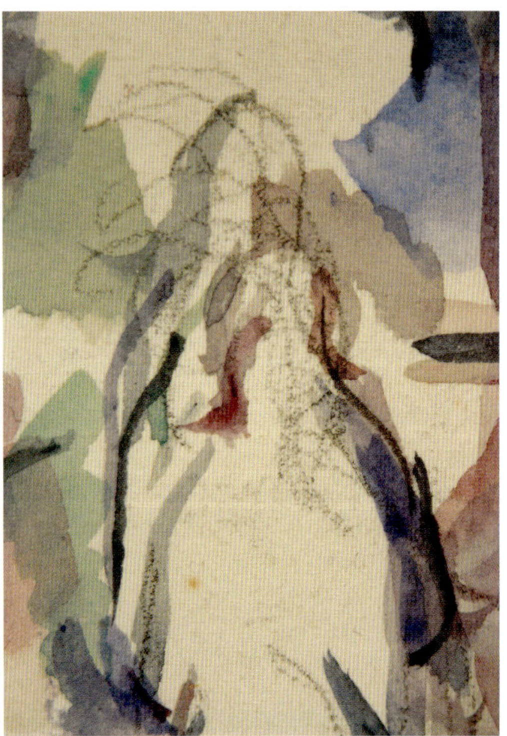

It is perhaps not surprising that in his recorded theoretical statements Cézanne emphasised the construction of relationships between carefully placed discrete strokes or patches of colour in his work and made little mention of the role of line. His project evidences a concern to 'draw with colour' and it is this that he appears to have wished to articulate verbally. He was also keen to distance himself from academic notions of drawing, based on outline. Rivière and Schnerb state, "Cézanne vigorously declared his horror of the photographic eye, of the precise and automatic drawing taught in the Ecole des Beaux-Arts".[34] Whatever his theoretical statements, in a practical sense line was not redundant for Cézanne. The way in which he used it, however, was as much a challenge to the Ecole des Beaux-Arts as was his drawing with colour. Initial coloured brush drawing in his oils did not represent a contour to which Cézanne was committed, but was instead an initial proposition for the edge of something, which would be repeatedly adjusted as the painting process proceeded. Roger Fry observed that Cézanne "dreads any slight final statement of the contour, and rather adumbrates its exact situation than defines it".[35] Reiteration of both graphite lines and blue and purple coloured lines can also be seen in *Statue under Trees* (fig. 28). The painted lines in *Route tournante* (cat. 10) would almost certainly have become less prominent and their positioning altered had Cézanne chosen to continue with this painting.

A reality constructed with colour alone may have been Cézanne's ideal, but line, whether pencil or coloured paint, plays a major role in the complex and often rhythmic web of relationships underpinning his paintings. Cézanne's appreciation and close visual study in his frequent visits to the Louvre of "the greats", as he called the Venetians and Spanish Old Masters in a letter to Bernard in July 1904, would have contributed significantly to his understanding of colour and drawing.[36] Lawrence Gowing has described how the convex and concave arcs of colour (which may refer to both patches of colour and coloured line) in *Apples, Bottle and Chairback* help to create form: "There is a ceremonious elaboration about them, yet innumerable hours in the Louvre spent on the study of how the spring and recoil of rhythm made volume manifest must have contributed to such an image".[37] The cool cobalt blue lines on the edges of the warmly coloured fruit also recede and as a result help to create form (fig. 26). In the oil painting *La Montagne Sainte-Victoire* horizontal and vertical coloured lines lead the eye into the distance and there are also lines with a rhythmic quality indicating bushes (fig. 29). Darkly coloured rhythmic lines, applied fairly late in the painting process, are also present in *Le Lac d'Annecy* (fig. 58).

Cézanne's paintings convey a sense of becoming, emerging or of being formed, which could not have been achieved with colour modulation alone. His use of line and colour was as much about the process of making a painting as it was about the act of looking.[38] Cézanne used both to adjust and modify his paintings as he constructed them. In his essay 'Cézanne's Doubt' Maurice Merleau-Ponty suggested that Cézanne's use of modulated colours and reiterated outlines approached the act of looking the more closely because, "rebounding among these, one's glance captures a shape that emerges from among them all, just as it does in perception".[39] But the doubt involved in the construction of his paintings is not primarily about perception. The many visible *pentimenti* (eg. fig. 30) in Cézanne's studio compositions as well as those painted in front of the motif cannot simply be attributed to direct perceptual experience.[40] In the context of late nineteenth-century views on the observer, Jonathan Crary argues that Cézanne made the creative discovery in the 1890s that "perception can take no other form than the process of its formation". He goes on to claim that for Cézanne looking at any one thing intently "led to its perceptual disintegration and loss, its breakdown as intelligible form; and that breakdown was one of the conditions for the invention and discovery of previously unknown relations and organizations of forces".[41] 'Drawing' in both the Courtauld oils and watercolours could usefully describe the formation of these newly invented relations between all parts of the painting's surface.

Cézanne was sensitive to the part that all stages in his painting process might play in the final surface. This included the paper support in the case of the watercolours and the off-white, grey or white oil ground in that of the oils,[42] as well as his coloured strokes and patches, diluted initial washes, underdrawing and overdrawing in graphite and

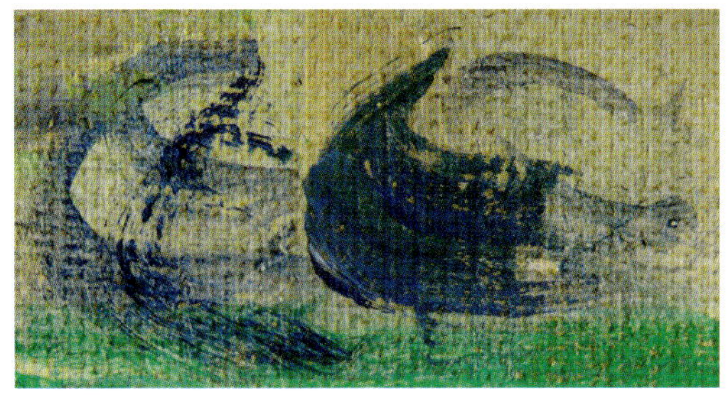

FIG. 29
Lines with a rhythmic quality indicating bushes in a detail of *La Montagne Sainte-Victoire* (cat. 4)

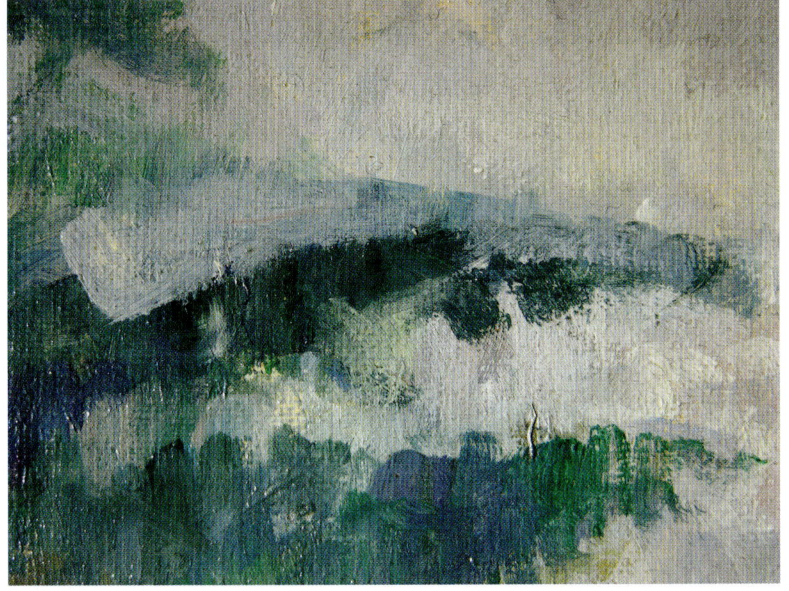

FIG. 30
Detail of a *pentimento* in the foliage of *Tall Trees at the Jas de Bouffan* (cat. 3)

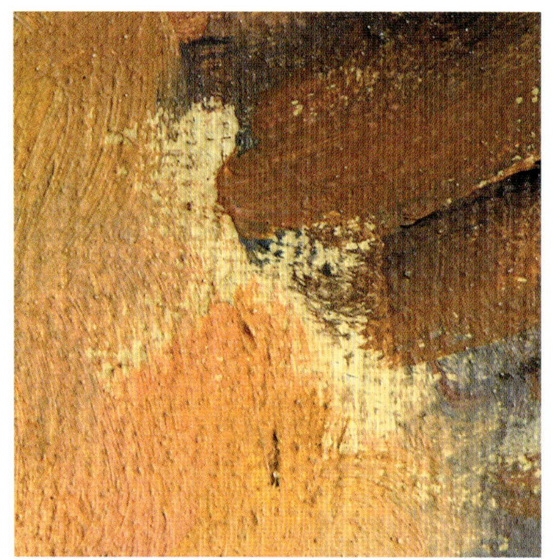

FIG. 31
Bare ground visible in the knuckles of the
left-hand figure in *The Card Players* (cat. 6)

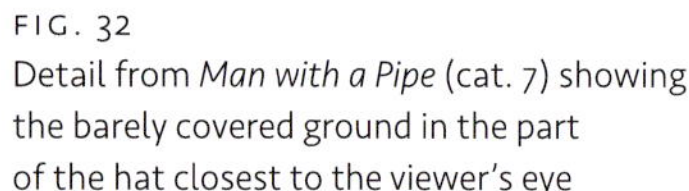

FIG. 32
Detail from *Man with a Pipe* (cat. 7) showing
the barely covered ground in the part
of the hat closest to the viewer's eye

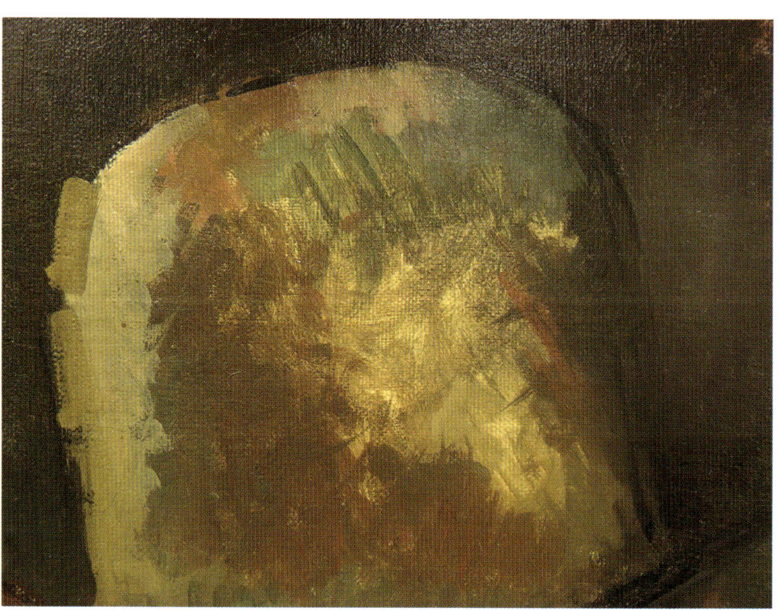

paint. At the outset of an oil painting, when initial relationships were established, the bare ground might serve Cézanne as a colour value. For example, in the unfinished *Route tournante* the white ground functions as the sky value. In oil paintings that he worked on for longer the use of the ground as a colour value is rare. Although the bare ground in the knuckles of the left-hand figure in *The Card Players* (cat. 6) works representationally as a highlight, it is very possible that – as in the documented case of his portrait of Ambroise Vollard[43] – Cézanne had not yet found the right colour (fig. 31).

In watercolour, however, the white of the paper is more integral to the design and moves more effortlessly between its dual role as support surface and depicted surface or image. This has much to do with inherent differences between a bare support (the paper) and a coated support (the oil ground applied to the canvas) as well as the greater degree of transparency possible using watercolour. To leave bare patches of white, or near white, ground was a more radical and conscious act than leaving bare paper; paper had occupied this dual role in drawings for centuries. Transition in Cézanne's watercolours is achieved through the qualities of the colour that separate areas of bare paper. The paper becomes the pediment in *Statue under the Trees* (cat. 16) and forms part of the fruit in the more resolved *Apples, Bottle and Chairback* (fig. 26). In the Courtauld oils it is more common to see a thin wash of dilute oil paint covering the exposed ground. This is the case in the hat of *Man with a Pipe* (fig. 32), where the barely covered ground functions as a 'culminating point', or the part of a form that is closest to the viewer's eye because the form is convex.[44]

In *Le Lac d'Annecy* exposed ground with a greenish wash represents light reflected on the water (fig. 33).

Bernard was the first to suggest, when describing Cézanne painting a watercolour of the Montagne Sainte-Victoire, that the colour relationships that Cézanne established were the result of a pre-conceived system. However, the colour relationships observable in Cézanne's Courtauld oil paintings and watercolours do not support this notion. Bernard wrote that Cézanne "began with the shadow and with a touch that he covered with a second broader touch, and then a third, until all these colours, creating screens, modelled and at the same time coloured the object".[45] He then gave the following interpretation: "I then understood that the laws of harmony guided his work and that all these modulations had a goal, determined in advance in his mind. He worked, in fact, in the way early tapestry makers must have worked, arranging related colours in a sequence until they met their contrasting colour opposites."[46] Gowing offered a less rigid interpretation of Cézanne's painting process in the Courtauld watercolour *La Montagne Sainte-Victoire* (cat. 14), when he described "an emergent logic in the order" of the diluted tints "rather than anything one can imagine observing on the spot".[47] Cézanne used colour and line to enquire into the nature of picture making and its complex relationship to the observed world. His colour was at times metaphoric and at others more local or specific to the subject he was depicting.

Many of the colour relationships visible in Cézanne's paintings had been used by artists for generations, but had only more recently been written about in more theoretical and scientific terms.[48] Amongst these relations were the simultaneous contrast of complementary colours and the juxtaposition of warm and cool colours. The complementary colour oppositions are red–green, orange–blue and yellow–violet. These pairings also each comprise a warm and a cool colour. According to Rivière and Schnerb, Cézanne believed: "It is through the opposition of warm and cool tones that the colours used by the painter – without any absolute luminous quality in themselves – come to represent light and shadow".[49] These colour relationships are key to Cézanne's construction of form and space and his representation of light through modulated colour. The French chemist Chevreul experimented extensively with optical mixtures of complementary or near-complementary colours. His book *The Law of Harmonious Colour* was published in 1839 and became perhaps the most widely used colour-manual of the nineteenth century.[50] It is likely therefore that Cézanne would have been aware of Chevreul's work, but scrutiny of the Courtauld oils and watercolours suggests that his approach was not systematic or formulaic in character. It was founded upon a profound practical understanding of the possibilities intrinsic in colour relationships, supplemented by exposure to contemporary colour theory and scientific and physiological ideas about vision and perception.

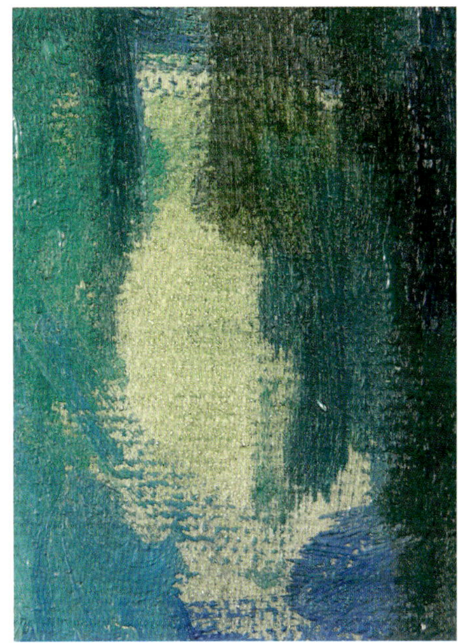

FIG. 33
Detail from *Le Lac d'Annecy* (cat. 9), where exposed ground with a greenish wash represents light reflected on the water

Cézanne's use of complementary contrast was sometimes explicit, for instance in the red and green strokes in the tree trunk in *Le Lac d'Annecy* (fig. 34). Shadow and light is represented in part by patches of yellow and violet in *Statue under Trees*. The pink and blue patches in *Route tournante* (fig. 35) are examples, however, of the juxtaposition of warm and cool colours that are not strictly complementary. Depending upon the colour context Cézanne was also able to manipulate whether a particular colour appeared warm or cool. His colour 'relations' are subtle and often unconventional because the visual thinking behind them was extremely complex. His use of strokes of the same warm red in the tree trunk and house directly behind in *Tall Trees at the Jas de Bouffan* (fig. 36), for instance, contradicts a construction of space whereby warm colours, which tend to advance, are reserved for the foreground. The order of the application of colour in the Courtauld works is not predictable. Similar colour mixtures might be seen at various stages in the painting process.

Cézanne did not apply uniform covering layers as he developed his paintings. That facilitated the creation of relationships between underlying partial washes, strokes and lines and the marks on the surface. The role of all the stages of his painting process was not defined in advance and the degree of visibility of underlayers on the surface of

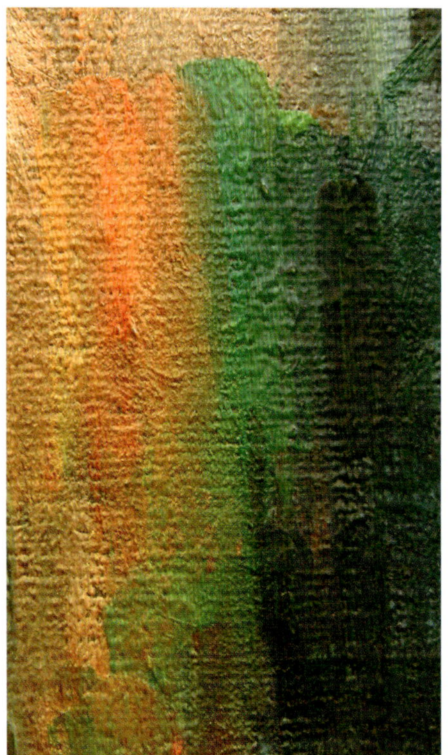

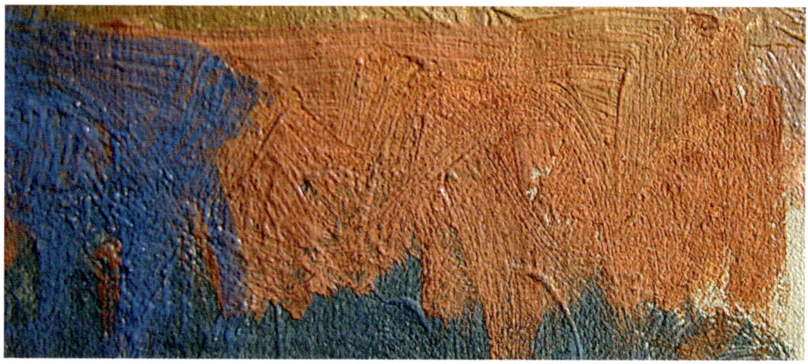

FIG. 34
Complementary colours juxtaposed in
the tree trunk in *Le Lac d'Annecy* (cat. 9)

FIG. 35
Warm and cool colour patches
juxtaposed in *Route tournante* (cat. 10)

TRANSPARENCY OF MEANS

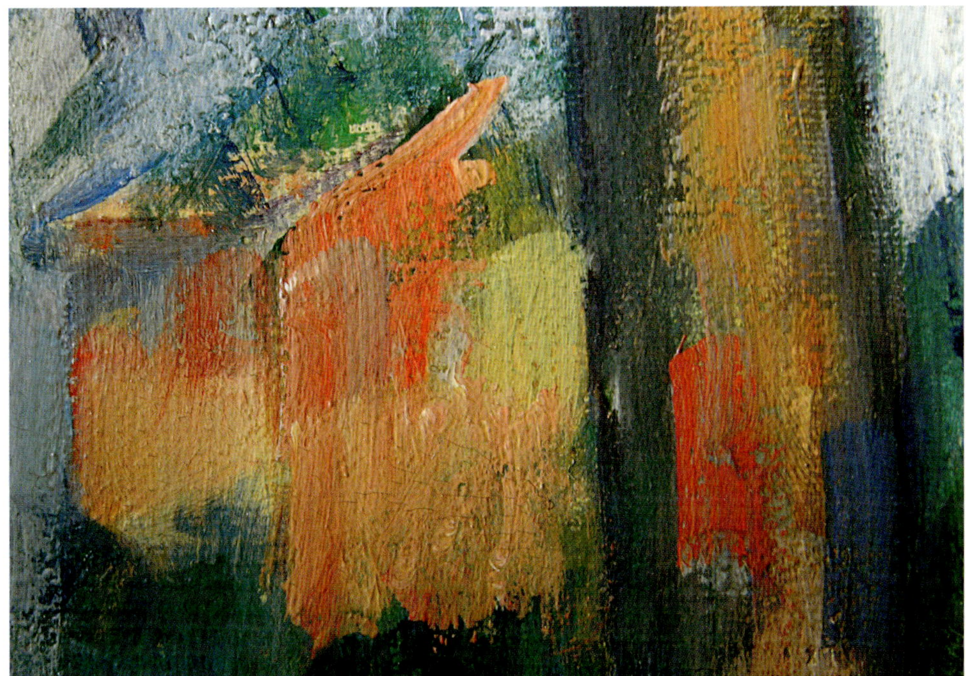

his completed paintings was not consistent. Often the result is a complex multi-layered surface, where heavily painted areas are juxtaposed with bare or scarcely painted areas of ground, for example in the treetops in *Tall Trees at the Jas de Bouffan* (fig. 37). Cézanne appears to have been looking for the point when he had done enough or perhaps come close enough to 'realise' his *sensation*. The tip of the right-hand figure's nose in *The Card Players* and the cast shadow for one of the apples in *Still Life with Plaster Cupid*, both rendered with a diluted blue wash, are examples of Cézanne's improvisatory approach (figs. 38, 39). In both cases an initial lay-in finds a place in the painting's surface at the point that Cézanne chooses to stop working on it.

The relationship between Cezanne's oils and watercolours is significant but not straightforward. John Rewald suggested that "even when Cézanne treated analogous subjects in oils and watercolours, he proceeded in such different ways and developed such dissimilar techniques of execution – inherent to each of these media – that it seems preferable to consider them as works more or less independent of each other".[51] Gowing, however, speculated upon Cézanne's willingness to transpose what he learned in one medium to the other. He saw the watercolours as the place where Cézanne evolved the colour patch which became the "unit of his later style",[52] but he also pointed out that the straight-edged colour patches, applied with a palette knife, in *L'Etang des*

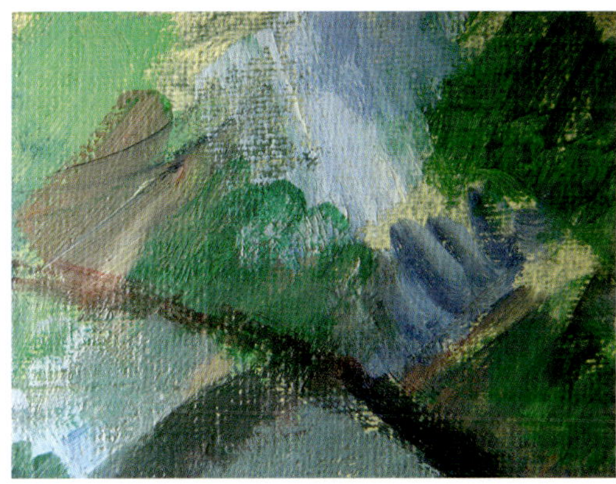

FIG. 37
Detail of the treetops in *Tall Trees at the Jas de Bouffan* (cat. 3) showing a complex multi-layered surface, where heavily painted areas are juxtaposed with bare or scarcely painted areas of ground

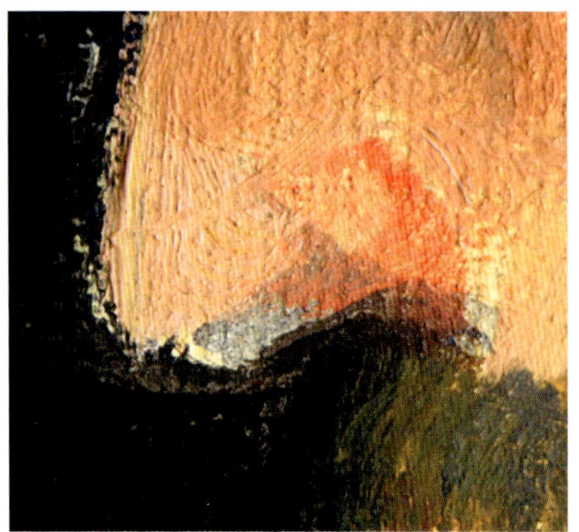

Detail of the tip of the right-hand figure's nose in *The Card Players* (cat. 6)

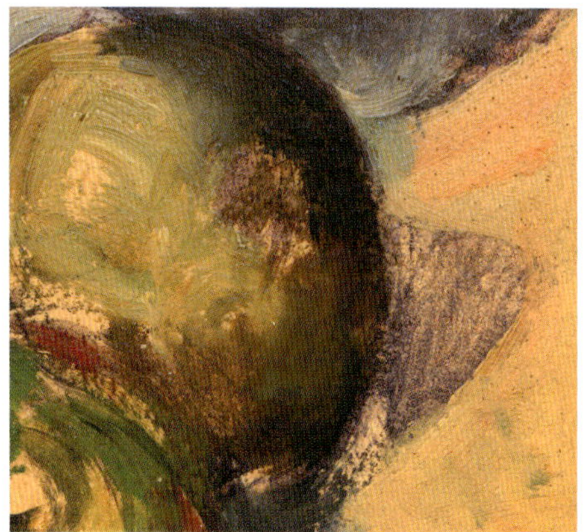

Detail of the cast shadow for one of the apples in *Still Life with Plaster Cupid* (cat. 8)

Sœurs (fig. 44) predated his use of colour patches in his watercolours at the beginning of the 1890s.[53] Armstrong writes that watercolour "seems to have provided Cézanne with a model for painting more lightly in oil, for allowing the ground to show through and using its white and cream as a colour in itself".[54]

There is much to link the Courtauld oil paintings and watercolours in terms of approach and use of materials. Cézanne was, it seems, keen to break down a traditional hierarchy that placed oil painting above watercolour in importance, and both media provide the space for both experimentation and more realised statements. *Apples, Bottle and Chairback* is executed in a manner and on a scale incompatible with a conventional watercolour preparatory sketch. Cézanne's practice is underpinned by a newly expanded notion of drawing, and dialogues between colour and line, as his use of both evolves, are evident in both media. Colour is used to perform many of the functions that had been reserved for linear constructions, thereby blurring a clear distinction between colour and drawing. The blocks of colour, first seen in the oil paintings in the variously shaped slabs of colour applied with a palette knife in *L'Etang des Sœurs*, facilitate modulating the paint in order to create space and represent light. This could be termed 'drawing with colour'. There are a few colour blocks formed by a continuous zigzag movement of the brush in paintings in the next decade but they are seen most clearly in late paintings such as *Route tournante*. However, despite these similarities, Ambroise Vollard's description of Cézanne applying in his oils "one layer of paint as thin as watercolour over another" encourages perhaps too great an elision of the two media.[55] Close study of the works also shows very clearly the differences in the media as Cézanne used them – particularly in the way his colour mixes were achieved and in degrees of transparency.

The oil paintings in The Courtauld Gallery include the following pigments: emerald green, viridian, cobalt blue, ultramarine, Prussian blue, chrome yellow, cadmium yellow, vermilion and at least two organic reds.[56] The colours that Cézanne created are the result of subtle variation in the proportions of these pigments in a matrix of white with the addition of small quantities of earths and carbon black.[57] Individual strokes of paint examined in cross-section are generally composed of three to five pigments. Colours rarely comprise unmixed pigments straight from the tube. Occasionally there is a patch of purer green or red but even these accents are usually slightly modified by a greyish stroke applied wet-in-wet (fig. 36). There is a tendency for the brushmarks to be differentiated, but they are not discrete. Cézanne's technique in the last thirty years of his life was not explicitly wet-in-wet but wet brushstrokes frequently cut into strokes that were applied earlier and had not yet dried.

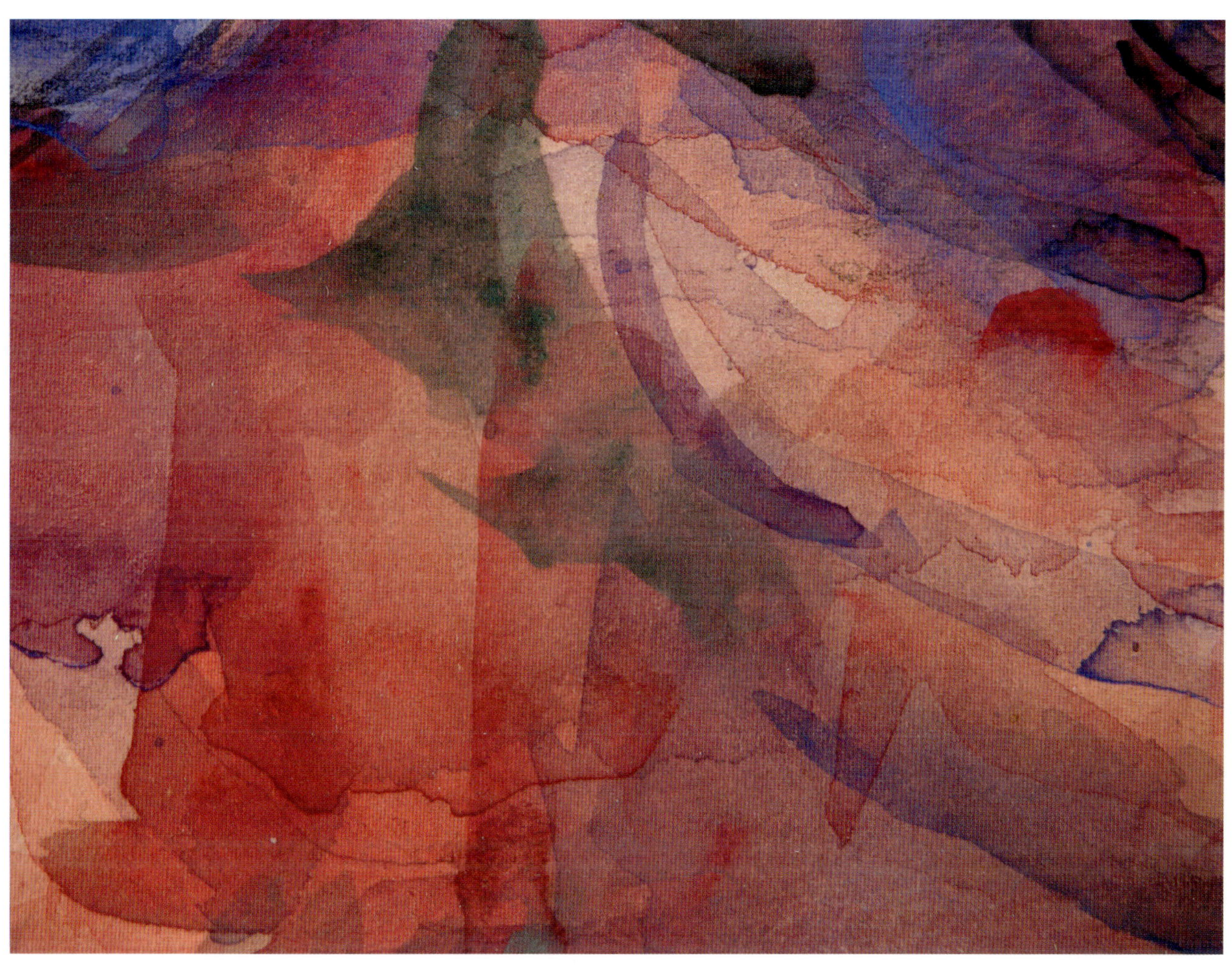

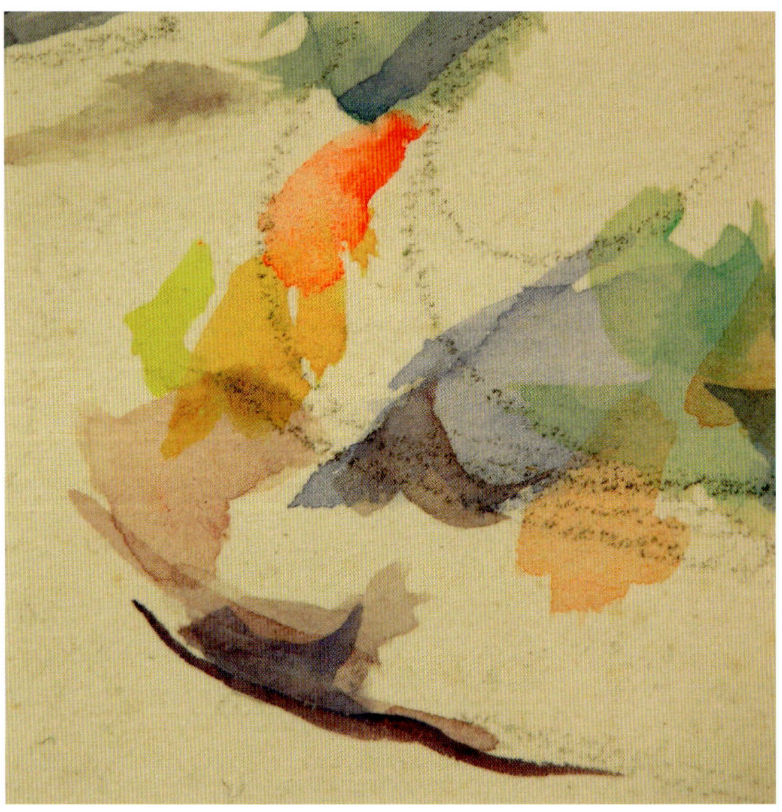

The range of pigments identified in the Courtauld watercolours and oil paintings is broadly similar, apart from the dark blues. The indigo found in *Apples, Bottle and Chairback* is exclusive to the watercolours and Prussian blue was only found in the oil paintings. No evidence was found for the use of black in the watercolours, apart from graphite used in the drawing that is occasionally picked up by superimposed patches of watercolour. This is visible in the watercolour *La Montagne Sainte-Victoire* (cat. 4) and *Armchair* (cat. 15). In the Courtauld watercolours some of the colours were created by mixtures of pigments. There is a mixed grey, for instance, in *Armchair* and mixed purples comprising cobalt blue and red lake were found in *La Montagne Sainte-Victoire*, *Statue under Trees* and *Apples, Bottle and Chairback*. It is also likely that Cézanne made mixed greens comprising cobalt blue and chrome yellow.[58] The subtle range of purples, oranges and greens was, however, achieved largely by the superimposition of pure red, blue, green and yellow and ochre pigments (fig. 40). Cézanne's method allows us to see the components of the mix where there is no overlap (fig. 41). Although there are instances of wet-in-wet blending on the paper, where the individual strokes have not completely dried, most of the patches of colour are discrete.

Cézanne's manipulation of the opaque and transparent qualities
of pigment suspended in medium in his watercolours and oils was to
some extent founded upon an understanding of the chromatic effects
that could be achieved by the layering of oil paint in the canvases that
he studied in the Louvre, but it was not at all restricted by precedent
or convention. Joachim Gasquet recorded Cézanne's appreciation of
Veronese's use of grey priming.[59] His exploitation of these qualities was
also subject to adjustment and change. The early evolution of oil-painting
technique involved the development of the medium so that its qualities
of opacity and transparency could be used to create the illusion of form.
The capacity of white or slightly off-white grounds and underlying layers
to reflect light was recognized as a means of increasing the intensity of
the colour of layers of translucent paint applied over them. The overall
effect was more luminous. The degree of transparency is a result of the
refractive index of the oil medium and the pigment being very close.[60]
Only a few pigments are actually transparent when mixed with oil,
though transparency of a range of pigments can be achieved by adding
oil or diluent. The relationship between the refractive indices of most
pigments and oil results in opaque colour. The inclusion of lead white
in a paint mix also generally leads to opacity.

Watercolour, only established as an autonomous medium during the
course of the eighteenth century, made use of broad washes of pigment
in a medium of gum Arabic diluted with water.[61] The medium of watercolour is not inherently transparent, but transparent effects are more
readily achieved in watercolour than in oil.[62] It can be rendered more or
less transparent depending upon the way in which the artist uses it. The
thickness of the layers of watercolour is the most important variable in
the execution of watercolour because the thicker the layer, the greater
the likelihood of dullness.[63] The inclusion of gouache and use of body
colour or distemper are also ways in which a watercolour technique can
be made more opaque.[64] Unlike oil paint, watercolour does not form a
uniform paint layer, so its transparency is not the result of the refractive
index of the pigment and the gum Arabic being very close. The particle
size and colour intensity of the pigments play a part because the transparency occurs between pigment particles. Smaller, more intense particles leave more gaps for the luminous white paper or underlying paint
to show through; they also permit the application of very thin, coloured
layers. The reflecting properties of white paper, like the white grounds
in oil paintings, increase the colour intensity of the watercolour.

Study of the techniques used for the Courtauld watercolours suggest
Cézanne's growing interest in maximising effects of transparency and
extending the possibilities of the watercolour medium. A major part in
this was his development of a technique that involved the application of
a very thin patch of colour which was allowed to dry before the application of the next. Although in *Armchair* opaque lead white pigment has

been identified in the purplish area behind the chair, towards the end of the 1870s Cézanne reduced his use of gouache.[65] In both the oils and watercolours, when colour is physically mixed this is a subtractive process. Isaac Newton first described the phenomenon that when all the colours of the spectrum are mixed in material form they combine to make black. The creation of colour through the superimposition of discrete strokes of watercolour is also subtractive, but the experience of the colour produced in this way is often more luminous or intense. Cézanne's method of paint application tends to maximise the reflection of light from the paper. He generally avoided the dulling of colour or increase in opacity resulting from too many superimposed layers, or upper strokes picking up colour below, that is visible in the floor tiles in *Armchair*. Occasionally, however, he exploited the opaque possibilities of watercolour, seen for instance in the spot of pigment-dense emerald green in the centre of the chairback in *Apples, Bottle and Chairback* (fig. 42).

Cézanne was not constrained by prevailing notions of the way the transparency of watercolour could be exploited. Nor did he rely upon the traditional build-up of opaque paint followed by transparent paint in order to construct form and space in his oil paintings. The colour effects in these works are generally due to light reflected from the surface of predominantly opaque paint fairly thinly applied (although considerably more thickly than in his watercolours). This is largely a consequence of the opaque lead white that he added to most of his paint mixtures. Occasionally he used true glazes of red and possibly yellow lake.[66] Paint strokes of non-traditional glazing pigments such as yellow ochre, rendered translucent through the addition of oil medium or diluent,[67] are also visible. His practice did not rely on glazes to modify colour as a final stage of finishing a painting. The final, uppermost stroke is not necessarily the most medium-rich or transparent. Late opaque strokes sometimes skip across lower more medium-rich layers. In *The Card Players* the red glaze visible in the background is in an underlayer.

The grounds in Cézanne's oil paintings consist of lead white modified by barium sulphate, quartz and chalk extenders and the addition of small amounts of yellow ochre and black.[68] Only *Le Lac d'Annecy* has a grey ground, rather than a white or creamy one, owing to a larger proportion of carbon black. *Still Life with Plaster Cupid* is painted in oil on paper which has been commercially primed with a ground comprising chalk and lead white plus small amounts of yellow ochre and carbon black. Light reflects from the ground in these paintings where patches of it are exposed or barely covered with paint. This effect is clearly visible in the foreground of *Pot of Primroses and Pears* and the background of *The Card Players*. The ground colour of *Route tournante*, now greyish in appearance, would originally have been the whitest of the paintings examined, owing to the greater proportion of lead white and absence of yellow ochre or black in its composition. Cézanne appears to have favoured

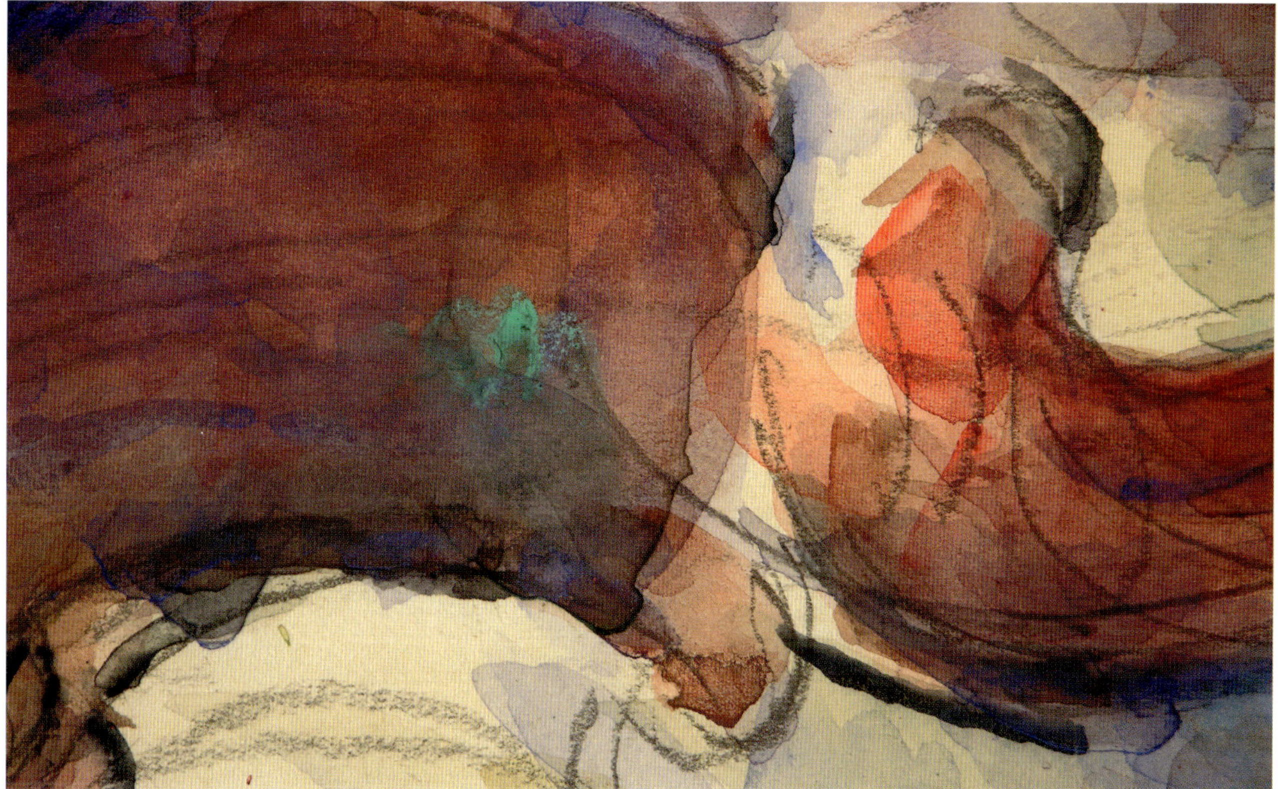

whiter grounds towards the end of his career:[69] this may have been because of an interest in their reflecting properties, but transparency of means in relation to the oils describes better the partial visibility of all stages in the painting process – achieved without reliance upon transparency of the paint.

A definitive description of the relationships between colour and line in Cézanne's paintings is as elusive as his broken, reiterated, equivocating contours. For all the increasing transparency of means in his paintings, Cézanne's version of reality towards the end of his life is not readily pinned down. Close study of nature was not for Cézanne something that could be represented by an artist following a clearly defined path towards a finished painting. Cézanne used colour and line to enquire into the nature of picture making and its relationship to the observed world. His paintings manifest to the viewer the contingency of looking and making. Attempting to understand them can be likened to the experience of following a pencil line in his watercolours as it weaves through colour, in and out of visibility.

Table 1: Supports and grounds in the oil paintings

PAINTING	SUPPORT (dimensions in cm)	COMPOSITION AND MEDIUM OF GROUND*
The Etang des Sœurs (CAT. 1)	O # ‡ 73.5 × 60	Lead carbonate, barium sulphate, zinc oxide or sulphide, calcium carbonate and iron oxide in oil
Tall Trees at the Jas de Bouffan (CAT. 3)	O # ‡ 81 × 65	Two layers: The lower calcium carbonate in protein and the upper lead white, barium sulphate, zinc oxide or sulphide, carbon black and iron oxide in oil
The Montagne Sainte-Victoire (CAT. 4)	O # ‡ 92.3 × 66.8 Later restoration has slightly increased its size	A thin calcium carbonate and protein initial layer is likely, with a main layer containing lead carbonate, barium sulphate, carbon black and iron oxide in oil
Pot of Primroses and Fruit (CAT. 5)	O # ‡ 56.2 × 46 There is the picture-liner's stamp on the stretcher bar	Lead carbonate, barium sulphate, calcium carbonate, silica, carbon black and iron oxide in oil
The Card Players (CAT. 6)	O ≈ ‡ 73 × 60	Lead carbonate, zinc oxide or sulphide, barium sulphate, silica and iron oxide in oil
Man with a Pipe (CAT. 7)	O # ‡ 73 × 60	Lead carbonate, barium sulphate, zinc oxide or sulphide, zinc carboxylate and carbon black and iron oxide in oil
Still Life with Plaster Cupid (CAT. 8)	Paper † ≡ 70.6 × 57.3	Calcium carbonate, lead carbonate, iron oxide and carbon black in oil
The Lac d'Annecy (CAT. 9)	O ‡ 81 × 65 The letter 'F' is stencilled onto the reverse	Lead carbonate, barium sulphate, calcium sulphate, lead carboxylate and carbon black in oil
Route tournante (CAT. 10)	§ # ‡ 92 × 73 A stamp of the colour merchant Chabod is on the reverse	Lead carbonate, barium sulphate and calcium carbonate in oil

* See Table 2 for a description of the methods of identification. Where zinc oxide or zinc sulphide is noted the white pigment is likely to comprise a mixture of lead carbonate with either barium sulphate or lithopone (barium sulphate with zinc sulphide) or alternatively, zinc oxide may be present. Where calcium carbonate (chalk) is noted and there are also black pigment particles, the black could be calcium phosphate (bone black).

O The support is medium weight, fairly loose, open weave linen canvas with weave counts ranging from 12 × 12 to 14 × 21.

§ Finely woven linen canvas, weave count 38 × 32.

This painting has been lined. Only *Pot of Primroses and Fruit* has a stamp on the stretcher advertising Charles Chapuis. Chapuis was apparently the only 'picture doctor' that Degas trusted and he recommended him to Vollard, Cézanne's dealer. Vollard began to use Chapuis for relining and stretching of canvases in February 1894. See *Cézanne to Picasso*, New York *et al.* 2006–07, p. 275.

≈ The painting has been loose lined.

† The paper has been adhered to a wooden panel.

‡ A standard, commercially available 'figure' size. In the Courtauld oil paintings Cézanne uses: figure 10 (55 × 46 cm) figure 20 (73 × 60 cm), figure 25 (81 × 65 cm), figure 30 (92 × 65 cm). The unlined *Lac d'Annecy* has the letter F standing for the standard 'figure' size stencilled to its reverse. *Route tournante* has the canvas stamp of Chabod, a supplier of colours and canvases. For other instances of the Chabod stamp see the forthcoming *National Gallery Technical Bulletin*, vol. 29, E. Reissner, 'Ways of Making: Practice and Innovation in Cézanne's Paintings in the National Gallery'.

≡ The paper support could have been cut from a *'grande aig'* (105 × 75 mm) standard size ready-primed paper. Such paper was commonly sold for oil paintings in either yellow or grey in a variety of textures. See A. Callen, *The Art of Impressionism*, New Haven and London 2000, p. 25.

Table 2: Pigments identified in the oil paintings and watercolours*

PAINTING	Lead white	Zinc white	Carbon black	Iron oxide	Chrome yellow	Cadmium yellow	Vermillion	Organic red	Emerald green	Viridian	Green earth	Cobalt blue	Ultramarine	Prussian blue	Indigo
The Etang des Sœurs (CAT. 1)	●	●		●	● ◊		●		●	●			●	●	
Tall Trees at the Jas de Bouffan (CAT. 3)	●		●	●	●	●	●	●	●	●	●		●	●	
The Montagne Sainte-Victoire (CAT. 4)	●	●		●	● ◊		●	● ∞	●	● ◊		●	●	●	
Pot of Primroses and Fruit (CAT. 5)	●	●	●	●	● ◊		●	● ◎	●	● ◊		●	●	●	
The Card Players (CAT. 6)	●		●	●			●	● ◎	●		●		●		
Man with a Pipe (CAT. 7)	●	●	●	●			●	● ∅	●						
Still Life with Plaster Cupid (CAT. 8)	●	●		●	●		●	●	●			●	●		
The Lac d'Annecy (CAT. 9)	●		●	●	● ◊		●	●	●	●		●	●	●	
Route tournante (CAT. 10)	●			●			●		●	● ◊		●	●		
A Shed (CAT. 12)				●				●		●		●			
The Montagne Sainte-Victoire (CAT. 14)				●	●		●	●	●	● ◊		●			
Armchair (CAT. 15)	●			●	● ◊		●	●	●	● ◊		●			
Statue under Trees (CAT. 16)					●		●	●	●			●			
Still Life with Apples, Bottle and Chairback (CAT. 17)				●	●		●	●	●			●	● ¤		●

* The identifications were made using two kinds of portable X-ray fluorescence (XRF) equipment and Infrared reflectance spectroscopy, analysis of paint samples using Light microscopy (LM) and Energy dispersive X-ray microanalysis in the scanning electron microscope (SEM-EDX) and also Fourier transform infrared microscopy and spectroscopy (FTIR) (in combination with Direct temperature resolved mass spectrometry (DTMS), Gas chromatography mass spectrometry (GCMS) and SEM-EDX) (see forthcoming paper describing these techniques fully – A. Burnstock, 'Analysis of inorganic materials from paintings and watercolours by Paul Cézanne from the Courtauld Gallery using two methods of non-invasive portable XRF with light microscopy and SEM/EDX spectroscopy').

∞ Two types of red lake

◎ Non-fluorescing

∅ Madder high in pseudopurpurine with some purpurin and a little alizarin was identified by using high-performance liquid chromatography (HPLC).

◊ This identification was made using XRF. When chrome is identified using this method it is often difficult to be certain whether this is indicating the presence of a chrome green such as viridian or chrome yellow.

¤ Aluminium was identified by XRF. It could indicate the presence of cobalt aluminate blue or possibly a mixture of cobalt blue and ultramarine.

ACKNOWLEDGEMENTS

My thanks to the Caroline Villers Fellowship which made this research possible, to Aviva Burnstock (The Courtauld Institute of Art, Department of Conservation and Technology) for her considerable support and also expertise in the identification of pigments, to the staff of The Courtauld Gallery who facilitated my access to the paintings, to Rachel Billinge (National Gallery, London) for capturing infrared reflectograms of the paintings, to Klaas Jan van de Berg and Suzan de Groot (Instituut Collectie Nederlands, Amsterdam), Jo Kirby (National Gallery, London), Bill Luckhurst (King's College, London), Federica Presciutti, Aldo Romani, Francesca Rosi, Costanza Miliani, Brunetto G. Brunetti and Manuela Vagnini (Centro di Eccellenza SMAArt, Dipartimento di Chimica, Università di Perugia) for contributing their expertise in the identification of pigments and ground materials, to Rica Jones and Piers Townsend (Tate, London) and Jacqueline Ridge and Lesley Stevens (National Gallery of Scotland, Edinburgh), who allowed me to examine the Cézannes in their care, and to Caroline Campbell and Stephanie Buck (The Courtauld Gallery), Greg Ward (Canterbury Christ Church University), John House (The Courtauld Institute of Art) and Anne Robbins (National Gallery, London) for the stimulating discussions we had in front of the paintings.

NOTES

1 House 2004, p. 146. House adds that these methods "were a visible realisation of the superiority of abstract ideas over sensory experience".

2 The French term *dessin* means drawing and line, but also more broadly draughtsmanship.

3 For Joachim Gasquet's account, 'Cézanne', first published in 1921, see Doran 2001, pp. 132, 142. Cézanne refers there to Ingres and Delacroix in discussions about drawing and colour.

4 Gowing in *Watercolour and Pencil Drawings by Cézanne*, Newcastle and London 1973, p. 7.

5 Adriani 1983, p. 64.

6 Angela Eames used this term in her lecture 'From Drawing to Computing and Back Again' delivered at the 'Drawing Across Boundaries' conference, Loughborough University, 1998 (see www.angelaeames.com). She writes: "Drawing as visual thinking, unconstrained by means or method, is both rudimentary and vital in developing human awareness of 'reality' in a synthesis of natural and artificial". See also C. de Zegher (ed.), *The Stage of Drawing Gesture and Act*, London and New York, 2003.

7 Shiff 1984, p. 299, note 23. Technical analysis has shown that Pissarro's palette at this time also contained black and earth colours; for an outline see L. Milsom, 'The Relationship of Camille and Lucien Pissarro considered through technical Examination of their Works from The Courtauld Collection', unpublished Courtauld Institute of Art Diploma dissertation, 2007, pp. 58–59.

8 For the pigments identified in the Courtauld oil paintings and watercolours see Table 2 at the end of this essay.

9 The painter Louis le Bail wrote in his unpublished, private notes that he had received advice from Pissarro in 1896–97 (significantly later than the period when Cézanne and Pissarro were working alongside one another): "Do not define too closely the outlines of things; it is the brushes' stroke of the right value and colour that should produce the drawing". See Rewald 1961, p. 458.

10 See Rewald 1984, Doran 1978, Doran 2001.

11 Hippolyte Taine's survey of modern theories of the mind, *On Intelligence* (1870), ran to a dozen editions during Cézanne's lifetime. See Gage 1993, p. 210.

12 Maurice Denis visited Cézanne in 1906 and in his journal recalled Cézanne saying that light must be represented by colours and not reproduced: "*La lumière n'est pas une chose qui peut être reproduite, mais que doit être représentée par autre chose, par des couleurs*': Doran 1978, p. 93, or Doran 2001, p. 93.

13 P. Smith, *Impressionism beneath the Surface*, London 1995, p. 156.

14 Emile Bernard in *L'Occident*, July 1904, pp. 17–30, reprinted in Doran 1978, p. 36, and Doran 2001, p. 38, and translated here by John House. "*Lire la nature, c'est la voir sous le voile de l'interprétation par taches colorées, se succédent selon une loi de harmonie. Ces grandes teintes s'analysent ainsi par les modulations. Peindre c'est enregistrer ses sensations colorées*'. See also House's discussion of the term *sensation* as an individual's 'sensory experience' in his essay in this catalogue.

15 Smith 1996, p. 48.

16 For a discussion of this debate see House 2004, Chapter 5, p. 146.

17 Bernard records these terms in one of the 'opinions' that he attributes to Cézanne. See Bernard 1904, reprinted in Doran 1978, p. 36, and Doran 2001, p. 39: "*On ne devrait pas dire modeler, on devrait dire moduler*".

18 Letter B5.

19 Joachim Gasquet, 'Cézanne', first published in 1921 , reprinted in Doran 1978, p. 108, and Doran 2001, p. 110.

20 Bernard 1904, reprinted in Doran 1978, p. 36, and Doran 2001, p. 38: "*Il n'y a pas de ligne, il n'y a pas de modelé, il n'y a que des contrastes. Ces contrastes, ce ne sont pas le noir et le blanc qui les donnent, c'est la sensation colorée. Du rapport exact des tons résulte le modelé. Quand ils sont harmonieusement juxtaposés et qu'ils y sont tous, le tableau se modèle tout seul*". The English translation here provided by John House.

21 R.P. Rivière and J.F. Schnerb, 'L'Atelier de Cézanne', in *La Grande Revue*, December 1907, pp. 811–17, reproduced in Doran 1978, p. 87, and Doran 2001, p. 88: "*Cézanne ne cherchait pas à représenter les formes par une ligne. Le contour n'exis-tait pour lui qu'en tant que lieu où une forme finit et où une autre forme commence … Point de trait en principe, une forme n'existe que par les formes voisines. Les traits noirs qui cernent souvent ses peintures n'étaient pas pour Cézanne un élément destiné à s'ajouter à la couleur, mais simplement une manière de reprendre plus facilement l'ensemble d'une forme par le contour avant de modeler par la couleur*." The English translation here provided by John House.

22 See, for instance, Smith 1996, p. 61.

23 Bernard 1904, reproduced in Doran 1978, p. 36, and Doran 2001, p. 39: "*Le dessin et la couleur ne sont point distincts; au fur et à mesure que l'on peint on dessine; plus la couleur s'harmonise, plus le dessin se précise. Quand la couleur est à sa richesse, la forme est à sa plénitude. Les contrastes et les rapports de tons, voilà le secret du dessin et du modelé*." The English translation here provided by John House.

24 Gowing 1973, p. 18.

25 Adriani 1983, p. 64.

26 During the course of the research project the author examined the oil paintings in infrared light using a Hamamatsu vidicon camera. In 2007 Rachel Billinge, Research Associate in the Conservation Department at the National Gallery, carried out further infrared reflectography, including the watercolours, using the National Gallery's new digital infrared scanning camera SIRIS (Scanning InfraRed Imaging System), which uses a indium gallium arsenide (InGaAs) array sensor. These infrared reflectograms are reproduced in this catalogue. For further details about the camera see D. Saunders, R. Billinge, J. Cupitt, N. Atkinson and H. Laing, 'A New Camera for High-Resolution Infrared Imaging of Works of Art', in *Studies in Conservation*, vol. 51, 2006, pp. 277–90.

27 See Simms 2002 for an alternative reading of Cézanne's challenge to the traditional additive relationship between drawing and colour in watercolours. His practice is described in terms of a separation of the drawn and painted halves of the medium where each level of the image offers the same visual information but in different languages.

28 *Cézanne in the Studio*, Los Angeles 2004, p. 108.

29 See the description of the function of the graphite drawing in relation to colour in cat. 17.

30 *Cézanne in the Studio*, Los Angeles 2004, p. 122.

31 *Cézanne in the Studio*, Los Angeles 2004, p. 112. The term '*tache*' refers to a patch of colour.

32 Ratcliffe 1960, pp. 282–83: 'The crucial areas in every attempt at that elusive realisation must be located ultimately at the contours, the meeting places on the canvas of the objects represented".

33 *Pioneering Modern Painting*, New York 2005, p. 52.

34 Rivére and Schnerb 1907, reprinted in Doran 1978, p. 87, and Doran 2001, p. 86: "*Cézanne déclarait avec vivacité son horreur de l'eoeil photographique, du dessin d'exactitude automatique enseigné dans cette Ecole des Beaux-Arts …*".

35 R. Fry, 'On Some Modern Drawings', in
    Transformations, London 1926, pp. 203–04.

36 Rewald 1984, p. 299. See also cat. 17 for
    more detailed references.

37 *Watercolour and Pencil Drawings by Cézanne*,
    Newcastle and London 1973, p. 21.

38 Cézanne's *Bathers* in the National Gallery,
    London (fig. 8) is a studio composition, so
    the repeated contour lines visible in this
    paintings can not be attributed to direct
    perceptual experience.

39 M. Merleau-Ponty, 'Cézanne's Doubt'
    in *Sense and Non-sense*, Evanston, Illinois,
    1964, p. 15.

40 Evelyn Benesch gives examples of problem-
    atic tension between networks of lines and
    patches of colour in Cézanne's work, which
    may have led to his abandoning some of
    his works, in 'From the Incomplete to the
    Unfinished', in *Cézanne. Finished – Unfinished*,
    Vienna and Zurich 2000, p. 51.

41 J. Crary, *Suspensions of Perception*, Cambridge,
    Mass., and London, 2000, pp. 287–89.

42 See Table 1 at the end of this essay for
    the materials used in the grounds of the
    Courtauld oil paintings.

43 Vollard 1924, first published in 1914 and
    reprinted in Doran 2001, p. 10.

44 Cézanne uses the term *"un point culminant"*
    in his letter to Bernard of 25 July 1904
    (Letter B5).

45 Bernard, 'Souvenirs', in *Mercure de France*,
    reprinted in Doran 1978, p. 59, and Doran
    2001, p. 60: *"Il commençait par l'ombre et avec une
    tache qu'il recouvrait d'une seconde plus débordante,
    puis d'une troisième, jusqu'à ce que toutes ces teintes,
    faisant écrans, modelassent, en colorante, l'objet".*
    The English translation here provided by
    John House.

46 *Ibid.*, p. 59 and p. 60 respectively: *"Je compris
    de suite que c'était une loi d'harmonie qui guidait son
    travail et que toutes ces modulations avaient une
    direction fixée d'avance, dans sa raison. Il procédait
    en somme comme ont dû l'observer les tapissiers
    anciens, faisant se suivre les couleurs apparentées
    jusqu'à ce qu'elles rencontrassent leur contraste dans
    l'opposition."*

47 L. Gowing, 'The Logic of Ordered
    Sensations', in *Cézanne. The Late Work*,
    New York and Houston 1977, p. 58.

48 Gage 1993, p. 173, discusses the analysis of
    colour contrast by artists and writers,
    starting from Aristotle.

49 Rivière and Schnerb 1907, reprinted in
    Doran 1978, p. 88, and Doran 2001, p. 87:
    *"C'est par l'opposition des tons chauds et froids que
    les couleurs don't dispose le peintre, sans qualité
    lumineuse absolue en elles-mêmes, arrivent à
    représenter la lumière et l'ombre".*

50 Gage 1993, p. 173.

51 Rewald 1983, p. 237.

52 Gowing 1973, p. 12.

53 Gowing 1977 (cited in note 47), p. 56.

54 *Cézanne in the Studio*, Los Angeles 2004,
    p. 76 note 3.

55 Vollard 1924, p. 129.

56 See Table 2 at the end of this essay.

57 Larger amounts of carbon black were
    present in *Man with a Pipe* and *The Card Players*.

58 Mixed greens comprising cobalt blue and
    chrome yellow were identified in the study of
    nine watercolour paintings by Cézanne in
    the collection of the Philadelphia Museum
    of Art. Mixed purples were also identified.
    See Zieske 2002, pp. 89–100.

59 Gasquet 1921 (cited in note 19), reprinted in
    Doran 1978, p. 132, and Doran 2001, p. 133.

60 Refractive index describes numerically the
    angle at which a substance deflects a ray
    of light when it enters obliquely from a
    medium of a different density – air, varnish,
    medium, pigment particle. The less scatter
    of light, caused by the pigment at the
    boundary of medium and pigment, the
    more transparent and saturated the paint
    layer. This is because the majority of light
    penetrates and is absorbed. It is absorption
    of light that gives rise to colour. Pigments
    and medium each have a numerical
    refractive index.

61 Adriani 1983, p. 15.

62 For an in-depth description of the properties
    and practice of watercolour see Bruce
    MacEvoy www.handprint.com.

63 S. Rees Jones, 'The History of the Artist's
    palette in terms of Chromaticity', in the
    proceedings of the seminar *Application of Science
    in Examination of Works of Art*, Boston Museum
    of Fine Arts Research Laboratory, 1967, p. 73.

64 There is some confusion over the terms
    gouache and body colour or distemper.
    Traditionally gouache is the method of
    mixing watercolour pigment with an
    opaque white pigment in gum Arabic.
    Body colour is traditionally a mix of
    concentrated watercolour pigments with
    fish or animal glue, without the addition
    of any white pigment. Both gouache and
    body colour are opaque watercolour paint.

65 Adriani 1983, p. 16.

66 Yellow lake was identified in the National
    Gallery, London's, *Hillside in Provence* (*c*. 1886–
    90) but not in the Courtauld oils. See A.
    Roy, 'The Palettes of Three Impressionist
    Paintings', *National Gallery Technical Bulletin*,
    no. 9, 1985, p. 19. Yellow lake is, however,
    very difficult to identify so its presence
    cannot be ruled out.

67 It is not possible to identify the presence
    of turpentine as a diluent; however, the
    appearance of Cézanne's paint, particularly
    in the early stages of a painting's execution,
    points to its use. For a slightly expanded
    discussion of this and his possible use of
    Haarlem siccative, see in the forthcoming
    National Gallery *Technical Bulletin, no. 29*, 2008,
    E. Reissner, 'Ways of Making: Practice and
    Innovation in Cézanne's Paintings in the
    National Gallery'.

68 Three of the Courtauld oil paintings were
    primed after stretching – *L'Etang des Sœurs,
    La Montagne Sainte-Victoire* and *Man with a Pipe*.
    There is nothing to suggest that these
    grounds were applied by Cézanne rather
    than by a manufacturer or colour merchant.
    The grounds applied before stretching were
    commercial.

69 Supported by technical analysis of Cézanne's
    The Gardener Vallier (*c*. 1905–06; Tate, London)
    and *La Montagne Sainte-Victoire* (*c*. 1900–02;
    National Gallery of Scotland, Edinburgh).

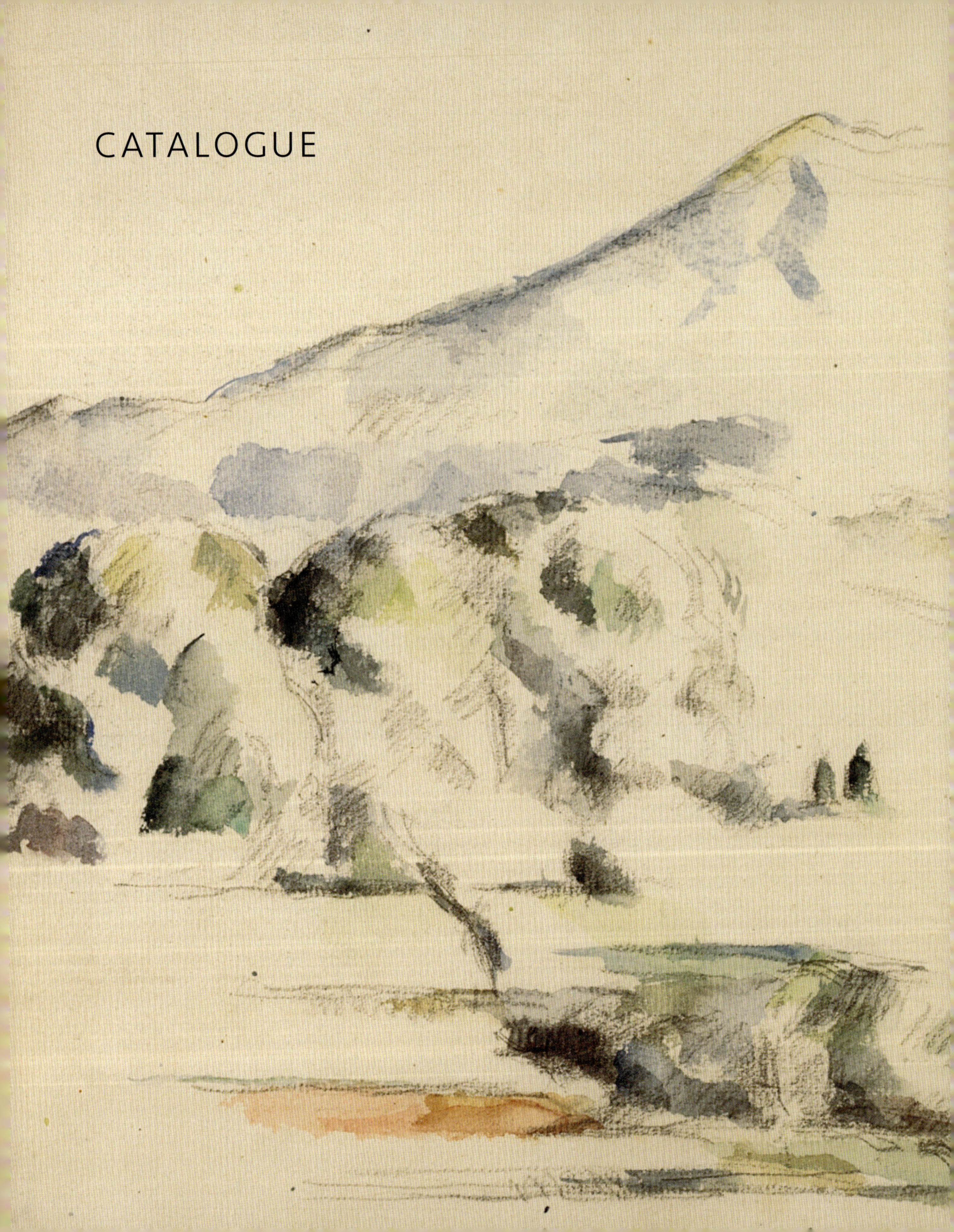
CATALOGUE

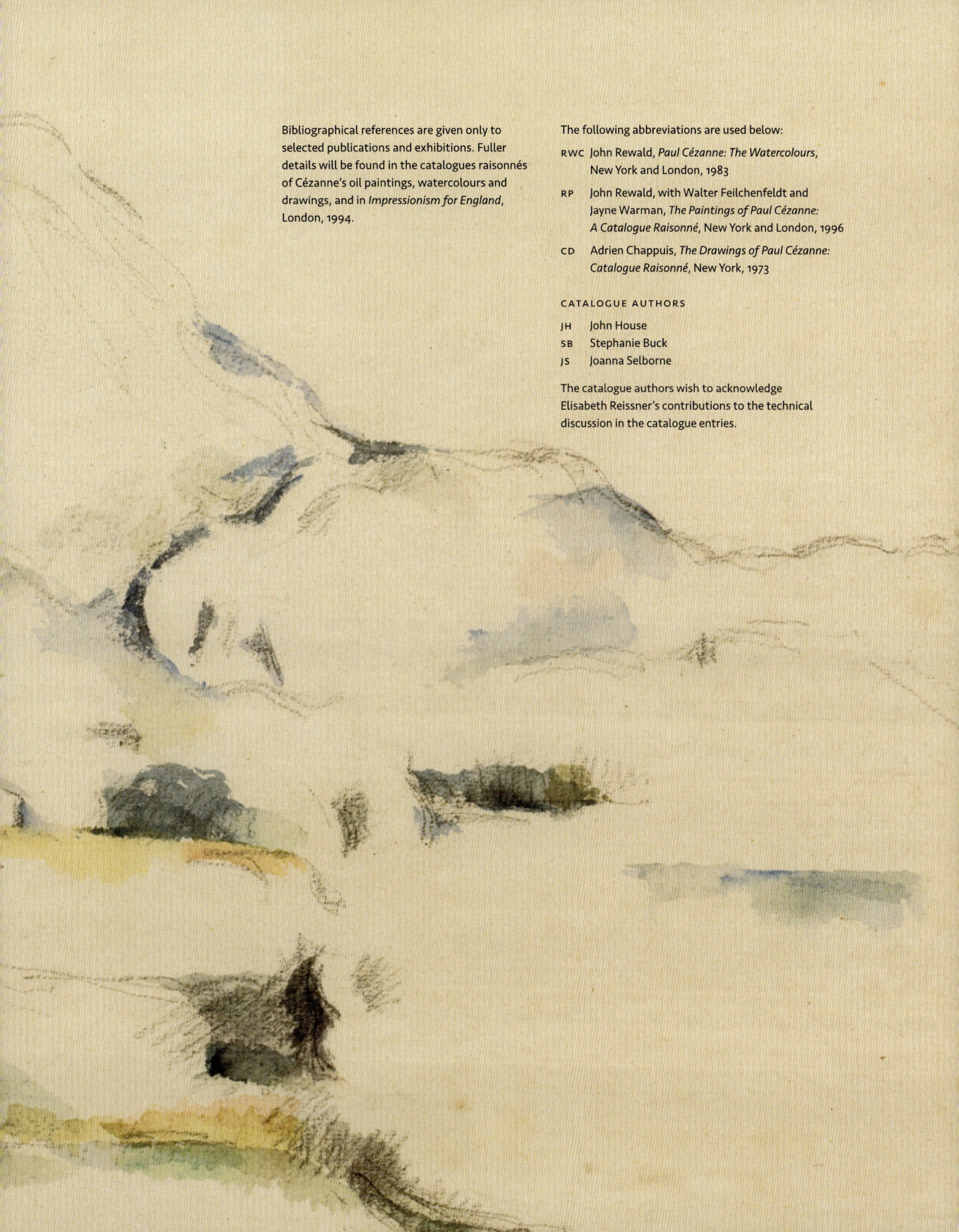

Bibliographical references are given only to selected publications and exhibitions. Fuller details will be found in the catalogues raisonnés of Cézanne's oil paintings, watercolours and drawings, and in *Impressionism for England*, London, 1994.

The following abbreviations are used below:

RWC John Rewald, *Paul Cézanne: The Watercolours*, New York and London, 1983

RP John Rewald, with Walter Feilchenfeldt and Jayne Warman, *The Paintings of Paul Cézanne: A Catalogue Raisonné*, New York and London, 1996

CD Adrien Chappuis, *The Drawings of Paul Cézanne: Catalogue Raisonné*, New York, 1973

CATALOGUE AUTHORS

JH John House
SB Stephanie Buck
JS Joanna Selborne

The catalogue authors wish to acknowledge Elisabeth Reissner's contributions to the technical discussion in the catalogue entries.

1 **L'Etang des Sœurs, Osny, près de Pontoise**, *c.* 1875

The Etang des Soeurs, Osny, near Pontoise

Oil on canvas, 60 × 73.5 cm
The Courtauld Gallery, London (Samuel Courtauld Trust)
P.1932.SC.53
Courtauld Gift, 1932

Osny is a village near the town of Pontoise, about twenty miles north of Paris; Camille Pissarro lived in Pontoise in the 1870s, and Cézanne worked with him in that region on several occasions during the decade. This painting has normally been dated to 1877, on the basis of the recollections of Pissarro's son Lucien, who was then a boy; however, as first suggested by Kathleen Adler, it should very probably be dated to 1875 on stylistic grounds. Although there is no report of Cézanne visiting Pontoise that year, he was in the north of France, and a visit to Pissarro might well have passed unrecorded. Cézanne had initially worked with Pissarro in 1872–74 in order to learn the discipline of painting from closely observed natural effects (see pp. 31–32, and figs. 11 and 13), but by around 1874 both men began to build up their paint surfaces with denser, more tightly structured zones of colour, and in several paintings dated 1875 Pissarro made extensive use of the palette knife. *L'Etang des Sœurs, Osny* is one of a group of paintings by Cézanne which are closely comparable to these; indeed, it seems very possible that it was painted at the same time, and shows the same site, as Pissarro's *Small Bridge, Pontoise* (fig. 43); Pissarro himself was the first owner of the canvas, though we do not know when he acquired it. By 1877 Cézanne, like Pissarro, was again working only with the brush, and with a far more broken touch.

Use of the palette knife in these years was a clear marker of an artist's rejection of academic methods, and in the mid-1870s this technique carried a specific association with Gustave Courbet, the celebrated master of knife-work, who was then in political exile in Switzerland. The knife is used here to build up the composition in bold swathes of paint, particularly in the foliage of the trees (fig. 44). In some places the paint is applied in denser blocks of colour, but the rhythm of the foliage is achieved by broad movements with the knife, creating a strong directional movement across the central area. Some sweeps of paint cover considerable areas of the picture with great simplicity, but others are applied so thinly that they set up complex relationships with the underlying layers seen through from below. Individual areas also acquire distinctive shapes of their own, rhyming with other similar shapes, most notably in the bands of dark leaves that lie over the sunlit foliage beyond. The apparent breadth of this knife-work belies the delicacy with which the knife is used. The brush is also employed on occasion, particularly in some of the narrower trunks and branches, but in the principal trunks the paint is largely built up from complex, superimposed knife strokes, sometimes, it seems, subsequently feathered with the brush. Overall, the effect of the work with the palette knife has been somewhat affected by

PROVENANCE

Camille Pissarro, Paris; Alphonse Kann, Saint-Germain-en-Laye; (Galerie Barbazanges, Paris?); Hugo von Reininghaus, Vienna; Galerie Barbazanges, Paris; Alexander Reid, Glasgow; Thomas Agnew & Sons, London; Samuel Courtauld, London (bought in 1923)

SELECTED EXHIBITIONS

Französische Kunst des XIX. und XX. Jahrhunderts, Kunsthaus, Zurich, 1917, no. 19; *Masterpieces of French Art of the 19th Century*, Thos. Agnew & Sons, London, 1923, no. 4; *Paintings and Drawings*, London 1925, no. 15; *Samuel Courtauld Memorial Exhibition*, London 1948, no. 5; *Landscape in French Art*, London 1949–50, no. 310; *Cézanne*, Edinburgh and London 1954, no. 16; *Impressionism for England*, London 1994, no. 4; *Pioneering Modern Painting*, New York, Los Angeles and Paris 2005–06, no. 63; *Cézanne in Britain*, London 2006–07, no. 16

SELECTED LITERATURE

RP 307
Dormoy 1929, p. 20; *Home House* 1935, no. 74; Cooper 1954 (2), no. 6; *Cézanne: The Late Work*, exh. cat. New York and Houston 1977–78, p. 56; Kathleen Adler, 'Aspects of Camille Pissarro *c.* 1871–1883', MA Report, Courtauld Institute of Art, London, 1969, pp. 40–42; Callen 2000, p. 138; House 2004, pp. 169–71

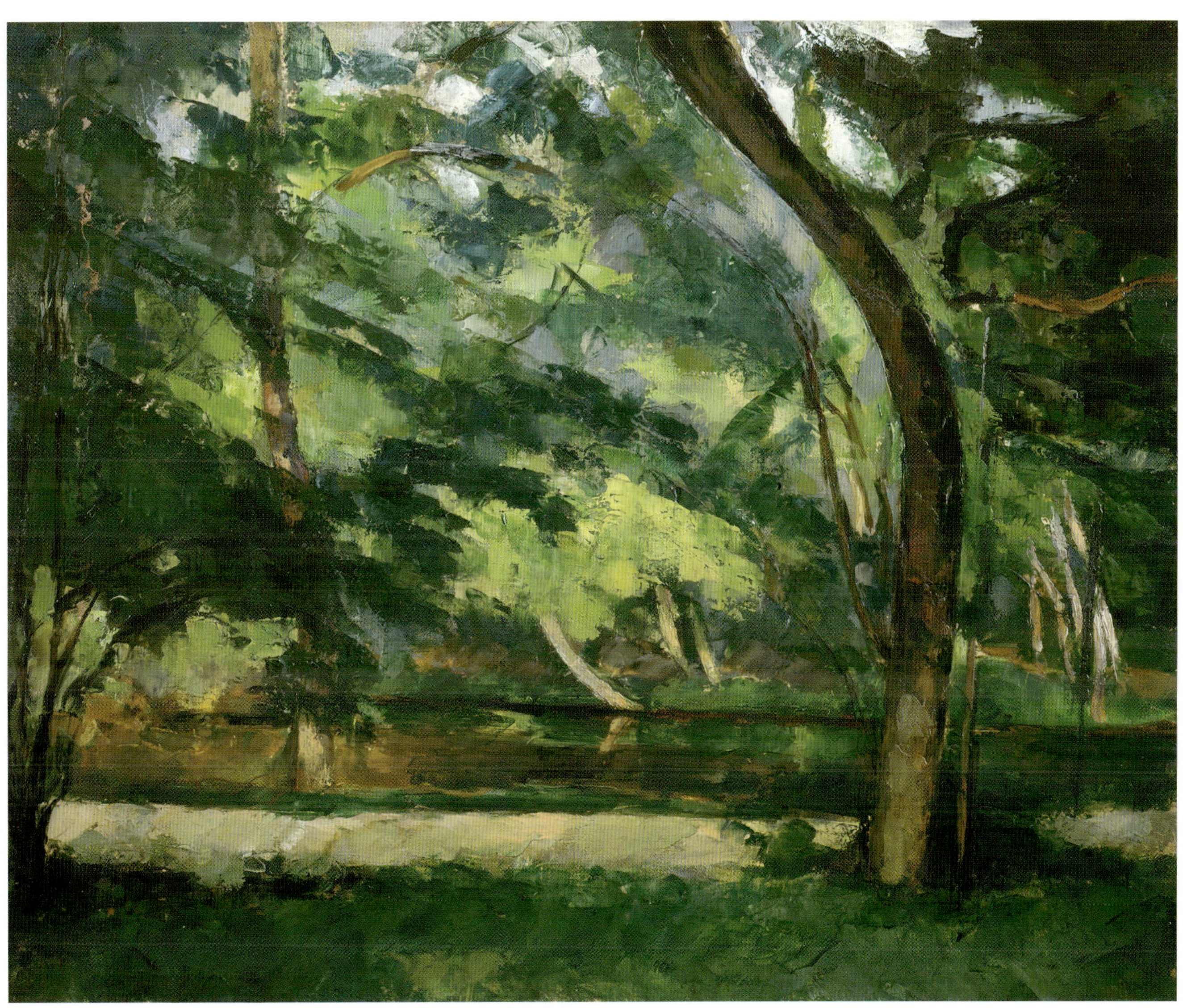

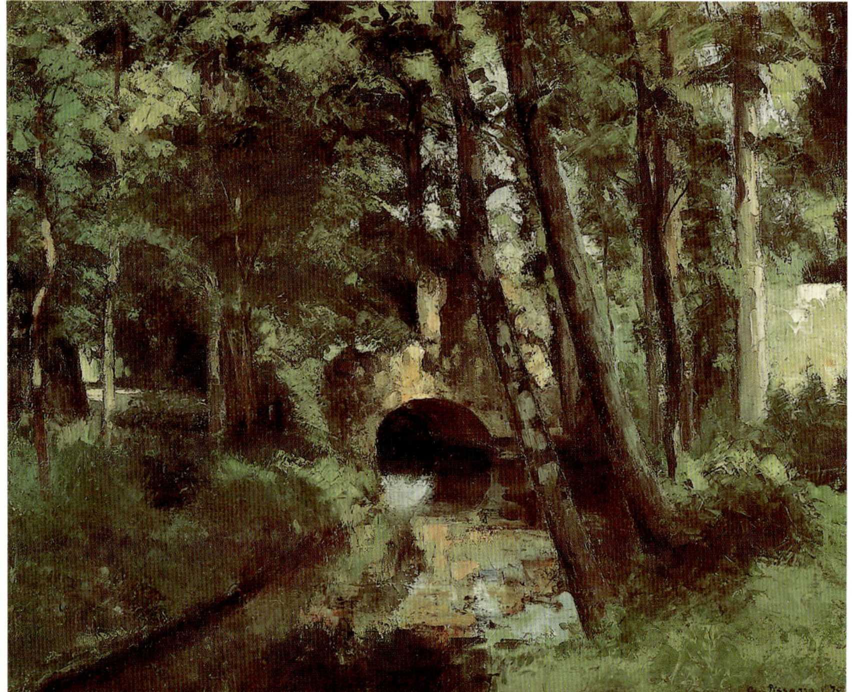

flattening of the paint surface during the later relining of the canvas.

Green is the dominant colour of the picture, containing mixtures of viridian and emerald green (see table 2, p. 69); vivid yellow-greens appear in the sunlit foliage across the water, and strong clear greens are used in other areas, while the more shadowed zones that act as *repoussoirs* are suggested in part by darker greens, in part by the mixture of ultramarine blue with the colour, thus combining tonal and colouristic methods of modelling. The sharp contrast between these zones was, it seems, only established in the later stages of the execution of the painting. Small warm-hued accents enliven the composition, and at certain points, such as on the main tree trunks and along the far edge of the water, juxtapositions of blue with warm oranges, reds and

browns create a more complex effect. This is particularly striking beneath the small diagonal sunlit tree trunk at the centre of the canvas; directly below this trunk, the water's edge is marked by a clear blue horizontal stroke, added late in the picture's execution, whereas to its right the water's edge is marked by a stroke of orange-red.

We have no clear evidence of how far Cézanne worked out-of-doors on paintings such as this, but it is very likely that it was, in part if not entirely, executed in front of the subject. However, the forms are simplified and rather stylised, with the arcs of trunks and branches framing the broad sweeps of the foliage. As with so many of his canvases, Cézanne stopped work on *L'Etang des Sœurs* when the definition of some of the forms was still in a provisional state. Here, the post or sapling immediately to the right of the principal trunk is overpainted with green touches that seem to belong to foliage beyond the tree-trunk, though the post itself appears to be standing immediately to its right; moreover, it is unclear to what tree the curling branches above this post belong. There is a further indication that Cézanne did not see the canvas as fully realised, or at least that it was not a work that he treated with care; the areas of exposed brownish stained canvas, where the paint layer has been lost in a roughly vertical band a few inches in from the left edge of the picture, suggest that at some time it was stored unstretched with its edge crudely folded. The canvas is primed with a light cream tone; the variations in the density of this ground around the cusped weave of the canvas edges indicate that it was applied when the painting was already stretched.

By the early 1880s Cézanne was working with the brush, in delicate parallel strokes of colour, but in the trees in *Tall Trees at the Jas de Bouffan* (cat. 3), for instance, these finer strokes are grouped so as to create rhythms and patterns whose overall effect is comparable to the foliage here, though the detailed surface effect of the canvas is very different. It is in lightly worked canvases from late in his career, such as *Route tournante* (cat. 10), that we find blocks of colour, applied with the brush, that are comparable to the palette-knife strokes here.

JH

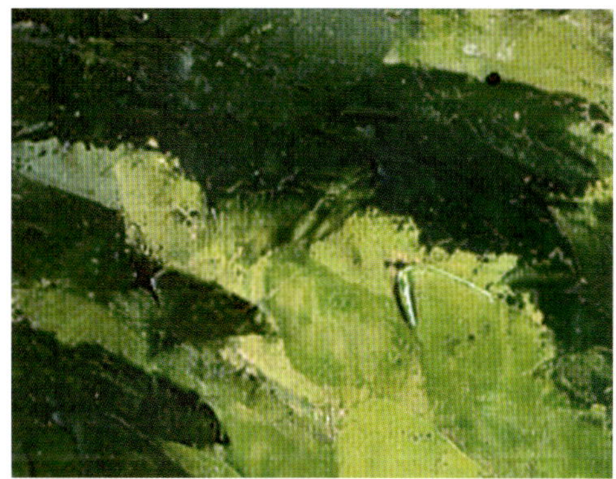

FIG. 44
Detail of cat. 1 showing the use of
the palette knife

2 **Ferme Normande, été (Hattenville)**, 1882 (?)

Farm in Normandy, Summer (Hattenville)

Oil on canvas, 49.5 × 65.7 cm
Private collection
(on extended loan to The Courtauld Gallery)

In 1882 the wife of Cézanne's principal patron, Victor Chocquet, inherited a farm at Hattenville near Yvetot in Normandy, and Cézanne very probably visited the Chocquets there that summer; as John Rewald has shown, this is one of a group of four closely related paintings of Normandy orchards, all of them originally in Chocquet's collection, which presumably show the place.[1]

Though *Farm in Normandy* is comparatively small and not elaborately finished, Cézanne built up a composition of great monumentality, framed by the arching branches from the left trees, and structured by the rhythm of the background trunks. Work on the painting ceased at a point when some areas were more fully worked than others. At the top left the background is blocked in with simple patches of colour, thinly applied, and the grass is treated in broad sweeps of quite uniform colour; but at certain points in the foliage the brushwork is far more broken and rhythmic, in crisp parallel strokes which suggest the texture of the foliage whilst at the same time giving the painting a taut surface structure. This type of brushwork appears again in *Tall Trees at the Jas de Bouffan* (cat. 3), and played a crucial role in the development of the most distinctive qualities of Cézanne's art (see pp. 33–37).

The greens which dominate the composition range from light and yellowish where the foliage is caught by the light, to duller hues with nuances of blue in the shadows throughout; against this play of cool colours are set successions of warm touches – heightened red accents which at times appear seemingly without naturalistic justification, on tree trunks and branches, and on the roof edge on the left, establishing links across the picture surface between elements located in different spatial planes. A similar function is served, less obtrusively, by a number of stronger blue accents that heighten the effect of shadow beneath the trees and stress the cool end of the picture's colour-composition. The lightest zone is the area seen between the tree-trunks at the centre of the canvas, but it is not clear what is represented by these cream-hued strokes, added very late in the execution of the painting.

The sticks or saplings in the meadow to the right reveal most clearly Cézanne's process of revising his compositions. Though this area is not thickly painted, their placing was altered at least twice. Both verticals are overpainted with a stroke of green across the top of the area of open grass, as if both were to be erased; moreover, the left of the two verticals was moved; its previous position can still be seen, not fully covered by reworking, at the same angle and about 2 cm to the right of its present position. In the area of foliage above and to the left of this, gently curved fine dark painted lines indicate the directions of the branches without being fully integrated with the green strokes that depict the foliage.

Perhaps in part because Cézanne did not have to rely upon selling his paintings in order to survive, he abandoned many when different areas of them were in different states of completion and certain parts were left unresolved. We cannot tell whether he regarded *Farm in Normandy* as a resolved canvas, since we do not know whether he sold it to Chocquet or simply left it with him when he left Hattenville. JH

PROVENANCE

Victor Chocquet, Paris; sale, Chocquet Collection, Galerie G. Petit, Paris, July 1–4, 1899, no. 11, as *L'Eté*; Alexandre Rosenberg, Paris; Bernheim-Jeune, Paris; Auguste Pellerin, Paris; Ambroise Vollard, Paris; Galerie E. Bignou, Paris; Reid & Lefevre, London; Samuel Courtauld, London (bought in 1937); Christabel Lady Aberconway, London; Private collection

SELECTED EXHIBITIONS

Landscape in French Art, London 1949–50, no. 316; *Samuel Courtauld Memorial Exhibition*, London 1948, no. 6; *Cézanne*, Edinburgh and London 1954, no. 30; *Impressionism for England*, London 1994, no. 5; *Cézanne*, Paris, London and Philadelphia 1995–6, no. 86

SELECTED LITERATURE

Rivière 1923, p. 214; Cooper 1954 (1), p. 378; Cooper 1954 (2), no. 7; Rewald 1985, p. 165

NOTE

1 Rewald 1983, pp. 151–52.

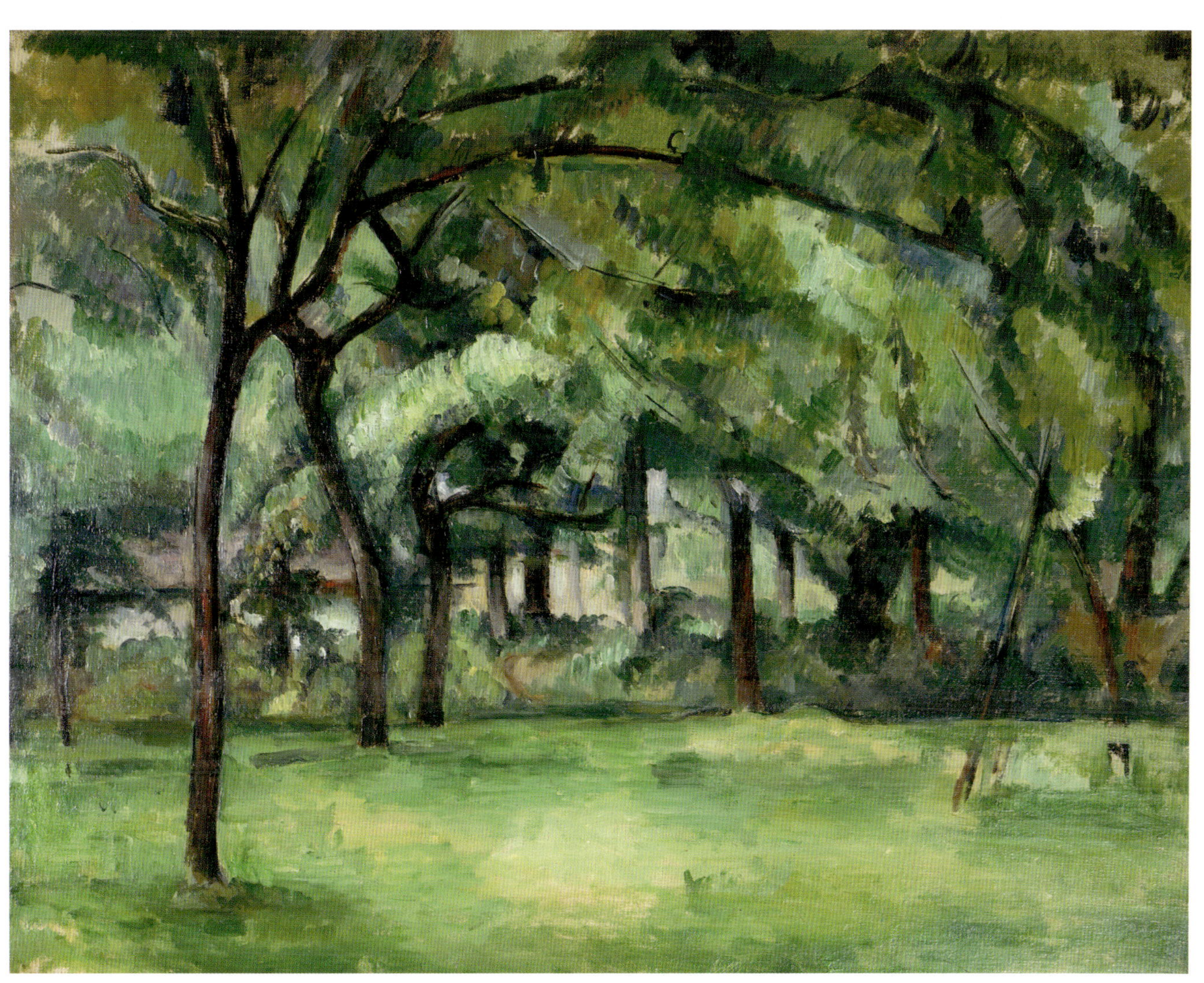

3 Les Grands Arbres au Jas de Bouffan, *c.* 1883

Tall Trees at the Jas de Bouffan

Oil on canvas, 65 × 81 cm
The Courtauld Gallery, London (Samuel Courtauld Trust)
P.1948.SC.54
Courtauld Bequest 1948

The Jas de Bouffan was the house and estate owned since 1859 by the artist's father, Louis-Auguste Cézanne, a wealthy banker. The house, a *manoir* dating from around 1700, lies about a mile and a half west of the centre of Aix-en-Provence. Cézanne painted many views of the house and grounds from 1866 until he sold the estate in 1899, and found there the solitude that he needed in order to work, both in the garden and in his studio in the house.

Tall Trees at the Jas de Bouffan is a particularly clear illustration of Cézanne's painting technique at the period. Working from a light creamy priming (visible in places, for instance near the bottom right corner), he first laid on comparatively simple, flat layers of colour, often thin and translucent, such as those seen in the lower right area of the canvas, to establish the essential planes of the composition. These were gradually refined by the addition of variegations of colour in crisper, more distinct brushstrokes; he did not work up the whole composition to a consistent degree of finish, but focused on certain salient points, leaving other areas scantily painted. In its more highly worked parts, the resulting painting is covered with a network of rhythmic strokes, often running in sequences parallel to each other.

This stroke is used here most consistently in the foliage, giving some sense of the natural textures represented, but, when viewed closely, the juxtaposed strokes gain a rhythm and a relative autonomy of their own (see pp. 33–37). Here, they are softer and more feathery than in his canvases of *c.* 1880 (figs. 12, 16), though they still give a distinctive sense of order to the picture surface, running mostly in diagonals in the foliage of the trees, but primarily vertical in the central bushes, thus serving to anchor the composition. In the foliage, their varied colour gives a shimmer and richness to the surface and a sense of light and atmosphere, but their ordered arrangement transcends the mobile effects of light on foliage that were Cézanne's starting point. This treatment of the surface in sequences of parallel brushstrokes can be compared with the evenly weighted, rhythmic handling adopted by his friend Pissarro in the same years (fig. 13), though Pissarro's strokes always retain a closer visual relationship to the textures of the scene represented.

The colour in the picture is clear and rich, with strong reds and oranges set off against the dominant network of blues and greens; even the more subdued areas of the picture, such as the tree-trunks amid the foliage, are enlivened by accents of stronger, warmer colour. The orange-red strokes on the tree-trunks, added late in the execution of the picture and seemingly arbitrary in representational terms, play a vital role in linking the upper parts of the canvas to the two principal sunlit areas below, namely, the view into distance on the right and the buildings beyond the trees at far left, which frame the scene. Between these luminous, warm zones a single stronger reddish accent, just below the bushes near the centre of the canvas, anchors the whole image. This heightened range of colours, adopted to evoke the rich coloured light of southern France (see also cat. 4), is a contrast to the rather denser greens of *Farm in Normandy* (cat. 2), painted in northern France in the same period.

PROVENANCE

Ambroise Vollard, Paris; Paul Rosenberg, Paris; Samuel Courtauld, London (bought in 1924)

SELECTED EXHIBITIONS

Paintings and Drawings, London 1925, no. 16; *Samuel Courtauld Memorial Exhibition*, London 1948, no. 11; *Landscape in French Art*, London 1949–50, no. 309; *Cézanne*, Edinburgh and London 1954, no. 33; *Impressionism for England*, London 1994, no. 7; *Cézanne in Provence*, Washington and Aix-en-Provence 2006, no. 23

SELECTED LITERATURE

RP 547
Sitwell 1925, p. 63, iii; Dormoy 1929, p. 19; Jamot and Turner 1934, no. 20; J. Rewald and L. Marschutz, *Forum*, no. 9, 1935, p. 253; Cooper 1954 (1), p. 379; Cooper 1954 (2), no. 11; Stokes 1978, pp. 266–67

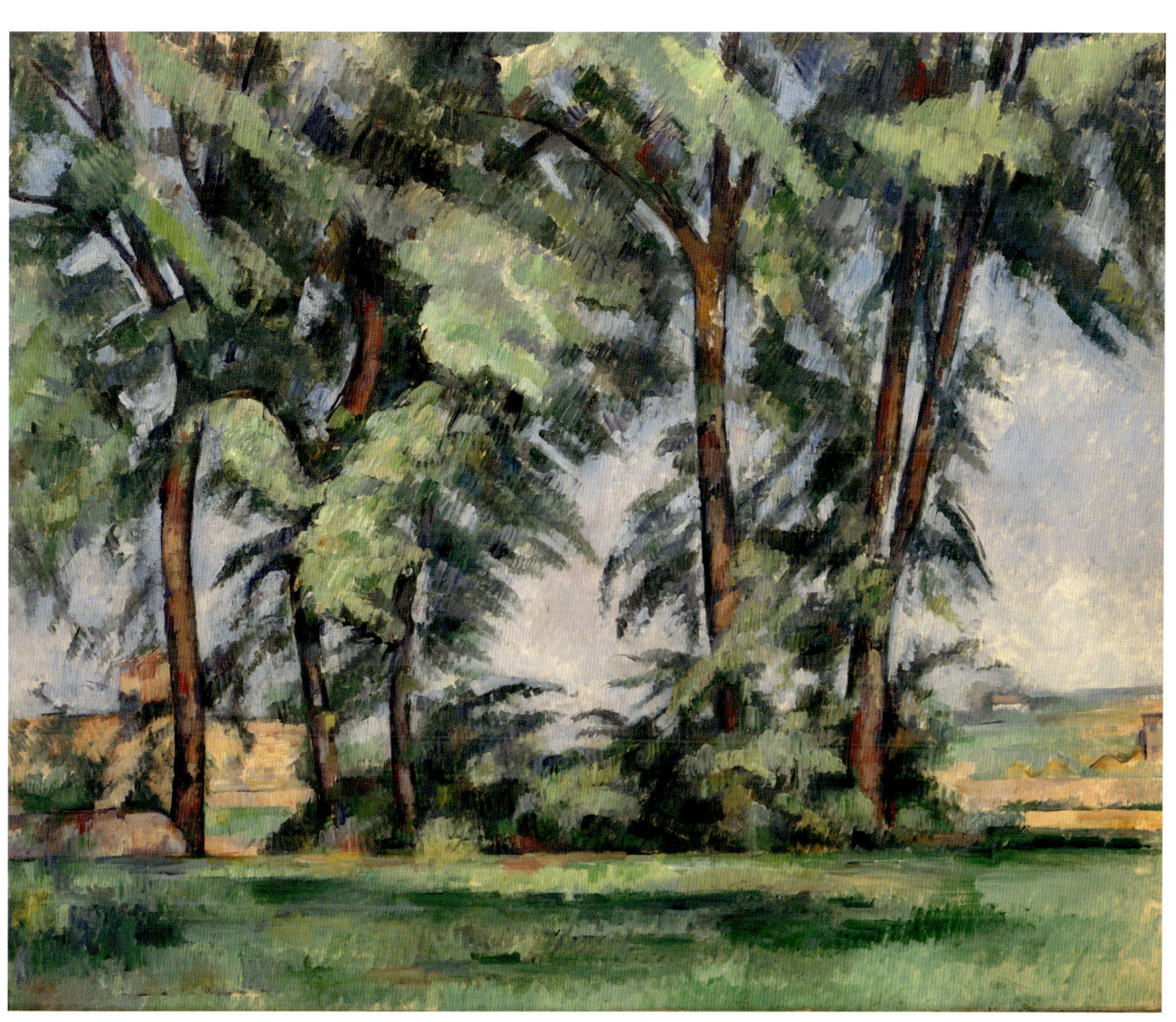

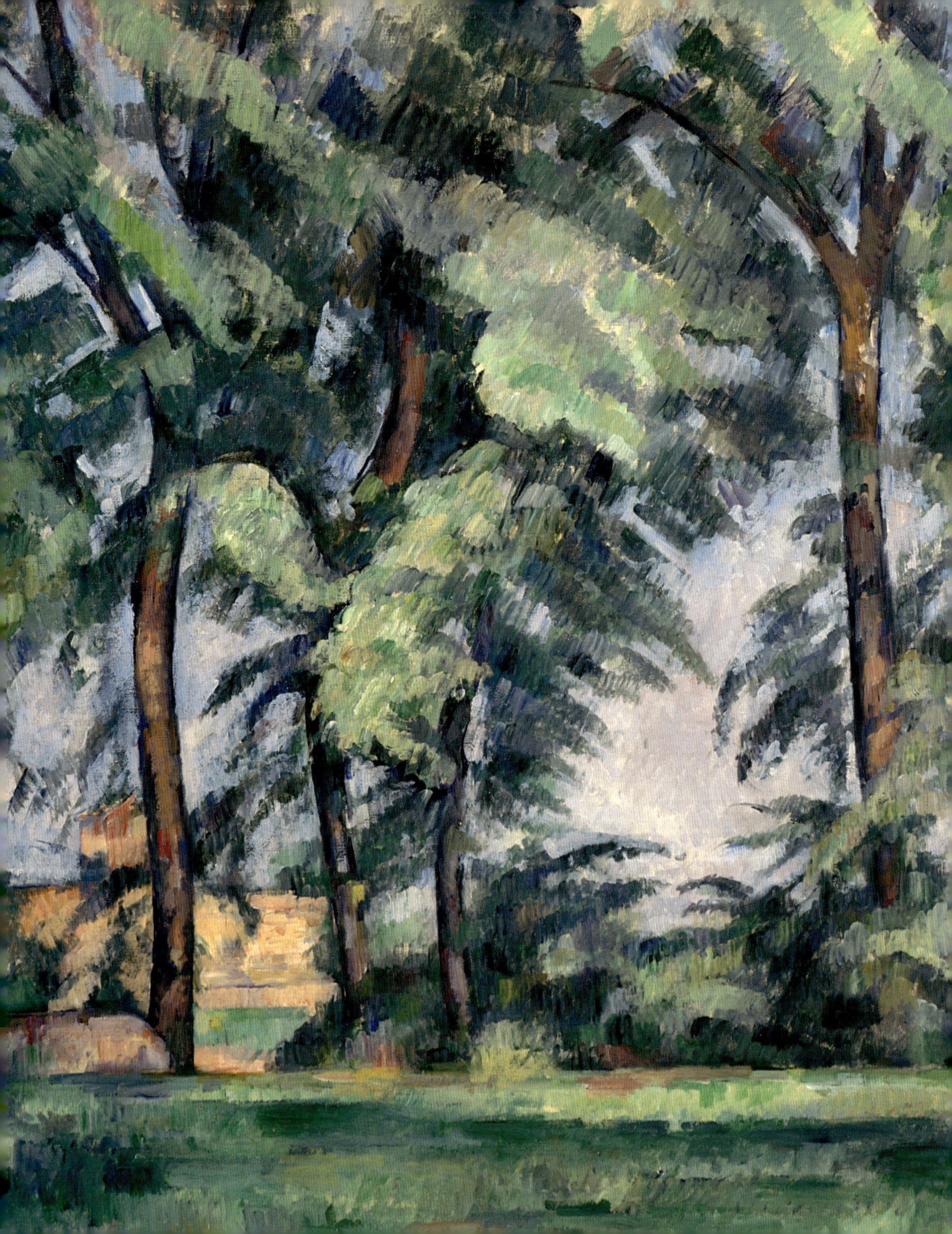

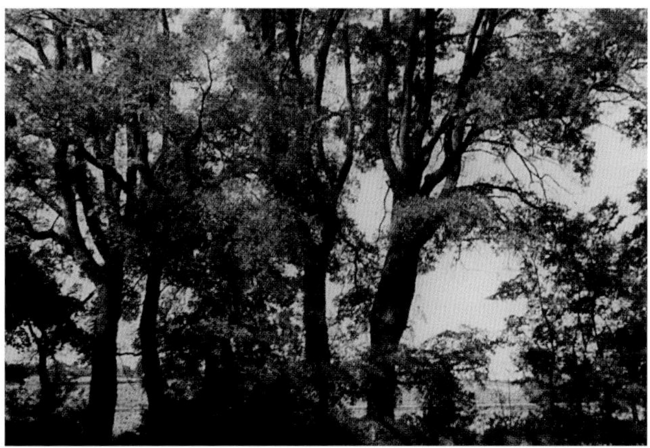

The composition of the picture is very tautly structured, in part by the tall tree trunks, but also by the colour and lighting. The forms of these trunks are somewhat simplified, creating a strongly articulated pattern across much of the canvas, but here, as elsewhere in Cézanne's art, there is nothing rigid or geometrical in the pattern they create. The care that Cézanne took over this particular composition is demonstrated by the existence of another canvas of the same group of trees, in a vertical format, with the trunks slightly closer together (RP 546), and a horizontal watercolour (RWC 244) in which the trees are more evenly spaced; it seems likely that the Courtauld canvas, the most elaborated and formally complex of these works, was the last in this sequence. John Rewald's photograph of these trees (fig. 45), taken around fifty years after the paintings were executed, confirms that Cézanne was working from an actual site, but at the same time highlights the simplifications he made to their forms. It seems likely that the picture was largely or entirely executed out of doors, though we have no conclusive evidence on the point.

Although the picture is quite elaborated in parts, Cézanne ceased work on it when not all its forms were clearly indicated; we are left uncertain of the structure of the building or wall behind the trees on the left, and of the spatial position of the alternating planes of warm and cool colour that lead into distance on the right. Such spatial ambiguities, combined with the rhymes of colour that link distinct zones of the scene, serve to emphasise the colour harmonies within the painting and the artifice of its making. JH

4 **La Montagne Sainte-Victoire au grand pin**, *c.*1887

The Montagne Sainte-Victoire with Large Pine

Oil on canvas, 66.8 × 92.3 cm
Signed, bottom right: *P. Cézanne*
The Courtauld Gallery, London (Samuel Courtauld Trust)
P.1934.SC.55
Courtauld Gift 1934

The Montagne Sainte-Victoire lies to the east of Cézanne's birthplace, Aix-en-Provence, and from many points of view its broken silhouette dominates the town. Cézanne painted it from numerous angles throughout his career, and it was clearly a subject to which he attributed great significance. The mountain itself had deep historical associations, with an ancient Roman military victory against the Teutons and with early Christian festivals, and, recently, with the erection on its crest of the Croix de Provence, to celebrate the fact that Provence had been spared from the recent Prussian invasion.[1] For Cézanne himself, the mountain evidently stood as an emblem of his home town and the landscapes of his home region.

In this composition the mountain is seen from a vantage point to the west of Aix, near the Bellevue property that belonged to his brother-in-law Maxime Conil, a short distance to the south west of Cézanne's family home, the Jas de Bouffan (see cat. 3), with the valley of the Arc in the foreground. The mountain peak lies about eight miles from this viewpoint, but Cézanne, by focusing on a comparatively small part of the scene in front of him, gave the mountain its dominant role in the composition. Although we now tend to see this scene as unspoiled and even timeless, the presence of the prominent railway viaduct at the far right would have been a strongly contemporary reference for the picture's original viewers.

When this painting, along with a *Champ de blé* (unidentified), was shown by invitation at the exhibition of the Société des Amis des Arts at Aix (a society of amateur artists) in 1895, it was received with incomprehension, but it attracted the admiration of the young poet Joachim Gasquet, son of a childhood friend of Cézanne. When Cézanne realised that the young man's praise was sincere, he signed the picture and presented it to him, initiating a friendship which lasted until around 1904. It is one of the very few paintings from after 1880 to which Cézanne added his signature. In 1908, two years after Cézanne's death, Gasquet sold it for the very high price of 12,000 francs to the dealers Bernheim-Jeune.

In comparison with *Tall Trees at the Jas de Bouffan* (cat. 3), the picture shows a simplification of Cézanne's painting technique. Elements of his system of parallel brush-strokes remain, particularly in some of the foliage, but elsewhere the paint areas are flatter and less variegated, with soft nuances of colour introduced to suggest surface

---

PROVENANCE

Joachim Gasquet, Aix-en-Provence; Josse and Gaston Bernheim-Jeune, Paris; Percy Moore Turner, London; Samuel Courtauld, London (bought in 1925)

SELECTED EXHIBITIONS

Salon Aixois, Aix-en-Provence, 1895, n. n.; *Französische Kunst des XIX. und XX. Jahrhunderts*, Kunsthaus, Zurich, 1917, no. 35; *French Art*, London 1932, no. 457; *Samuel Courtauld Memorial Exhibition*, London 1948, no. 10; *Landscape in French Art*, London 1949-50, no. 307; *Cézanne*, Edinburgh and London, 1954, no. 39; *Impressionism for England*, London 1994, no. 8; *Cézanne*, Paris, London and Philadelphia 1995-6, no. 92; *Cézanne in Provence*, Washington and Aix-en-Provence 2006, no. 69

SELECTED LITERATURE

RP 599
Revue Illustrée du Salon Aixois, 1895; *Cézanne*, ed. Bernheim-Jeune, Paris, 1914, pl. LIX; J. Gasquet, 'Ce qu'il m'a dit ... le motif', *L'Amour de l'Art*, December 1921, p. 262; Gasquet 1921/26; Rivière 1923, p. 215; Sitwell 1925, opposite p. 10; Dormoy 1929, p. 15; *Home House* 1935, no. 75; J. Rewald and L. Marschutz, *Le Point*, August 1936, p. 17; T. Duret, *Histoire des peintres impressionnistes*, Paris, 1939, p. 153; J. Rewald, *Art News*, 15–29 February 1944, p. 10; Schapiro 1952, pp. 74–75; Cooper 1954 (2), no. 12; Stokes 1978, II, p. 270; G. Hamilton, 'The Dying of the Light: The Late Work of Degas, Monet, and Cézanne', in *Aspects of Monet*, New York, 1984, p. 234; Musée Granet, exh. cat., Aix-en-Provence, 1990, figs. 160 and 181; *Cézanne and Poussin*, exh. cat., Edinburgh 1990, fig. 12; Kear 1998, pp. 234–36; Callen 2000, pp. 36, 44, 70, 184–85

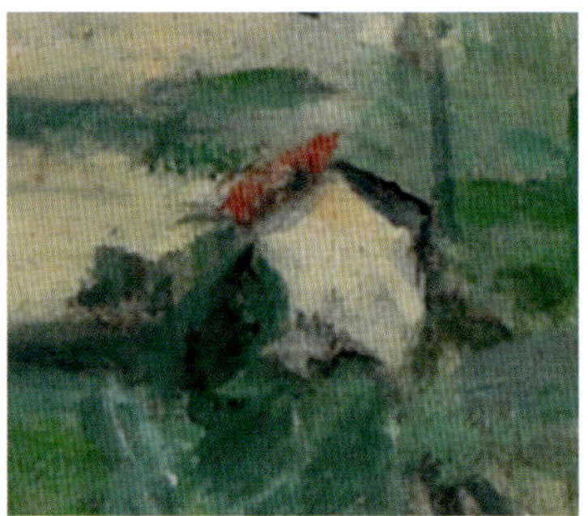

FIG. 46
Detail of cat. 4 (house at lower centre)

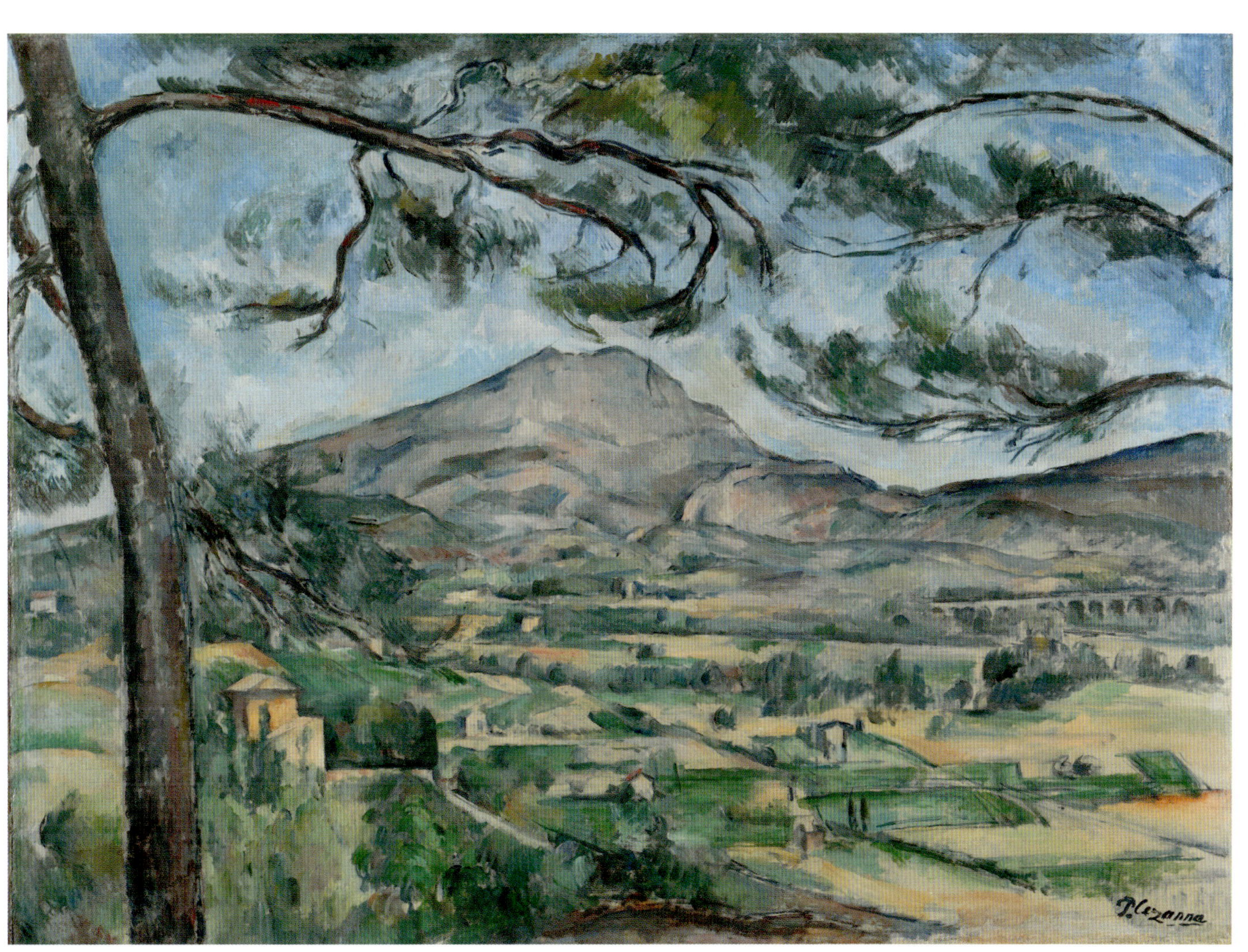

texture and the play of light. In places, especially in the lower right area of the canvas, the cream priming of the canvas is left bare or only covered with a thin wash, and its luminosity contributes to the overall tonality of the picture. Traces of the initial underdrawing, mostly in blue paint, are visible in the final state of the painting. The fact that Cézanne chose to exhibit the canvas in 1895 indicates that, despite its somewhat uneven degrees of finish, he regarded it as a resolved statement of his approach to painting.

Recession into distance is suggested in two ways, by both colour and line. There is a gradual transition from the clearer greens and orange-yellows of the foreground to the softer atmospheric blues and pinks on the mountain, but even the foreground foliage is repeatedly tinged with blues; and pinks and reds – notably on the branch silhouetted against the sky at upper left – knit the foreground forms to the far mountain. Small touches of red were added in several parts of the composition at a late stage in its execution in order to emphasise these interconnections, most conspicuously the crisp accents on the branch at upper left and the single sharp red stroke on the roof of the tiny building about 10 cm above the bottom centre of the canvas (fig. 46).

On the right side of this same roof, though, there is a crisp dark blue stroke, emphatically demarcating its edge. This is part of a network of quite linear contours, suggesting fences, walls and the edges of fields, which – along with the shifts in colour – lead the eye into the distance; some of these belong to an initial linear underpainting, but at certain points they were reemphasised at a late stage in the execution of the canvas. Across the foreground, many of the strokes are diagonal, leading the eye into the pictorial space across the fields in the valley, but near the bottom centre a few small crisp verticals were added late in the execution of the painting; these may suggest trees, but they also serve to halt the eye's movement into space and reassert the two-dimensionality of the image. On the mountain itself, a few distinct, slightly cursive linear strokes reinforce the use of colour contrasts to suggest its form, and along much of the top edge of the mountain ridge late-added, more linear blue strokes accentuate the demarcation between hills and sky.

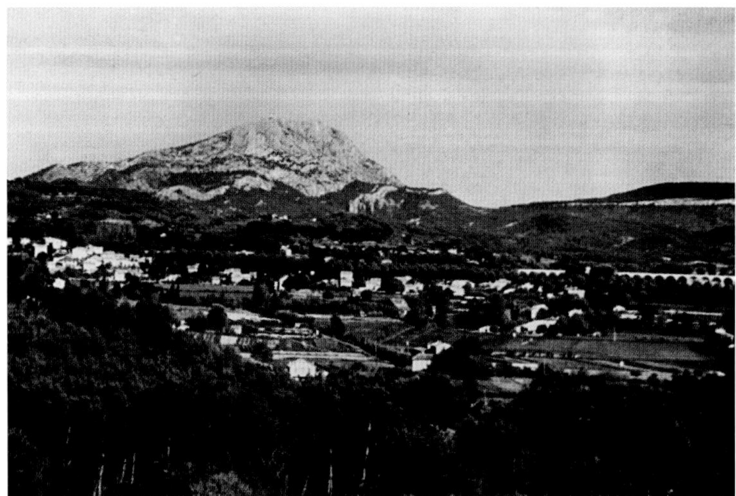

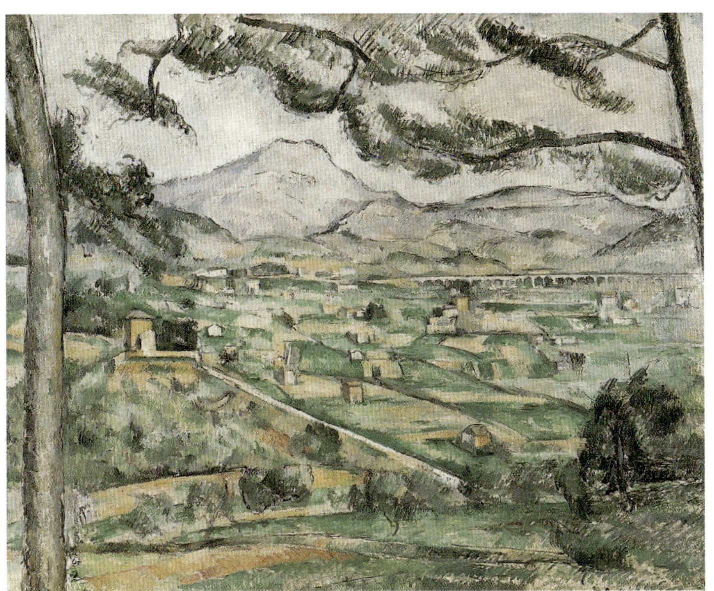

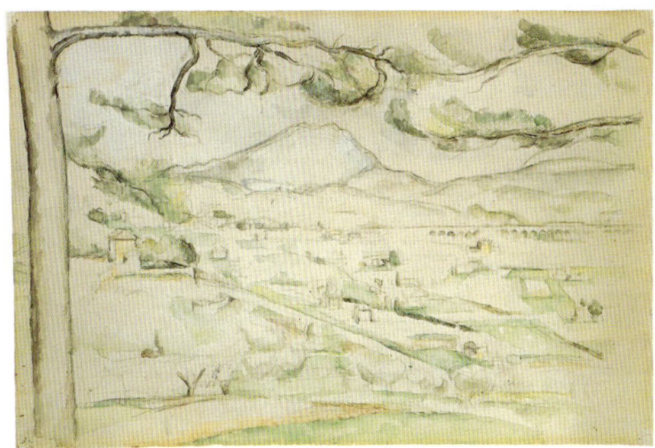

This surface coherence is enhanced by the placing of the branches, especially those on the right that stem from an invisible trunk and carefully frame the contour of the mountain. The picture's composition is particularly tautly structured, with darker trees acting as a *repoussoir* framing the central coloured vista, and the branches at top centre framing the mountain. Parallels for this can be found in the seventeenth-century landscapes of Nicolas Poussin. Cézanne's concern with such compositional devices seems to be an early stage in his search (as he is reported to have said in 1905) to "revivify Poussin in front of nature",[2] a comment that at one and the same time signals his respect for the classicising tradition in French art and his insistence that any valid art should be based on the direct study of nature.

A variant version of this subject includes part of the trunk of the pine tree whose branches appear on the right of the present composition (RP 598; fig. 48); in a closely related watercolour (RWC 241; fig. 49), the second trunk is omitted but otherwise the composition is similar to fig. 48; in the Courtauld canvas the foreground space is truncated and a little more is seen to the far left of the canvas, thus creating a more expansive horizontal format. Though the sequence of the three works cannot be firmly established, it seems likely that the Courtauld canvas, more assured in its composition, came last, and that the watercolour acted as an intermediate stage as Cézanne began to rethink the composition of his initial oil.

The play of light and shade is more specific than usual in Cézanne's landscapes, especially on the house at lower left, but, when the picture is viewed as a whole, the zones of cooler and warmer colour virtually alternating as the eye moves up its surface and into space, and the luminous space framed by tree-trunk and branches, transform the natural subject into a composition of great order and monumentality. JH

NOTES

1 See Athanassoglou-Kallmyer 2003, especially pp. 152–53

2 "*Vivifier Poussin sur nature*", I give the quotation in its first and most securely documented form, as published by Charles Camoin during Cézanne's lifetime, in Charles Morice, 'Enquête sur les tendances actuelles des arts plastiques', *Mercure de France*, 1 August 1905, p. 353. Cézanne's recorded comments on Poussin are discussed in Theodore Reff, 'Cézanne and Poussin', *Journal of the Warburg and Courtauld Institutes*, 1960, pp. 150ff.; Theodore Reff, 'Cézanne et Poussin', *Art de France*, 1963, pp. 302ff.; Shiff 1984, esp. pp. 175ff.; and *Cézanne and Poussin*, Edinburgh 1990. See also John House, 'Cézanne and Poussin: Myth and History', in Richard Kendall (ed.), *Cézanne and Poussin: A Symposium*, Sheffield 1993, pp. 129–49.

5 **Pot de primevères et fruits**, *c.* 1888–90

Pot of Primroses and Fruit

Oil on canvas, 46 × 56.2 cm
The Courtauld Gallery, London (Samuel Courtauld Trust)
P.1948.SC.56
Courtauld Bequest 1948

The apparent simplicity of this image is deceptive. The primary subject and its surroundings are knitted into a complex interplay of forms and colours; and, as the eye explores the picture, the configuration of shapes in the background becomes increasingly hard to read. Is the form on the right the stretcher bars of a canvas seen from the back, leaning against the wall, or a painter's easel, as its shape might suggest, were it not for the beige canvas tone between its bars? And what is represented by the three strips of colour on the background wall? Infrared reflectography reveals diagonal strokes of graphite drawing between the top of the flower and the leaf to its left; these may indicate an earlier idea of the placement of the forms in the background.

These uncertainties prevent us from reading the image as the depiction of an actual space, and force us to concentrate on the roles that the colours and shapes play in the overall composition. At the core of the composition the lavish curves of the plant are framed by the bars beyond, and the green of the leaves is set against the red bar behind them. Around the plant, the colouring is predominantly yellows and oranges alongside soft blues, variegated with great delicacy. However, small red accents recur throughout the picture, linking to the stronger reds of the bar on the wall and the fruit on the plate, and a soft pink flush is introduced into the table-top, the pot and the left background, to offset the dominant soft grey-blues of these areas.

In places the boundaries between forms are expressed by changes of colour, but elsewhere Cézanne added fine contour lines late in the execution of the picture, presum-

ably feeling that more emphatic demarcation was needed. Some of the plant's leaves were redefined with fine linear strokes, creating softly cursive rhyming shapes across the foliage, and the scalloped edge of the plate was deftly re-emphasised, without any distracting detail. The contours are also varied in terms of colour according to their position, with a mainly green outline separating the nearer fruit on the plate from the one beyond it, while a crisp deep blue line pulls the upper right side of the pear on the table forward from the flowerpot; however, the lower right and bottom edges of the pear are emphasised by contrasts of light against dark tone and warm against cool colour without any added contours.

As the picture now stands, the back edge of the table appears at four distinct levels; however, at the outset the edge to the right of the flowerpot was continuous with its level to the immediate left of the pot, and at the far right the edge appears at both the higher and lower level. Moreover, in the picture's final state, the position of the furthest fruit on the plate seems oddly insecure. The picture's ambiguities of form and space demonstrate Cézanne's relative disregard, as he worked up a canvas, for representational consistency, in favour of the exploration of nuances of colour and tone that allowed him to knit the painting together into a coherent whole. Though most of the canvas is quite fully covered, it is not thickly painted, thereby exploiting the luminosity of the priming; its brushwork is unemphatic, without any strong overall rhythm. This handling seems to fit a date at the end of the 1880s, not long after *La Montagne Sainte-Victoire* (cat. 4).

JH

PROVENANCE

Ambroise Vollard, Paris; Cornelis Hoogendijk, Amsterdam; Paul Rosenberg, Paris; Marquis de Rochecouste, Paris; Galerie Barbazanges, Paris; Galerie E. Bignou, Paris; Reid & Lefevre, London; Samuel Courtauld, London (bought in 1928)

SELECTED EXHIBITIONS

Moderne Kunst Kring, Stedelijk Museum, Amsterdam, 1911, n. n.; *Nineteenth Century French Painters*, Knoedler Galleries, London, 1926, no. 21; *Samuel Courtauld Memorial Exhibition*, London 1948, no. 12; *Cézanne*, Edinburgh and London, 1954, no. 40; *Classic Cézanne*, Sydney, 1998–99, no. 11; *Impressionism for England*, London, 1994, no. 9; *Cézanne in Britain*, London, 2006–07, no. 30

SELECTED LITERATURE

RP 639
Jamot and Turner 1934, no. 25; Cooper 1954 (2), no. 13; Bruce-Gardner 1987, p. 23; Kitschen 1995, pp. 127

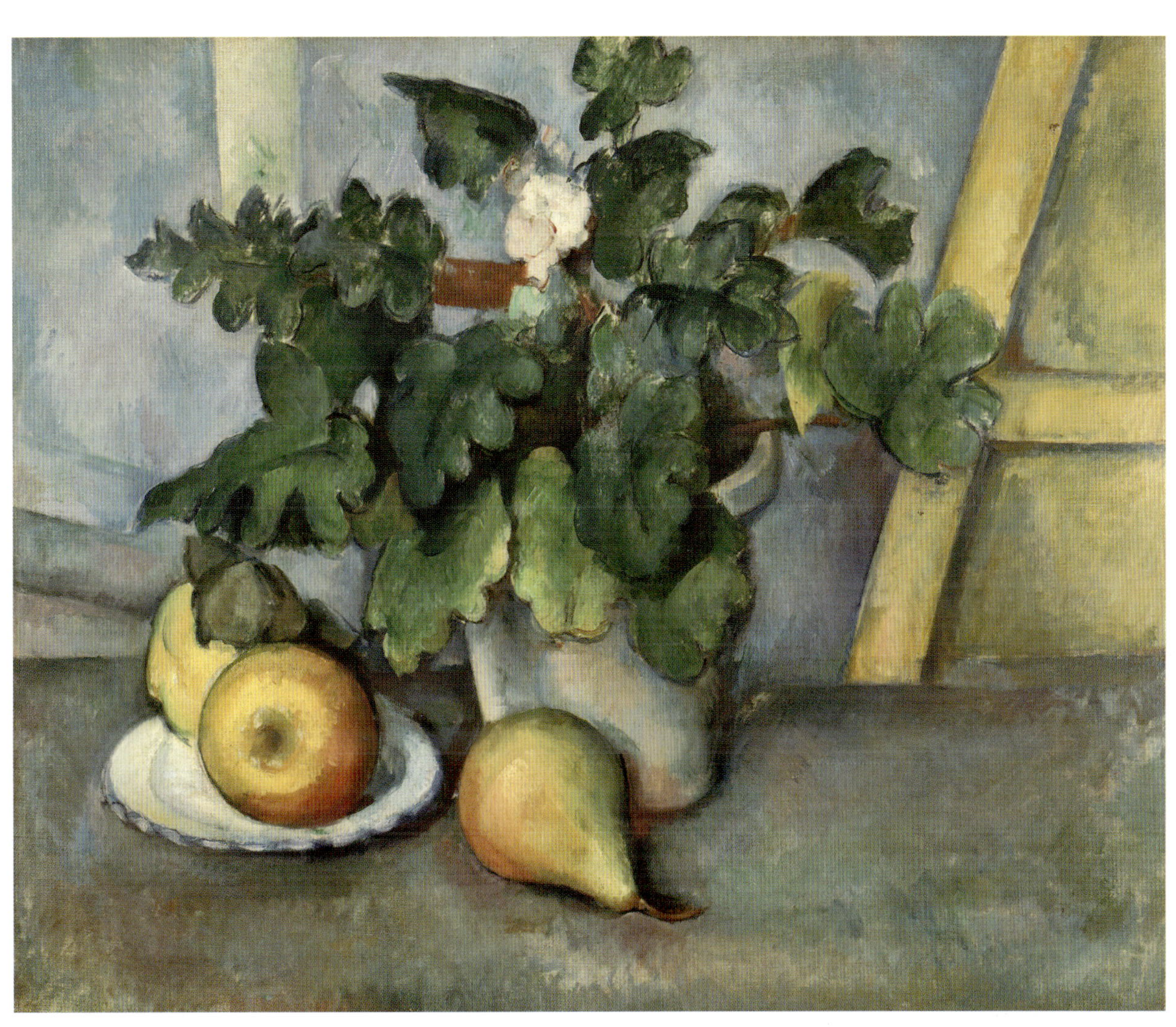

6 **Les Joueurs de cartes**, *c.*1892–95

The Card Players

Oil on canvas, 60 × 73 cm
The Courtauld Gallery, London (Samuel Courtauld Trust)
P.1932.SC.57
Courtauld Gift 1932

During the 1890s Cézanne painted a long sequence of canvases of peasants from his home town of Aix-en-Provence. The most ambitious of these show groups of men playing cards. Two show three card players, with spectators (RP 706; fig. 50; and RP 707; Metropolitan Museum of Art, New York), and were probably painted first; in the other three, which differ in size but are very similar in detail, the subject is distilled into a simpler form, with two figures facing each other, seen in profile (RP 710; private collection; and RP 714; Musée d'Orsay, Paris). The existence of a number of preparatory studies of individual figures shows the importance Cézanne attached to the theme, and suggests that the figures posed for him one at a time. According to Joachim Gasquet, the paintings were executed in Cézanne's home, the Jas de Bouffan, though the panelled background and the presence of a wine-bottle (though without glasses) in the Courtauld version may suggest that Cézanne intended the setting to evoke a café interior. However, Cézanne has minimised any associational detail in the scene.

The overall tonality of the present picture is quite subdued; at first sight the composition is built up of greys and browns. However, a wide range of subtly gradated colours is used to model the figures and their surroundings. Around the pivotal warm zone of the table-top, a succession of smaller warm touches knit the composition together, on the men's faces, hands and clothing and on the panelling beyond them, and a larger sharp red accent appears above the left figure at the top of the picture (we cannot tell whether this represents something on a background wall, or reflected in a mirror, or situated in a wider space beyond the figures). Against the warm hues are set the soft blues which model the figures and suggest the atmosphere of the room, but these cool hues are also very varied, with a few sharper accents of clear green, for instance above the head of the right-hand figure and on his collar. For the most part, the colour is simply and broadly brushed on to the canvas, but at certain points, particularly in the men's faces, crisper and very delicate accents are introduced in order to suggest their modelling more closely; elsewhere, for instance in the men's hands, small zones of unpainted cream-primed canvas act as highlights.

The treatment of the panelling (fig. 51) is a fine example of Cézanne's approach to building up the paint surface; on top of an initial bluish wash, a further, very partial, layer was thinly applied with loose brushwork, more reddish in places and perhaps thus closer to the local colour of the panelling. The darker more saturated paint on top of this was used to clarify the space between the background and the figures and to emphasise their contours, but it does not cover the whole area, thus allowing us to see the successive stages of its execution.

PROVENANCE

Ambroise Vollard, Paris; Dr Julius Elias, Berlin; Jorgen Breder Stang, Oslo; Alfred Gold, Berlin; Samuel Courtauld, London (bought in 1929)

SELECTED EXHIBITIONS

Paul Cassirer, Berlin, 1904, n. n.; *French Art*, London 1932, no. 392; *Samuel Courtauld Memorial Exhibition*, London 1948, no. 13; *Cézanne*, Edinburgh and London 1954, no. 52; *Cézanne Gemälde*, Tübingen 1993, no. 65; *Impressionism for England*, London 1994, no. 10; *Cézanne in Britain*, London 2006–07, no. 31

SELECTED LITERATURE

RP 713
Meier-Graefe 1918, p. 194; Rivière 1923, p. 218; Jamot and Turner 1934, no. 23; *Home House* 1935, no. 1; Cooper 1954 (2), no. 14; Stokes 1978, pp. 270–71; T. Reff, 'Cézanne's "Cardplayers" and their Sources', *Arts Magazine*, November 1980, pp. 104–17; *Cézanne*, exh. cat., Paris, London and Philadelphia 1995–96, p. 338; Kear 1998, pp. 142–50; Athanassoglou-Kallmyer 2003, pp. 207–15

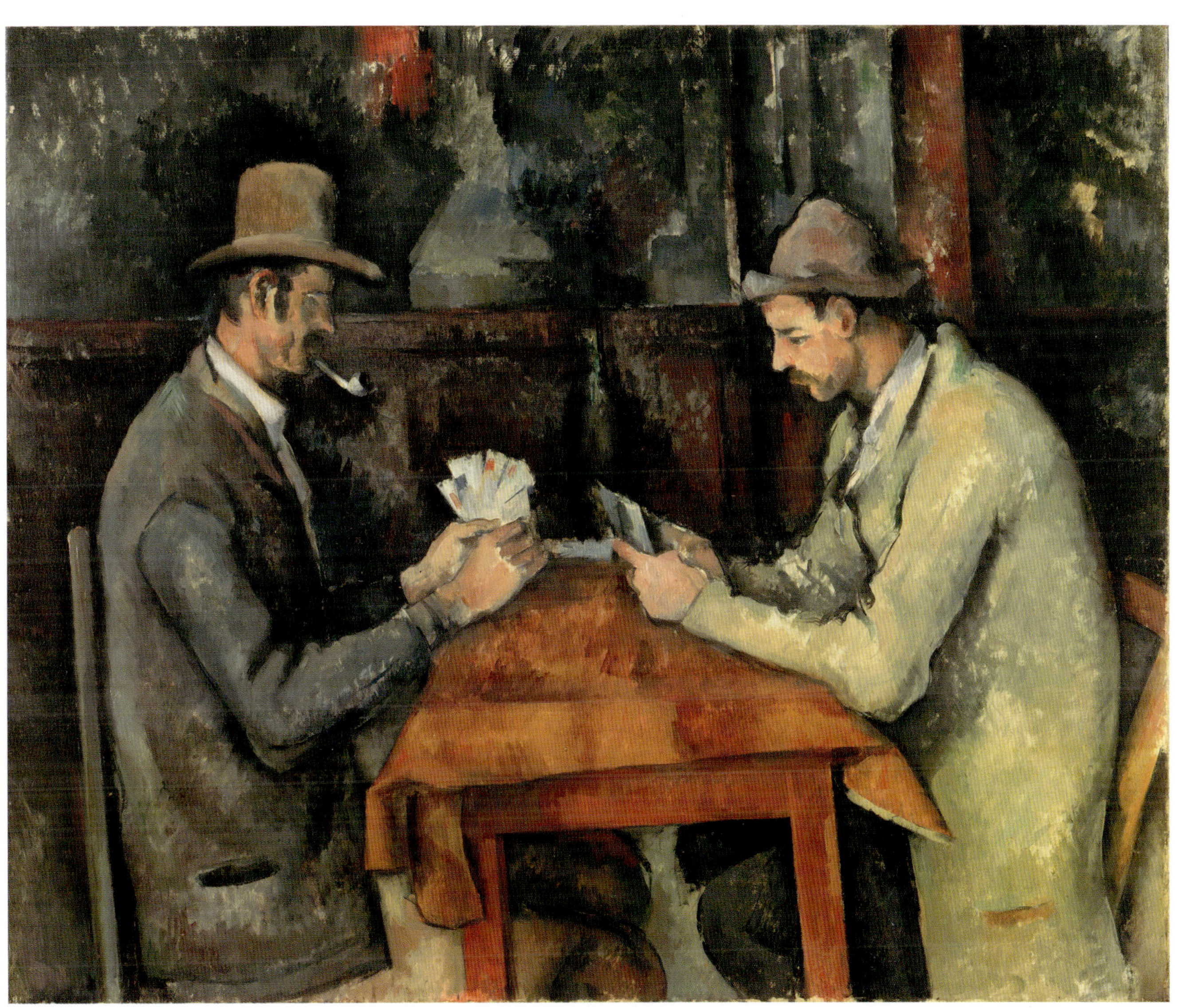

Numerous adjustments, for example to the contours of the hats, cards and knees, are visible in a good light; late in the execution of the canvas, dark contours in various colours were added to certain forms in order to reemphasise their position, for instance to the men's knees and of the left side of the right figure's sleeve.

In the painting's final state, there are certain clear discrepancies with 'normal' natural vision: the verticals of the table lean to the left, and the knees of the left figure extend unduly far to the right. Joachim Gasquet cited Cézanne's criticisms of artists who used plumb-lines to ensure the accuracy of their verticals[1] and Rivière and Schnerb recorded his disregard for precision and symmetry in the delineation of forms.[2] Such oddities were not, it seems, wilful and deliberate distortions, but rather emerged during the execution of the painting, as Cézanne concentrated on relationships of colour and

tone at the expense of the literal representation of the depicted subject (see pp. 43–44). The treatment of the cards that the left figure holds offer a further demonstration of Cézanne's determination to avoid illusionistic representation, since their edges blur into a single zone of variegated off-white paint where the player holds them.

His preoccupation with the organisation of his canvases does not mean that Cézanne was unconcerned about his subject matter. In his later art, he sought a reconciliation between working from nature and old master traditions; in the Card Player paintings he harnessed himself to a long tradition of images of figures seated around tables. Theodore Reff has weighed the claims of a whole range of images to be seen as 'sources' for the Card Player compositions, ranging from Paolo Veronese, the Le Nain brothers and Chardin to Honoré

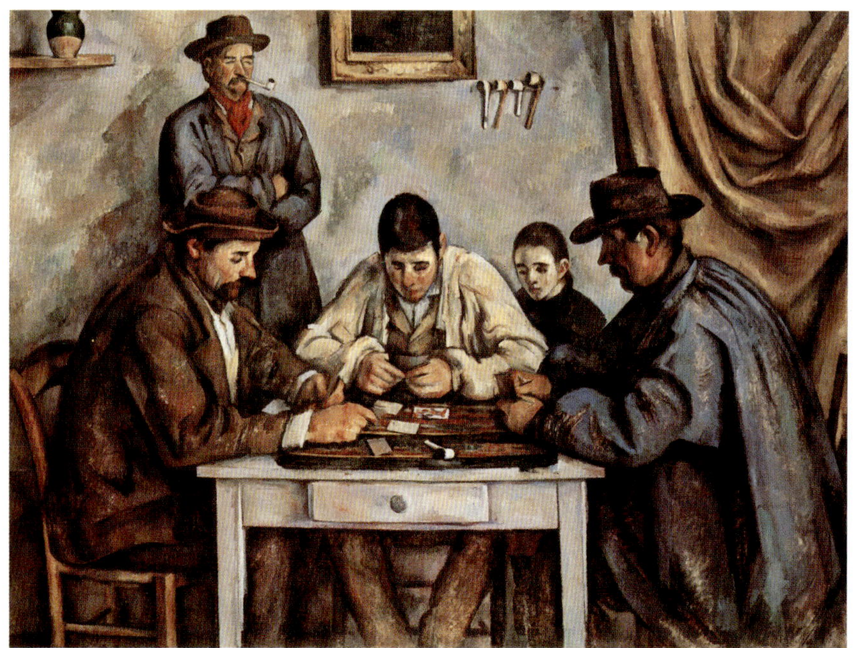

FIG.50
Paul Cézanne, *The Card Players*, 1890–92
Oil on canvas, 135 x 181.5 cm
Barnes Foundation,
Merion, Pennsylvania

Daumier.[3] Generically, Cézanne's paintings can indeed be linked to seventeenth-century peasant subjects such as those of the Le Nains (an example of which hung in the Musée Granet in Aix-en-Provence) of whom he spoke with admiration in the 1890s, rather than to the peasant paintings of the nineteenth century, in which indoor scenes with male figures are most unusual. However, his canvases differ from the work of his contemporaries because of their total avoidance of any signs of psychological or anecdotal interchange between the figures, through either gesture or facial expression.

The Card Player paintings have recently been discussed in the context of the problems facing French agriculture in these years, with the suggestion that they may also relate to the tax increase on playing-cards proposed in 1894 and implemented in 1896, as the result of government concerns about gambling.[4] However, the ways in which the figures are presented in the paintings give no hint of such topical concerns. Cézanne's peasants stand in more general terms as figures for a way of life that he saw as enshrining the basic values of his local region, which he viewed as threatened by contemporary urban fashions. At the end of his life, he told Jules Borély: "Today everything has changed in reality, but not for me, I live in the town of my childhood, and it is with the eyes of the people of my own age that I see again the past. I love above all else the appearance of people who have grown old without breaking with old customs."[5]

In this sense, the image of seated peasants, still and seemingly silent, concentrating on their game of cards, can be seen as the human counterpart to the landscapes of his home countryside, notably the Montagne Sainte-Victoire (see cat. 4), which held such iconic significance for him. JH

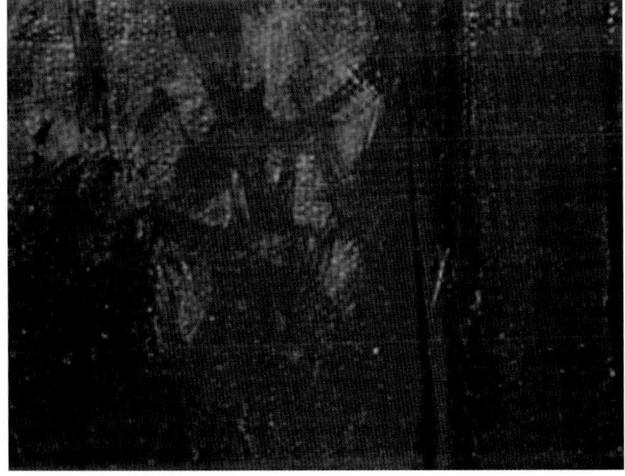

Detail of cat. 6 (panelling on back wall)

NOTES

1 Doran 1978, p. 153.
2 Doran 1978, p. 87.
3 Reff 1980, pp. 104–17.
4 See Athanassoglou-Kallmyer 2003, pp. 207–15.
5 Doran 1978, p. 21.

7 **L'Homme à la pipe**, *c.* 1892–95

Man with a Pipe

Oil on canvas, 73 × 60 cm
The Courtauld Gallery, London (Samuel Courtauld Trust)
P.1932.SC.58
Courtauld Gift 1932

This painting is one of five comparable canvases from this period which depict lone peasants smoking pipes (these include RP 705, private collection; and RP 757, State Hermitage Museum, St Petersburg). The model here is the same as that for the left-hand figure in *The Card Players* (cat. 6). The two paintings were probably painted at much the same date, since they are very similar in colour and handling. Here, dark coloured lines are used to underdraw and subsequently redefine the forms. The man's face, the prime focus of the composition, is more elaborated than any part of *The Card Players*: parts of the face are treated with successions of diagonal strokes (here running from upper left to lower right), reminiscent of the parallel strokes which Cézanne had employed a decade earlier (see cat. 2, 3), though more delicate and less assertive. Pivotal to the treatment of the face is the contrast between the dull blues of the shadow of the nose and the rich warm hues of its lit side; this contrast is heightened by two particularly crisp, bold strokes of red added down the ridge of the nose very late in the execution of the painting. Elsewhere, the relatively subdued colour acts as a foil to the face, but soft nuances of warmer and cooler colour are introduced throughout, with a few sharper blue accents, notably on the man's left cheek and, most strikingly, on his neck.

Late-added linear contours are scarcely used on the most highly worked zone, the face, but dark-coloured lines are introduced on the more thinly painted, broadly brushed jacket and especially on the waistcoat, thus giving a tauter, more emphatic structure to the lower parts of the composition and supporting its primary focus, the face. There is a provisional quality to some of these lines, notably the dark line that passes directly over one of the loosely indicated waistcoat buttons; on the left side of the hat, two emphatic strokes of beige paint are added across the contour, thus disrupting the previously established form of the hat.

As a painting of a single figure, facing the viewer, the canvas occupies an interesting position on the borderline between portraiture and genre painting. It clearly represents a specific individual with distinctive features, rather than the generic types so common in French nineteenth-century peasant painting, and, through Joachim Gasquet's later testimony, we know he sitter's name and profession. However, it cannot be seen straightforwardly as a portrait, for the individual is used, here, to stand for a type; as in *The Card Players*, and the other pipe smoker canvases the simple, monumental form of the figure is used to suggest the timeless, traditional values which Cézanne attributed to the peasants of the Aix region (see cat. 6). JH

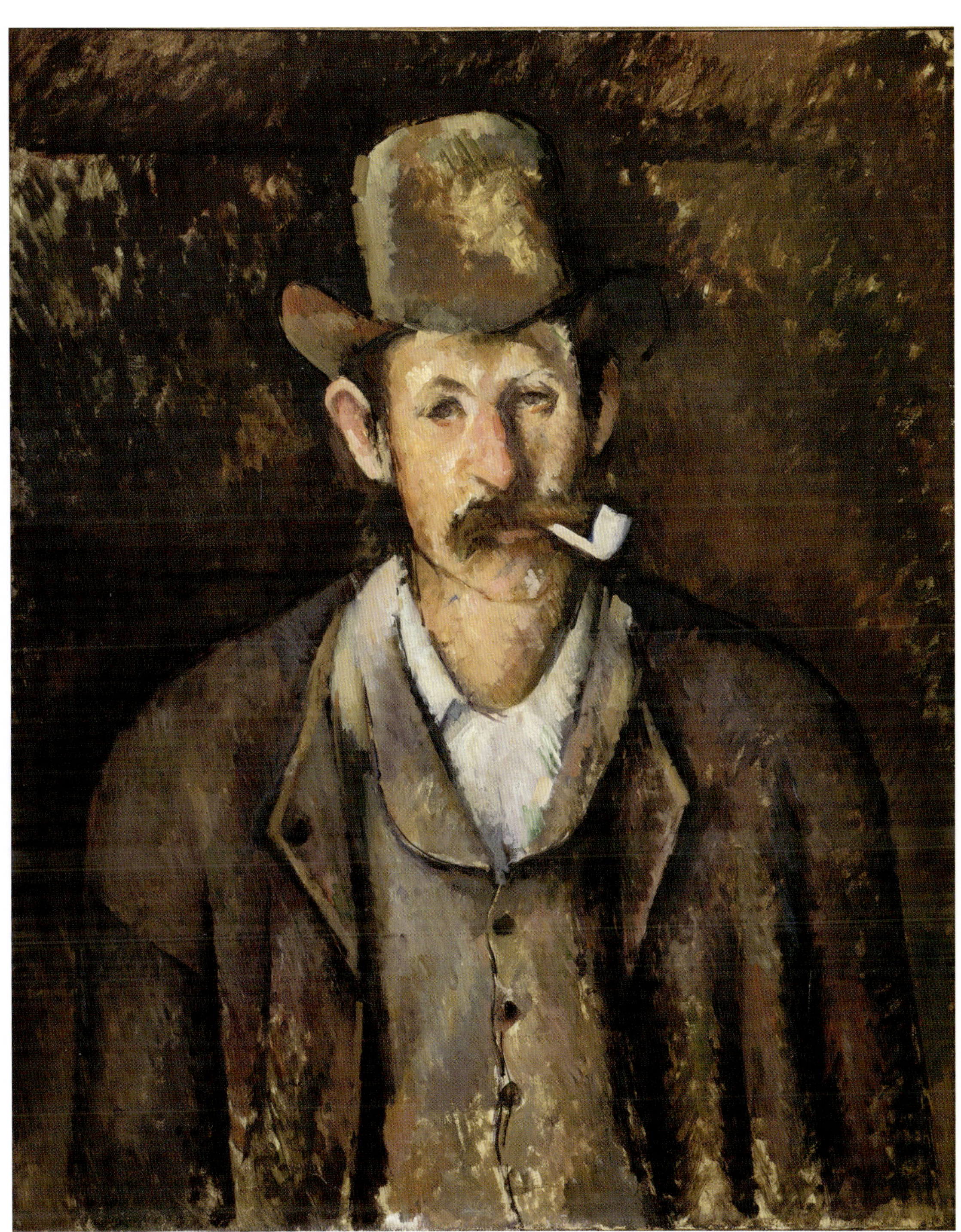

8 **Nature morte avec l'amour en plâtre**, *c.*1894

Still Life with Plaster Cupid

Oil on paper, laid on board, 70.6 × 57.3 cm
The Courtauld Gallery, London (Samuel Courtauld Trust)
P.1948.SC.59
Courtauld Bequest 1948

Cézanne's still life compositions perhaps reveal his changing preoccupations most fully, since still life gave him the freedom to choose and arrange the combinations of objects he wanted to depict. A witness described the complex business of setting up one such still life subject: "The cloth was arranged on the table, with innate taste. Then Cézanne arranged the fruits, contrasting the tones one against the other, making the complementaries vibrate, the greens against the reds, the yellows against the blues, tipping, turning, balancing the fruit as he wanted them to be, using coins of one or two sous for the purpose. He brought to this task the greatest care and many precautions; one guessed it was a feast for the eye to him."[1]

Still Life with Plaster Cupid is one of the most complex of Cézanne's late still lifes, both in its composition and through the inclusion of the cast and other works of art. It was the first work by Cézanne to enter Samuel Courtauld's private collection. Courtauld acquired it in May 1923, the year after his revelatory experience of Cézanne's paintings at an exhibition at the Burlington Fine Arts Club in London. The plaster cast of a Cupid (believed in the nineteenth century to be after the seventeenth-century French sculptor Pierre Puget, but perhaps after a work by François Duquesnoy) still remains in Cézanne's studio at Aix (see figs. 52, 53), as does the cast of a flayed man (traditionally attributed to Michelangelo; see fig. 53), represented in the painting (RP 785; private collection) that is seen propped up at the top of the present picture. Puget, a fellow Provençal, was important for Cézanne throughout his career; he made many copies of Puget's sculptures in the Louvre, evidently responding to their richly dynamic three-dimensional forms.

The Cupid cast is in reality 46 cm high, and it appears larger than life in the painting; the same is true of the canvas which is shown leaning against the wall on the left, *The Peppermint Bottle* (RP 772; fig. 55) which was painted at much the same time as this picture; the area of it that we see, which includes the red stripe and blue area at top left, is shown here larger than it is in the original canvas, although implicitly it is standing on the floor well beyond the foreground table. The far apple, apparently placed on the distant floor, appears as large as the fruit on the table.

There are ambiguities, too, in the relationships between the objects. The 'real' blue drapery at the bottom left merges into the drapery in the painted still life in the picture on the left; the foliage of the 'real' onion fuses with the table leg in the same still life; the back edge of the table top virtually dissolves into the floor to the left of this onion; the edge of the plate disappears just to the right of the green apple; and the base of the cast dissolves

PROVENANCE

Ambroise Vollard, Paris; Baron Denys Cochin, Paris; Bernheim-Jeune, Paris; Herbert Kullmann, Manchester; Bernheim-Jeune, Paris; Dr G. Jebsen, Oslo; Paul Rosenberg, Paris; Alexander Reid, Glasgow; Samuel Courtauld, London (bought in 1923)

SELECTED EXHIBITIONS

Masterpieces of French Art of the 19th Century, Thos. Agnew & Sons, London, 1923, no. 10; *Paintings and Drawings*, London 1925, no. 10; *Samuel Courtauld Memorial Exhibition*, London 1948, no. 15; *Cézanne*, Edinburgh and London 1954, no. 50; *Cézanne. Les Dernières Années*, Paris 1978, no. 17; *Impressionism for England*, London 1994, no. 12; *Cézanne*, Paris, London and Philadelphia 1995–96, no. 162; *Cézanne i blickpunckten*, Stockholm 1997–98, no. 27

SELECTED LITERATURE

RP 786
M. Denis, 'L'Influence de Cézanne', *L'Amour de l'Art*, December 1920, p. 279; Sitwell 1925, p. 78; Dormoy 1929, p. 52; Jamot and Turner 1934, no. 24; Cooper 1954 (2), no. 16; M. Schapiro, *Art News Annual*, 1968, pp. 37, 39, 47; *Cézanne: The Late Work*, exh. cat. New York and Houston 1977–78, p. 31; Stokes 1978, p. 269; T. Reff, 'The Pictures within Cézanne's Pictures', *Arts Magazine*, June 1979, fig. 31; Bruce-Gardner 1987–88, p. 23; Kitschen 1995, pp. 134–38, 153–56, 168–70, fig. 46; Callen 2000, pp. 26–27, 168

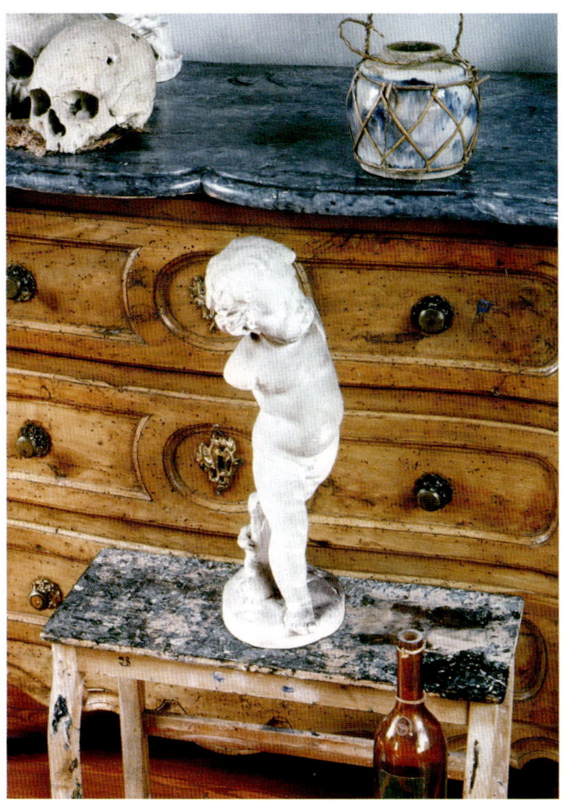

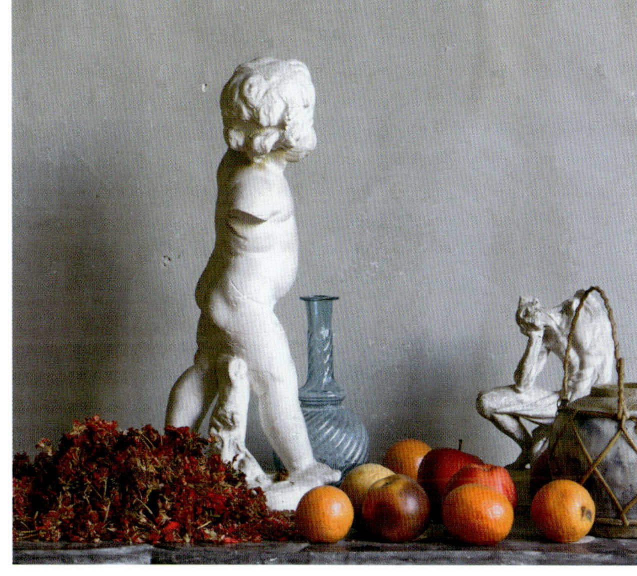

into the floor just to the right of the Cupid's leg. There is also real uncertainty about the arrangement of planes in the background, where the edges of the canvas depicting the flayed figure cannot be clearly determined. All of these devices combine to ensure that the image is not seen as a direct transcription of observed reality; rather, the viewer's eye is drawn to the relationships of colour and tone on the canvas, which coexist in a constant tension with the sense of physical presence that the brush-marks also evoke.

Exceptionally in Cézanne's oeuvre, *Still Life with Plaster Cupid* is painted in oils on paper, though its dimensions, complexity and ambition make it clear that it can in no way be seen as an academic study or as a preparation for a painting on canvas. There are a number of drawings and watercolours of the Cupid cast, and also three oil paintings, two of them very summary (RP 783–84), and one more ambitious (RP 782; fig. 56); none, however,

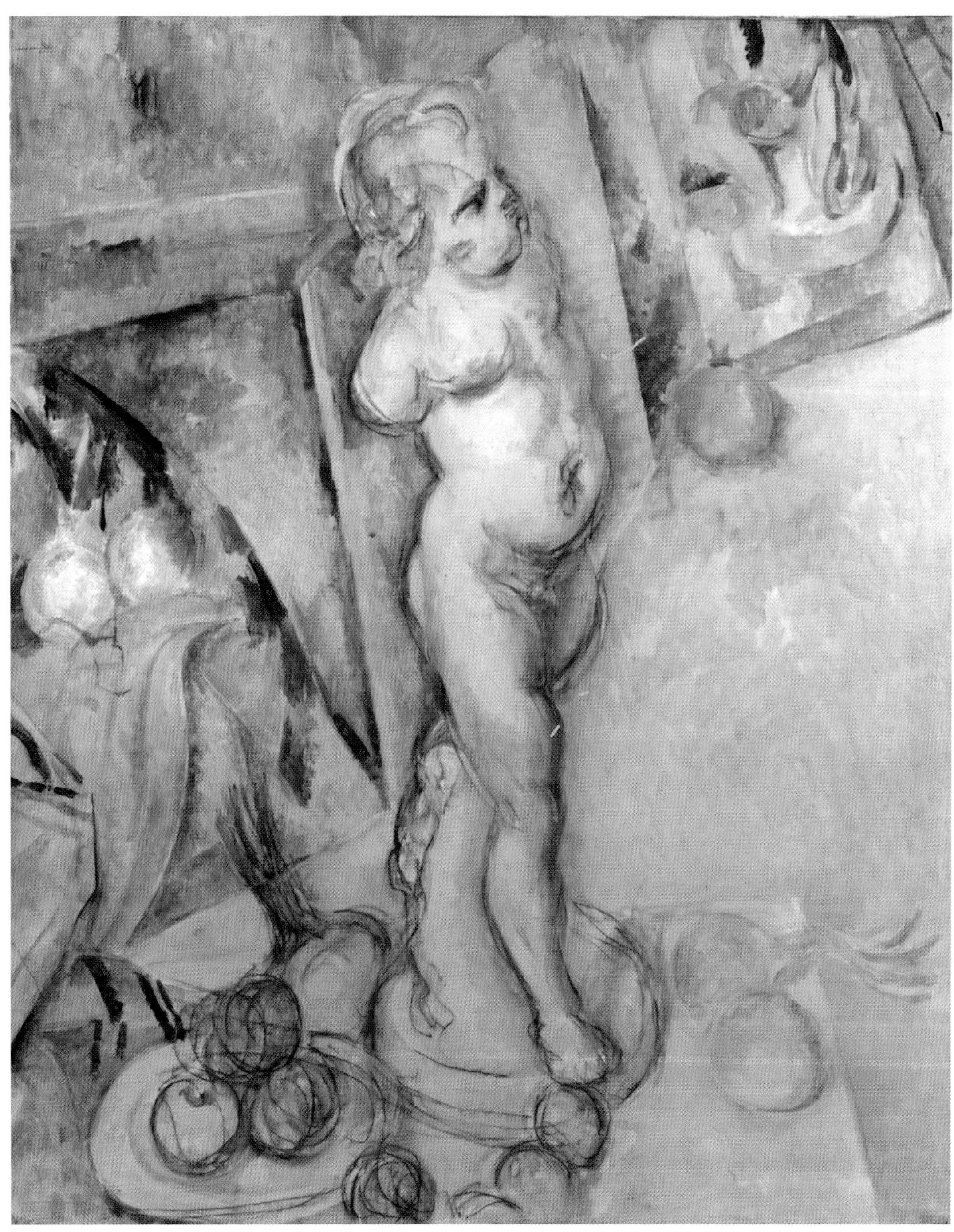

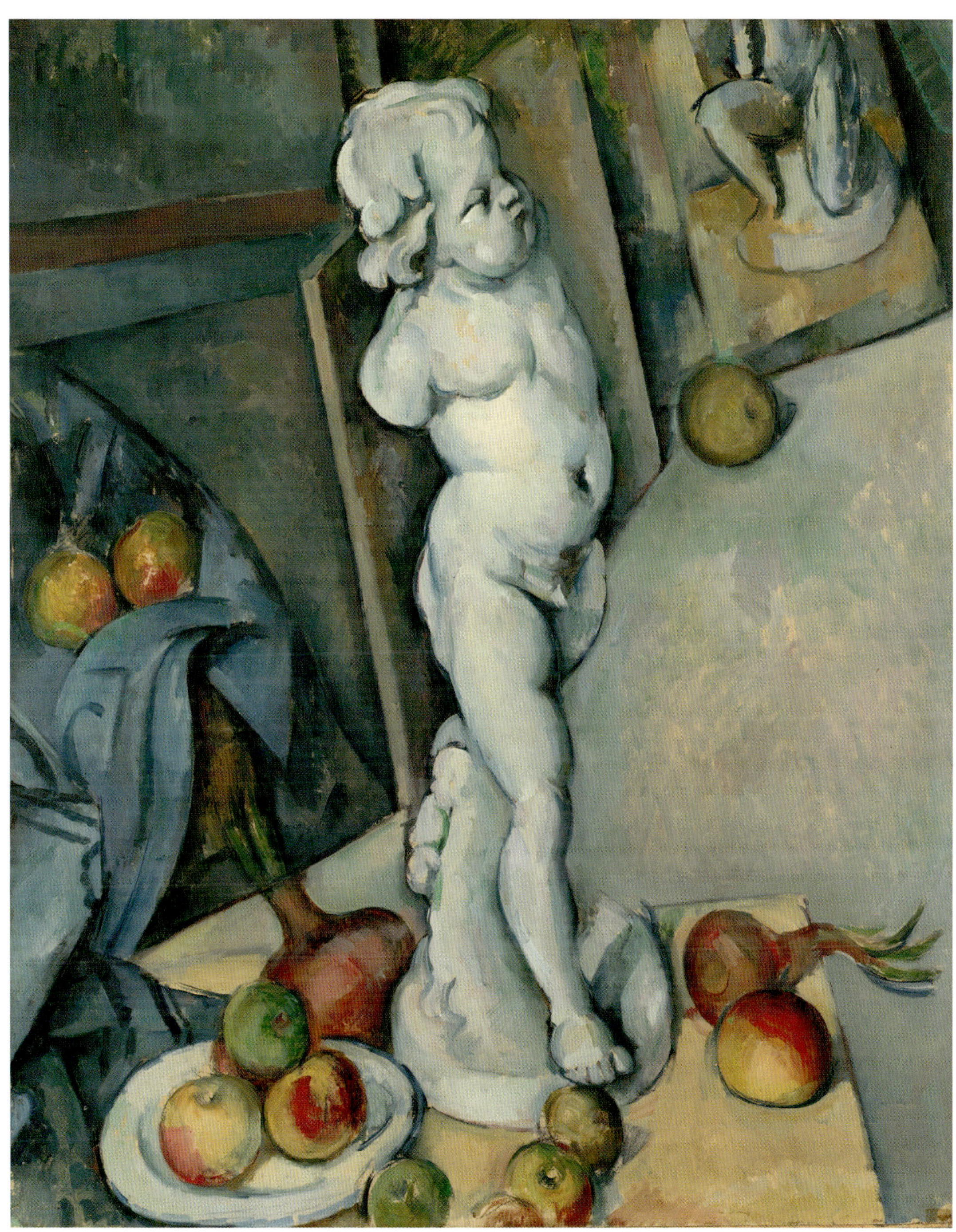

shows it from the same angle, and none presents it in such an elaborate and complex setting.

Some sketching, probably in pencil, is clearly seen in normal light as underdrawing for the apples, and infrared reflectography revealed more underdrawing (fig. 54); the paint does not closely follow these pre-established lines. Repeated contours appear for parts of the plate, the fruit and the plaster cast, showing that Cézanne revised the scale and placing of all these elements before beginning to paint. However, there are other areas, notably the background, where no under-drawing is visible and the image is started and finished in paint.

At a late stage, Cézanne added a gentle restatement of the principal contours on the margins and within the figure of the Cupid, in somewhat simplified curves that accentuate the flowing, mobile rhythm of the figure, which is set off against the sharply rectilinear canvas that is seen in perspective immediately beyond the cast. In a sense this emphasis of the cursive form of the Cupid recreates in paint the dynamic forms of the cast itself and its baroque original.

Throughout, the canvas is conceived in terms of contrasts between warm and cool colour. On the left side and at the base, this is presented in terms of the broadly local colours of blue drapes set against red and orange fruit and onions, but the contrasts are much softer on the right, with the light-toned floor shifting between pink and blue-green tones, with added luminosity lent to the image by the light-toned paper seen through the paint layers. The Cupid cast is modelled primarily with blue with some green accents, while the highlit

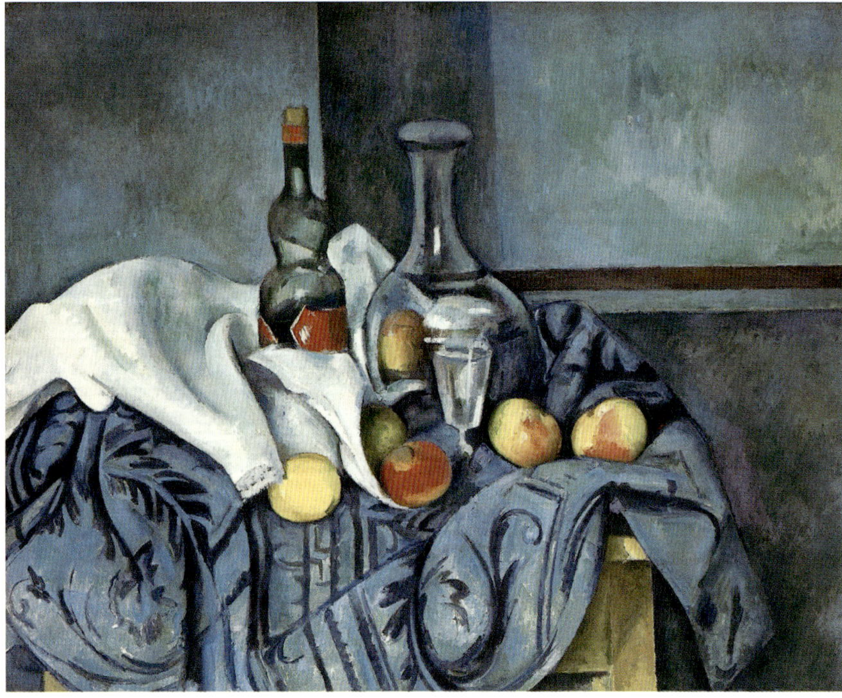

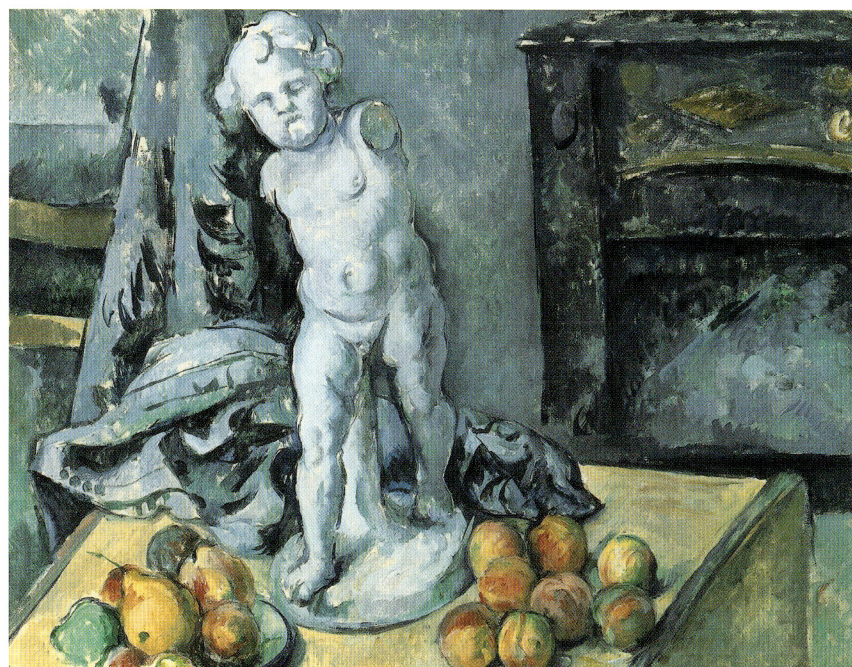

areas of the figure are treated in warm cream tones, creating yet another cool-warm contrast, very subtle this time, that weaves the figure, virtually colourless in reality, into the overall coloured play of the canvas.

The inconsistencies and paradoxes of the space are compounded by the multiple paradoxes about the nature of the reality depicted that recur throughout the picture: between 'real' and painted fruit and 'real' and painted drapery; between the 'real' fruit on the table and the Cupid figure – a cast of a statue; and between this cast and the flayed man beyond – a painting of a cast of a statue. All of these devices seem to stress the artificiality of the picture itself – of its grouping and of its making; of all Cézanne's still lives, this one reveals most vividly the artificiality of the idea of *nature morte*, an assemblage of objects, arranged in order to be painted, and, beyond this, it stands as a complex meditation on the artifice of the art of painting itself, and also, perhaps, on his own project to create a "harmony parallel to nature" without sacrificing the relative autonomy of the painted image. JH

NOTE

1 Quoted in John Rewald, *Paul Cézanne*, London, 1950, p. 174.

9 **Le Lac d'Annecy**, 1896

The Lac d'Annecy

Oil on canvas, 65 × 81 cm
The Courtauld Gallery, London (Samuel Courtauld Trust)
P.1932.SC.60
Courtauld Gift 1932

Le Lac d'Annecy is the only oil painting that Cézanne executed while staying at Talloires on the shores of this lake in Haute-Savoie in July 1896, during a trip undertaken at the request of his wife Hortense and his son Paul. The view is taken from the beach of Talloires, looking in a southerly direction across the narrowest point of the lake towards the Château de Duingt, half hidden by trees across the water (fig. 57). Cézanne wrote in a letter to Joachim Gasquet from Talloires: "This is a temperate zone. The surrounding hills are quite lofty. The lake, which at this point narrows to a bottleneck, seems to lend itself to the linear drawing exercises of young ladies. Certainly it is still a bit of nature, but a little like we've been taught to see it in the albums of young lady travellers." He was little more enthusiastic in writing to his Aixois friend Philippe Solari: "To relieve my boredom I'm doing some painting, it's not much fun, but the lake is very fine with big hills all around . . . it's not as good as our country. . .".[1] In this canvas, with its vibrant colour and monumental structure, Cézanne was clearly determined to transcend this commonplace picturesque.

The canvas is dominated by a cool colour range of blues and greens, sometimes quite deep and sonorous in tone, but its principal focuses are the succession of warm accents which runs across it, where the early morning sunshine strikes the objects in the scene – the left tree trunk, the buildings across the water, and the far hills. The pink under-layer in the background hills shows that Cézanne was thinking about the canvas in terms of warm-cool contrasts from an early stage in the execution of the painting. This contrast is brought into particularly sharp focus on the left edge of the castle tower: a vertical stroke of orange is set against the deep blues beyond, but, between the two, there is an extremely narrow band of very pale grey unpainted, primed canvas, with the result that the building is lifted forward from its surroundings both by the stroke of warm colouring and by this thread of light (fig. 59). The decision not to overpaint this fine streak at the point that he added colour on either side of it shows how tightly he controlled the colour effects he achieved.

The whole picture is tautly structured, with the massive bulk of the tree as a *repoussoir* on the left and its branches enclosing the top (see also *La Montagne Sainte-Victoire*, cat. 4); the composition is anchored in the centre by the tighter, more rectilinear forms of the buildings and their elongated reflections. The small building to the right of the castle with its vivid orange-red roof plays an especially important role in establishing a sequence of visual stepping stones that suggest recession into space; yet at the same time the rhyming colour-accents anchor our experience of the painting firmly on the canvas surface.

In reality, the castle is about one mile away across the water from Cézanne's viewpoint, but, by narrowing his visual field and focusing closely on it, he made it seem considerably closer (compare the treatment of the mountain in cat. 4). The form of the building is slightly

PROVENANCE

Ambroise Vollard, Paris; Cornelis Hoogendijk, Amsterdam; Paul Rosenberg, Paris; Marcel Kapferer, Paris; Bernheim Jeune, Paris; Percy Moore Turner, London; Samuel Courtauld, London (bought in 1926)

SELECTED EXHIBITIONS

French Art, London 1932, no. 505; *Samuel Courtauld Memorial Exhibition*, London 1948, no. 16; *Landscape in French Art*, London 1949–50, no. 311; *Cézanne*, Edinburgh and London 1954, no. 55; *Impressionism for England*, London 1994, no. 13; *Cézanne*, Paris, London and Philadelphia 1995–96, no. 174

SELECTED LITERATURE

RP 805
J. Gasquet, 'Ce qu'il m'a dit . . . le motif', *L'Amour de l'Art*, December 1921, p. 270; Rivière 1923, p.221; Dormoy 1929, p. 19; Jamot and Turner 1934, no. 27; Cooper 1954 (2), no. 17; *Cézanne. The Late Work*, exh. cat., New York and Houston 1977, pl. 68; Stokes 1978, pp. 267–68; Musée Granet, exh. cat., Aix-en-Provence, 1990, fig. 51; *Cézanne and Poussin*, Edinburgh 1990, fig. 58; Callen 2000, pp. 130–31

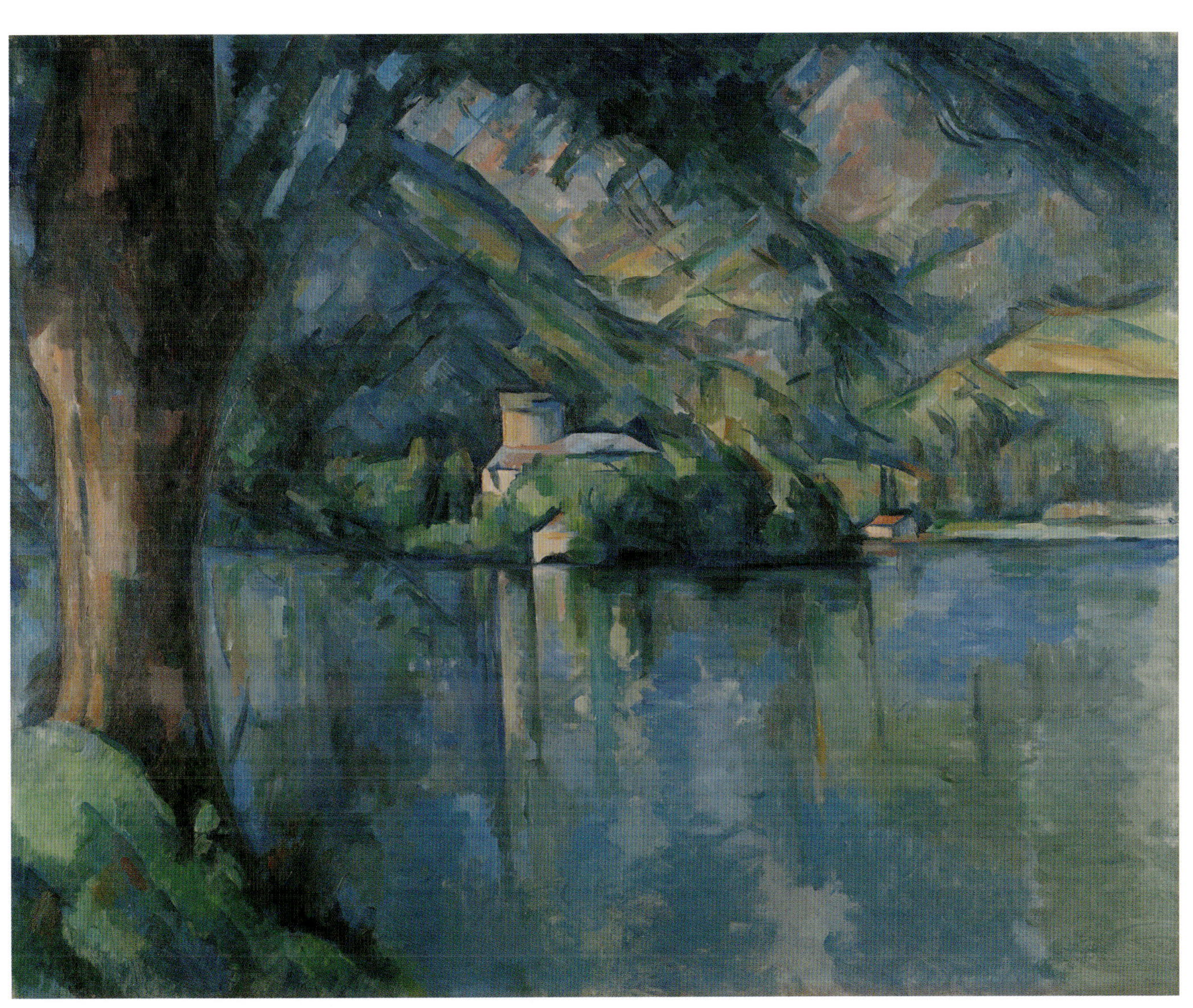

modified; in reality its turret – the focal point of Cézanne's canvas – is somewhat narrower than it appears in the painting (see fig. 57). The reflections in the water are slightly distorted – like the table legs in *The Card Players* (cat. 6), they are not exactly vertical; and the water surface is implausibly still; Cézanne took no interest in the specific play of reflections that played so central a part in the art of Claude Monet, whose work he nevertheless greatly admired.

The brushwork across the background builds up a sequence of planes of colour, which unite the nearby foliage to the far hillsides. Across the background, these are extremely varied in shape and scale, ranging from simple and relatively flat zones to smaller, loosely wedge-shaped accents and unobtrusive clusters of very small parallel strokes, reminiscent of, but far smaller and less assertive than, those in his canvases of the early 1880s (see cat. 2, 3). At certain points cursive, graphic arcs, virtually detach themselves from the foliage, and accentuate the sense of formal rhythm and pattern across the top of the picture. These were added relatively late in the execution of the canvas, but a number of strokes of more opaque paint were added after and across them in the lightest area of the far hillside, thus blurring the relationship between foreground and background (fig. 58). There is a similar blurring in the relationship between the water surface and the small branch to the right of the main trunk. In contrast to the complex treatment of the tree and the hills, the brushwork is much looser and broader in the water, and the light tone of the canvas priming is used to lend luminosity to this area of the canvas.

John Rewald has suggested that *Le Lac d'Annecy* may have been extensively reworked after Cézanne left

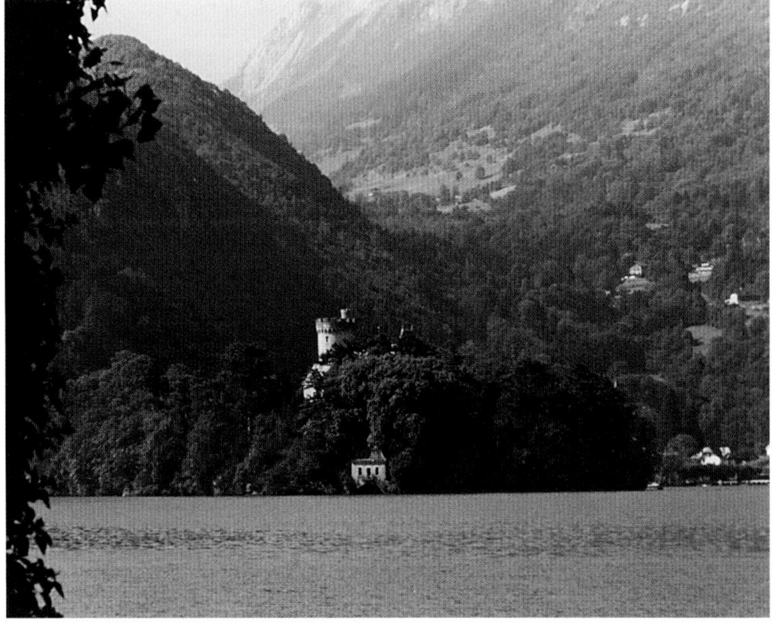

View across Lac d'Annecy, 1960s
Photograph : John Rewald
National Gallery of Art Library, Washington, Rewald Archive

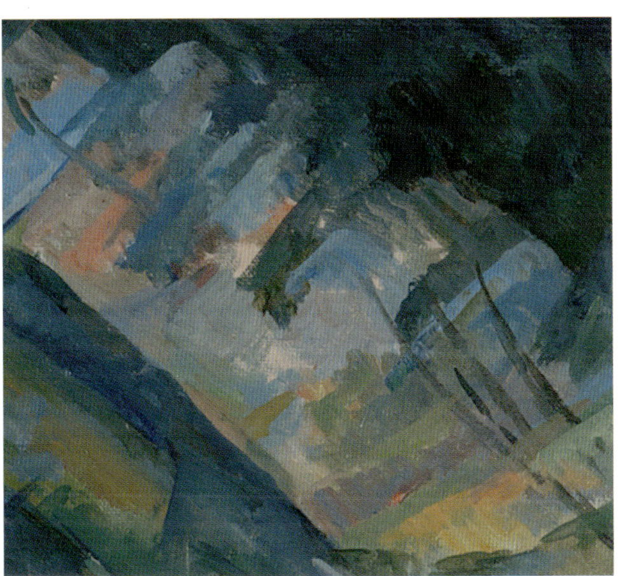

Detail of cat. 9 (darkly coloured rhythmic
lines, applied fairly late in the
painting process)

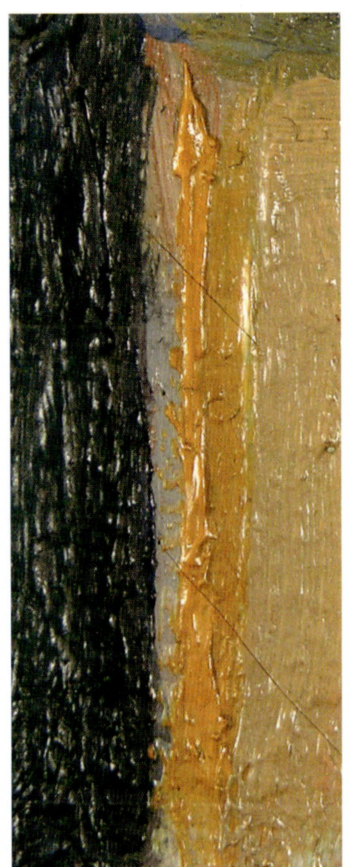

Detail of cat. 9 (left edge
of castle tower)

Talloires, because of his dissatisfaction with his
surroundings there;[2] however, there is nothing about the
execution of the canvas that differentiates it from other
landscapes of the same period. Despite the diversity of
mark-making, the picture's composition and the closely
interwoven sequences of colours give a strongly unified
structure to the whole picture-surface. Such coordination
became even more prominent in Cézanne's last works,
from this period until his death in 1906, but it was not a
means of rejecting nature; rather it was the expression
of the "harmony parallel to nature" that he was seeking
in his paintings; it was thus that he hoped to make
out of his experiences of the visible world a lasting,
coherent art. JH

NOTES

1 *Correspondance* 1978, pp. 252–54.
2 Rewald 1996, I, pp. 483–84.

10 **Route tournante**, *c.*1905

Turning Road

Oil on canvas, 73 × 92 cm
The Courtauld Gallery, London (Samuel Courtauld Trust)
P.1978.PG.61
Princes Gate Bequest 1978

The site represented in *Route tournante*, one of Cézanne's largest landscapes, has not been identified. It has been suggested that it is a scene near Cézanne's last studio, on a hill on the northern edge of Aix-en-Provence. However, it seems more likely to be a scene from northern France; Cézanne was painting near the Fontainebleau Forest, to the south-east of Paris, on his last visit to the north of France in the summer of 1905, and the canvas may well date from that trip. The flatness of the landscape depicted and the comparatively muted colour suggest a northern site, in contrast to the rocky landscapes around Aix and the stronger colour-contrasts by which Cézanne expressed the effects of the southern light. Warm and cool colours alternate throughout the canvas, in informally conceived zones of related colours, but the tonal range is extremely restricted, without the sharper contrasts of dark and light colour that he used to articulate many of his landscapes, such as *Le Lac d'Annecy* (cat. 9); however, viewed from close to, the canvas is enlivened by a number of more intensely coloured touches.

In contrast to its loose execution, the subject of *Route tournante* is conventional, with a village in the distance dominated by a church spire, and the composition framed by trees on the left. The picture is very lightly worked, with large areas of light-toned primed canvas left unpainted, especially in the sky, but also in many other parts of the canvas. Technical examination has shown that this ground was originally white (it has the whitest priming of all the Courtauld Gallery Cézannes) but has discoloured over time, muting its impact. In the second half of his career, Cézanne abandoned many

canvases at a similarly early stage of their execution, when in conventional terms they were clearly unfinished. However, he considered even some of his most highly worked paintings to be in some sense unsatisfactory and incomplete, while there are seemingly unfinished areas in many paintings that he seems to have felt to be fully resolved (see cat. 4).

We cannot tell why Cézanne did not continue to work on this painting. The turning road in the foreground is indicated only by a number of rapidly painted linear ultramarine marks; these were reinforced shortly before he ceased work on the canvas by two browner strokes, presumably intended to guide him towards further

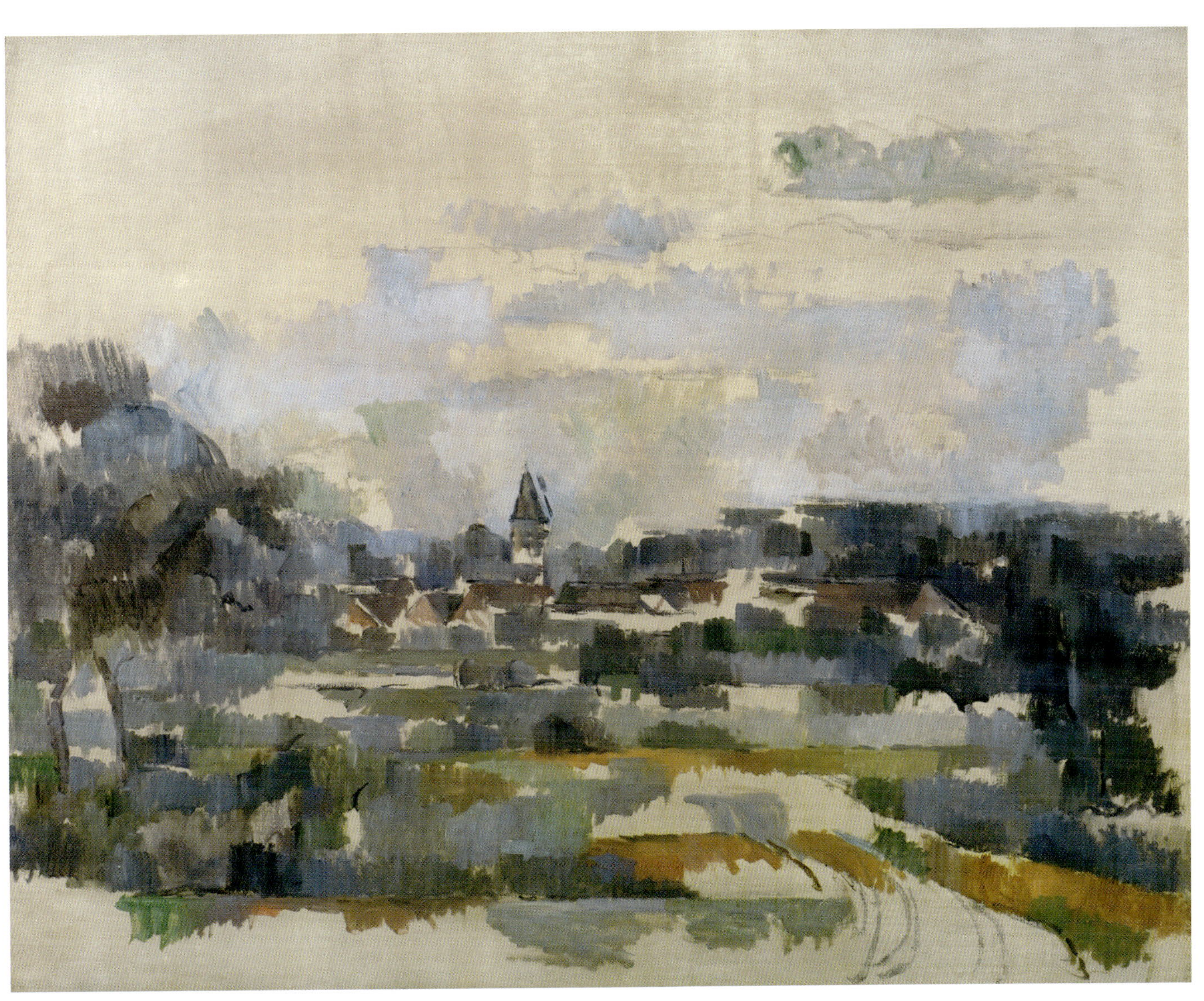

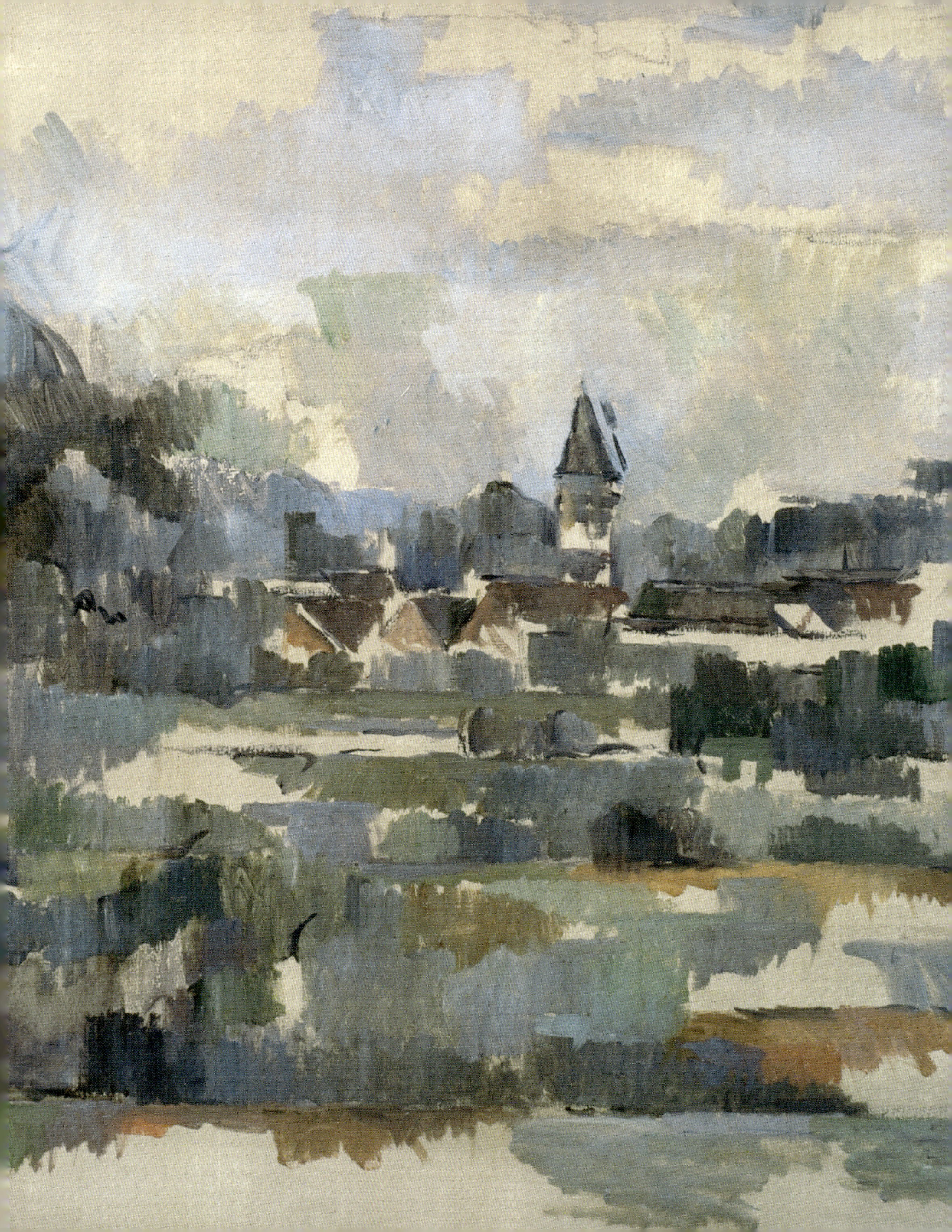

elaborations if he had continued work on the picture. Likewise, to the right of the church spire, linear strokes were added at a late stage on top of the intervening colour planes, seemingly as a prelude of enlarging or moving the spire. The extra outline to the right of it seems to indicate a reworking that Cézanne never completed (fig. 60). The lie of the land in the centre of the picture remains unclear. Our eye can imagine a progression into space across the sequence of horizontal bands of coloured strokes, which perhaps suggest a sequence of fields and hedges, with more linear blue strokes both beneath and on top of the broader touches; but the detail is nowhere clear, and the path of the road further into the landscape is not indicated. The linear strokes act as some sort of armature for the patches of colour, but without clarifying the spatial relationships represented. These planes at the centre of the canvas are presumably an example of the type of coloured marks that he demonstrated to the collector Karl Osthaus in 1906 where "the colour

remained colour without becoming the expression of distance" (see pp. 40–41). Likewise, the zones of unpainted canvas do not wholly dovetail into the image in representational terms.

Although by nineteenth-century standards the picture would have appeared unresolved, the lack of conventional finish in Cézanne's late paintings such as *Route tournante* has been a powerful inspiration for many artists in the twentieth century, in their search for an expressive personal style that rejected academic rules. *Route tournante* was one of a small group of Impressionist and Post-Impressionist paintings and drawings assembled by the celebrated Old Master collector Count Antoine Seilern. Seilern also owned two watercolours and a drawing by the artist (cat. 11, 15, 16). Like *Statue under Trees* (cat. 16), the present painting was acquired by Seilern from Sir Kenneth Clark, at the time director of the National Gallery, London. JH

 Portrait of Hortense Fiquet (Madame Cézanne Sewing), *c*. 1880

Graphite on pale cream wove paper, with laid and chain lines
472 × 309 mm
The Courtauld Gallery, London (Samuel Courtauld Trust)
D.1978.PG.239
Princes Gate Bequest 1978

Cézanne met Hortense Fiquet (1850–1922) in 1869, when
she seems to have been working as a bookbinder in Paris.[1]
Fearing the loss of his father's financial support, the
artist kept the liaison secret even after the couple's son
Paul was born in 1872; he did not legalise the relationship
until they married in 1886. Even though they lived apart
for long periods Hortense was Cézanne's most-often
depicted model, her portraits ranging from large oil
paintings to watercolours and quick pencil sketches.[2]

The majority of the paintings show Mme Cézanne
seated, with no occupation other than posing for the
artist. The exception is a portrait in the Nationalmuseum,
Stockholm, of about 1877 (RP 323; fig. 62) that shows her
sitting in a comfortably upholstered armchair sewing a
large cloth and taking no notice of the viewer – a pose
and an activity chosen previously by Cézanne in *Girl at the
Piano* (*The Overture to Tannhäuser*) of about 1869–70 (RP 149;
fig. 66). Two pencil sketches (CD 398, 728) also show
Hortense sewing but are not directly related to the
portrait and are usually thought to date after 1877. The
present drawing is generally considered the final one
of this group.

Of all the drawn portraits of the future Madame
Cézanne, this sheet is notable for its large format as well
as its ambitious composition, in which the sitter is shown
(unlike most of Cézanne's portraits, including the Stockholm painting) with various objects – a bed, a cabinet,

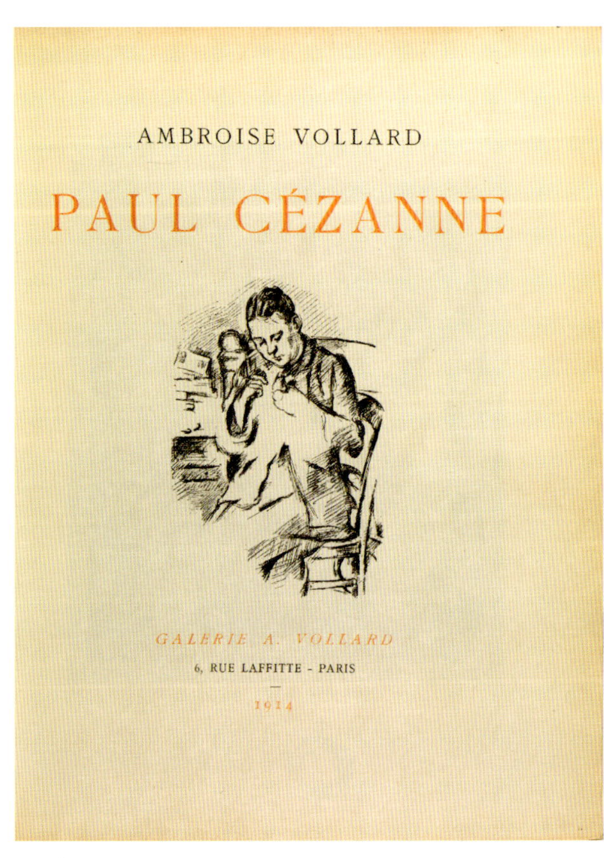

FIG.61
Title page of Ambroise Vollard,
Paul Cézanne, Paris, 1914

TECHNICAL NOTE

Sheet backed, two repaired tears at the
upper border

WATERMARK

INGRES and P L BAS imitated mechanically

PROVENANCE

Ambroise Vollard, Paris; Simon Meller, Munich;
Paul Cassirer, Berlin; H. von Simolin, Berlin;
Paul Cassirer, London; Count Antoine Seilern,
London (bought in 1941)

SELECTED EXHIBITIONS

Société des Artistes Indépendants. *Centenaire
du peintre indépendant Paul Cézanne*, Grand Palais,
Paris 1939, no. 44; *Watercolour and Pencil Drawings
by Cézanne*, Newcastle and London 1973, no. 66;
Princes Gate Collection, London 1981, no. 133;
Impressionist, Post-Impressionist and related drawings,
London 1988, no. 5

SELECTED LITERATURE

CD 729
Venturi 1936, no. 1466; Vollard, 1914, p. 177;
Meier-Graefe 1918, p. 37; Seilern 1961, p. 105,
no. 239; Andersen 1970, no. 67; Venturi 1978,
p. 76; *100 Masterpieces from The Courtauld Collection*,
London 1987, p. 212

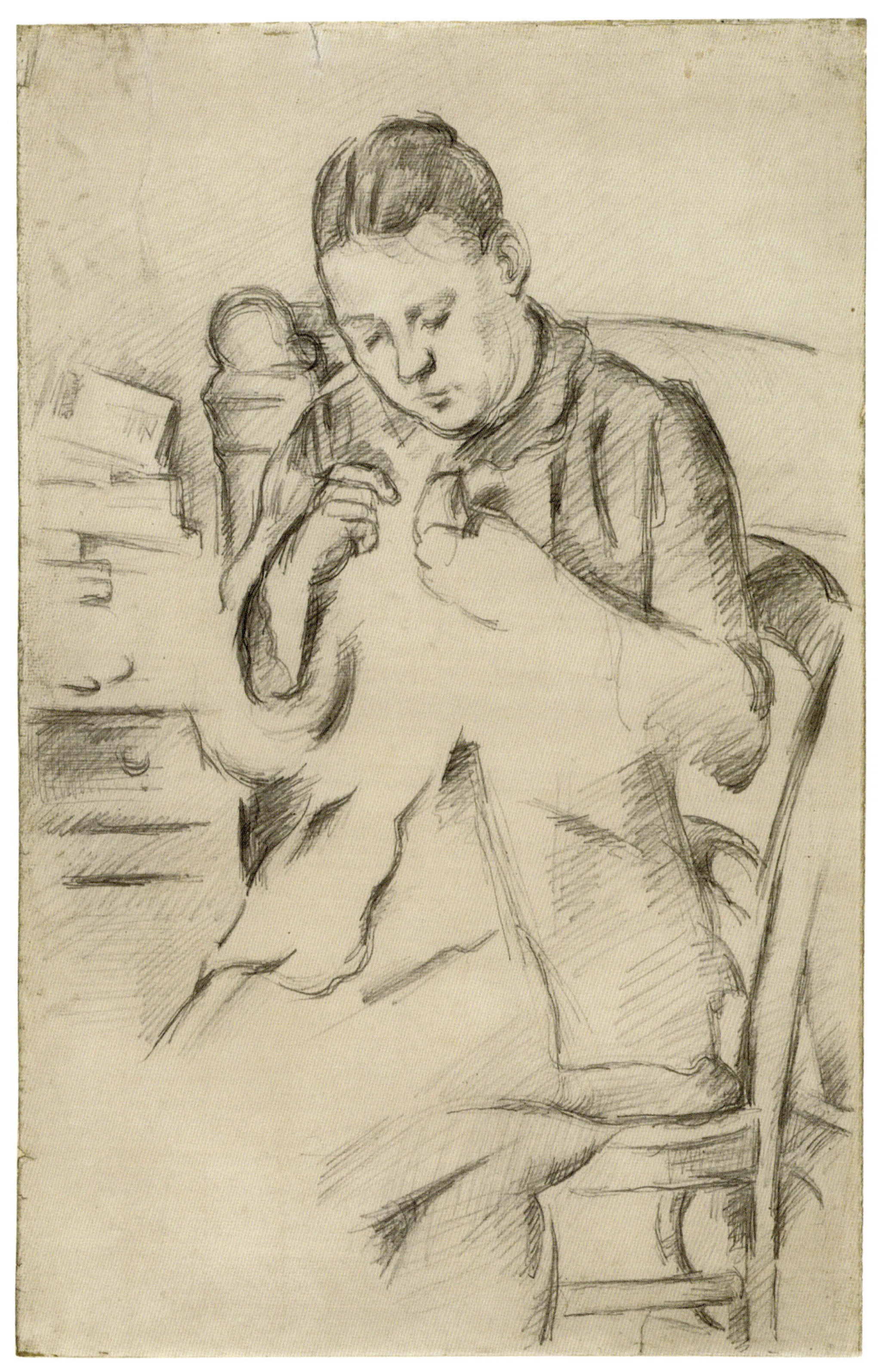

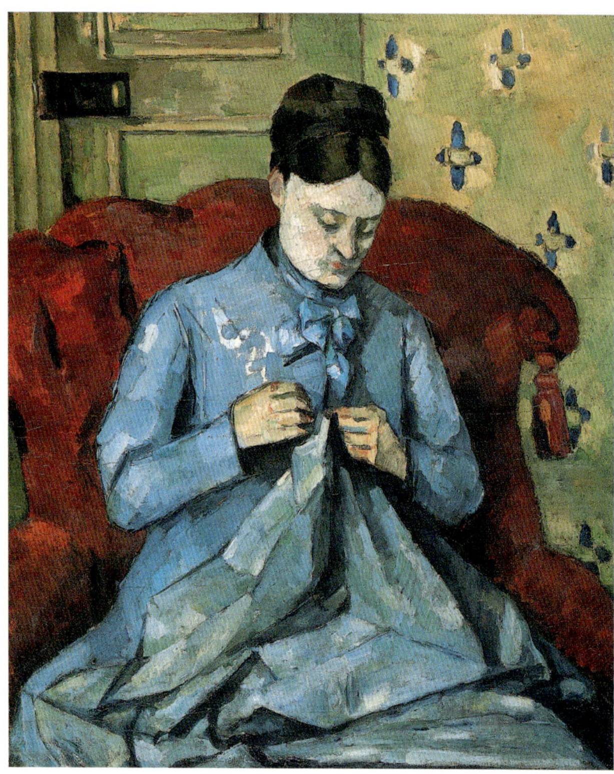

Ambroise Vollard's choice of this drawing as an illustration for the title page of his important early (1914) monograph on Cézanne (fig. 61) seems particularly appropriate. Tellingly, the dealer, who owned numerous portraits of Mme Cézanne,[5] gave this drawing the title *The Seamstress*,[6] implying a genre picture and indicating that the figure is so fully absorbed in her activity that all individual traits are transcended. The conventional distinction between genre painting and portrait is dissolved, as is the one between portrait and still life. As has often been pointed out, Cézanne is said to have asked his sitters to pose without moving at all. Describing his own portrait session with Cézanne in 1899, Vollard recalled how he fell asleep and toppled off the chair on which he was sitting, prompting Cézanne to scold him: "You have spoiled the pose. I am telling you, truthfully, you need to hold yourself like an apple. Would an apple move?"[7] Maurice Denis also described Vollard's portrait sessions, writing in his journal that Cézanne complained that the sitter's movement had "made him lose the line of concentration".[8]

In the Courtauld drawing the genres of portrait and still life are linked not only in the treatment of the figure but also because she is framed on the left by a still life of books, an unusual orchestration of a portrait that the artist did not take up again until the late 1890s in *Portrait of Gustave Geffroy* (RP 791; Musée d'Orsay, Paris) and *Boy with Skull* (RP 825; The Barnes Foundation, Merion, Pennsylvania). With regard to its structure, the still life echoes the figure of Hortense herself: the pile of books is topped by a small volume placed at a slight angle and as the spines of the books are merely indicated by a few curved pencil strokes the pile's centre is essentially left blank. On a compositional level, this bond links the individual elements of the picture. At the same time, the unusual book still life functions as a classic accessory, presumably referring to the sitter's work as a seamstress of handmade books and perhaps suggesting that she was educated.[9] Although such allusions are for the most part uncommon in Cézanne's portraits, they are not unique in drawings of his future wife executed in the early to

and a pile of books.[3] Sitting upright on a simple wooden chair, Hortense bends over her needlework, which falls into her lap. The texture and form of the cloth, however, are left unclear; it is defined only at its lower edges by multiple curved pencil strokes that differ from the straighter outline of her jacket. Needle and thread are not shown. Instead of a clear depiction of the subject, as would be expected in a traditional representation, the centre of the drawing is daringly left blank. Cézanne established the sitter's presence, her full mental concentration on the work, thus creating an intense portrait of her quiet occupation. In order to direct the viewer's gaze to the centre, the lower left corner is blank, thus inviting the eye to enter the composition. Following the contour of the cloth, the gaze reaches the crucial area between the seamstress's motionless hands onto which her lowered eyes are fixed. The attentive gaze parallels the concentrated exploratory look of the viewer – and in the first place, of the artist himself observing the sitter. It also characterises Cézanne's approach in general when submitting himself to sustained observation and the 'realisation' of his work.[4] Thus, the Courtauld drawing manifests a fundamental issue of Cézanne's artistic concerns.

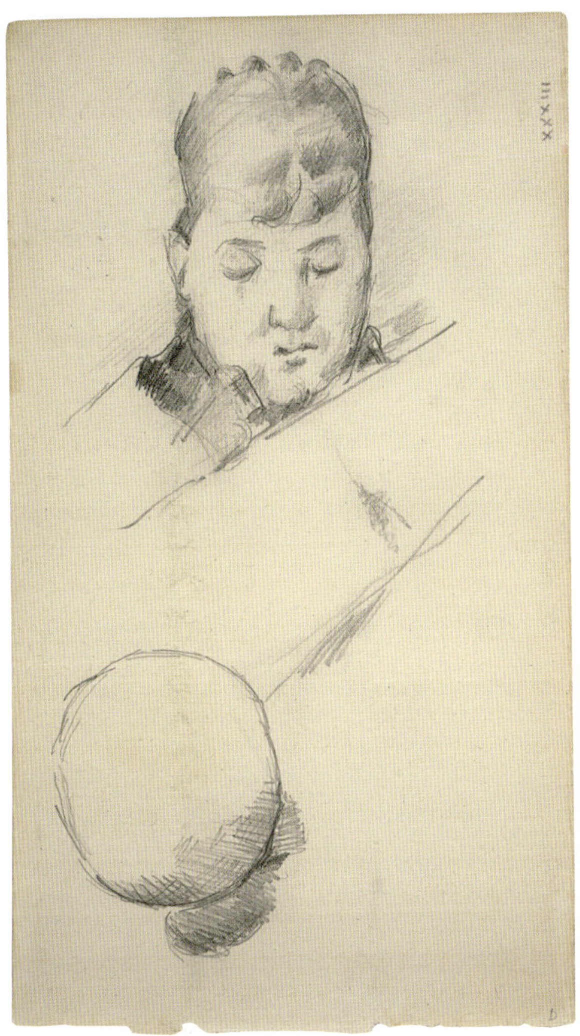

FIG. 63
Paul Cézanne, *Bust of Madame Cézanne*
c. 1884–85
Graphite on paper, 218 × 125 mm
National Gallery of Art, Washington
Collection of Mr and Mrs Paul Mellon

mid-1880s. One well-known example is the tender pencil portrait of Hortense reclining, juxtaposed with a watercolour of a hydrangea or, in French, *hortensia* (RWC 209; private collection, Zurich).[10] Another playful pun on her name is found in a sketch in the National Gallery, Washington (CD 840; fig. 63), which shows a restrained bust-length portrait of Hortense in the upper half of the sheet and a ball with a strongly cast shadow in the lower portion. While it is usually interpreted as an orange, the ball presumably refers to Hortense Fiquet's nickname, '*La Boule*'.[11] This reference might also explain the close juxtaposition of the remarkably round head of Hortense in the Courtauld drawing with the knob on the bedpost. Functioning as an important structural element in the composition, the bed also lends intimacy to this monumental portrait drawing and indicates the sitter's role as the artist's companion. Thus the various levels of artistic concern make this sheet a particularly ambitious, fully realised work and lend it a prominent status within Cézanne's drawn oeuvre. SB

ACKNOWLEDGEMENT

I am most grateful to Pamela Barr for her help with the editing of my entries.

NOTES

1 *Cézanne. Finished – Unfinished*, Vienna and Zurich 2000, p. 388; R. Butler, *Hidden in the Shadow of the Master. The Model-wives of Cézanne, Monet, and Rodin*, Yale University Press 2008 (forthcoming), Part I, ch. 1 (I am grateful to Ruth Butler for discussing Hortense Fiquet's biography with me).

2 For biographical details see *Cézanne in Provence*, Washington and Aix-en-Provence 2006, pp. 305–15.

3 One other pencil portrait of Madame Cézanne in the Museum Boymans-van Beuningen, Rotterdam (CD 1065; inv. F II 220), dated to 1887–90, has a comparable format, measuring 475 × 322 mm. For the importance of the drawings' sizes for the understanding of their status see W. Feilchenfeldt, 'Cézanne's works on paper. Towards a reclassification', in *Classic Cézanne*, Sydney 1998–99, p. 59. The large sheets which were not bound in a sketchbook "attain the high standard of the large-sized watercolours and are often of equal importance" (*ibid.*, p. 55).

4 For the relationship between Cézanne and his motif and the viewer see R. Shiff, 'Sensation, movement, Cézanne', in *Classic Cézanne*, Sydney 1998–99, p. 18. For Cézanne's understanding of *realiser* see John House's introduction to the letters to Bernard, below, p. 147.

5 RP 324, 387, 532, 533, 536, 582, 583 (?), 606, 607, 650, 651 (?), 652, 653, 655, 683, 685, 700, 703.

6 Vollard 1914, p. 177.

7 "*Vous dérangez la pose! Je vous le dis, en vérité, il faut vous tenir comme une pomme. Est-ce que cela remue, une pomme?*", Vollard 1914, p. 92. For the English translation see Garb 2007, p. 158. The portrait (RP 811) is today in the Musée du Petit Palais, Paris.

8 "*Vollard pose tous les matins chez Cézanne, depuis un temps infini. Dès qu'il bouge, Cézanne se plaint qu'il lui fasse perdre la ligne de concentration*": see Denis 1957, p. 157, diary entry for 21 October 1899. In the later scholarly literature it has often been stated that Cézanne treated portrait sitters not as subjects but like objects of still life: see Garb 2007, p. 158, with reference to earlier critics.

9 See P. Kathke, *Porträt und Accessoire. Eine Bildnisform im 16. Jahrhundert*, Berlin, 1997. Butler (see note 1) refers to two carefully written letters in Hortense's hand and concludes that she did have at least basic schooling.

10 *Cézanne. Finished – Unfinished*, Vienna and Zurich 2000, no. 8; *Cézanne in the Studio*, Los Angeles 2004, pp. 28–31; Garb 2007, p. 171.

11 *Cézanne in Provence*, Washington and Aix-en-Provence 2006, p. 305.

12 **Une cabane**, *c.*1880

A Shed

Graphite and watercolour on pale cream wove paper
314 × 475 mm
The Courtauld Gallery, London (Samuel Courtauld Trust)
D.1932.SC.109
Courtauld Gift 1932

This work is generally thought to be the earliest Cézanne watercolour in The Courtauld Gallery's collection. Lionello Venturi, presumably guided by the picturesque motif of a seemingly ramshackle building hidden under a dense canopy of leaves and overgrown by vegetation, dated it 1872–77, thus placing it in the artist's so-called Impressionist period. Believing that the even distribution of the watercolour on the sheet was incompatible with a very early work, Neumeyer proposed a date of around 1880.

Although this date has generally been accepted in recent scholarship, the drawing remains enigmatic in several respects: the motif is unique in Cézanne's oeuvre and the site cannot be identified: it is a matter of speculation whether it might have been situated on the family's estate, the Jas de Bouffan.[1] Moreover, the representation of the subject itself – variously described as a cottage,[2] a garden wall with a built-in shack,[3] a garden shed,[4] and an outhouse[5] – is ambiguous, as it is not clear which parts of the low, frontally viewed building are meant to recede in space and which are parallel to the picture plane. The continuous horizontal line, which ends abruptly on the left, possibly indicating a gutter, refers to a roof-like structure, supported by vertical stone walls. Within this framework the building lacks definition, as it remains uncertain whether the vertical lines in the centre indicate wooden planks, whether the shorter horizontal lines within this area refer to a door, and how the vaguely indicated central segments relate in space. Oblique lines, which usually help to define architecture, are absent and no more than a few details indicate the texture of the various materials.

The spatial ambiguity is also due to the inconsistent use of diagonal hatching in the extensive linear pencil drawing. As becomes especially evident in the digital infrared reflectogram (fig. 64), which shows the line drawing more clearly in places densely covered by watercolour, the hatching is used in some areas to project forms vigorously into relief, such as the stem of the climbing vine on the right. In other areas – for example, the corner of the wall segment on the left – equal series of lines are drawn over the verticals and thus flatten

TECHNICAL NOTE

Slight acid burns from an old mount at the lower and left edges; tear repaired at the upper edge, right of centre; verso: inscribed in pencil *+ vole* and numbered in blue crayon *66*; traces of pencil and blue-grey wash, apparently transferred from another drawing; the sheet unevenly trimmed at the bottom

PROVENANCE

Paul Cézanne *fils*, Paris; Bernheim-Jeune, Paris; Gottlieb Friedrich Reber, Barmen; Paul Rosenberg, Paris; Samuel Courtauld, London (date of purchase unknown)

SELECTED EXHIBITIONS

Les Aquarelles de Cézanne, Paris 1907, no. 73 (?); *Cézanne Aquarelle*, Berlin 1907, no. 65 (?); *Second Post-Impressionist Exhibition*, London 1912, no. 167; *Paul Cézanne, Exhibition of Watercolours*, London, Leicester and Sheffield 1946, no. 3; *Samuel Courtauld Memorial Exhibition*, London 1948, no. 48; *Landscape in French Art*, London 1949–50, no. 546; *Drawings and Engravings*, London 1959–60, no. 15; *Paul Cézanne*, Vienna 1961, no. 47; *Exposition Cézanne, Tableaux-Aquarelles-Dessins*, Pavillon de Vendôme, Aix-en-Provence, 1961, no. 21; *Watercolour and Pencil Drawings by Cézanne*, Newcastle and London 1973 , no. 142; *Mantegna to Cézanne*, London 1983, no. 98; *Impressionist, Post-Impressionist and Related Drawings*, London 1988, no. 4; *Impressionism for England*, London 1994, no. 71; *Classic Cézanne*, Sydney 1998, p. 106, no. 35; M.T. Benedetti, *Cézanne. Il padre dei moderni*, Complesso del Vittoriano, Milan, 2002, p. 132; *Cézanne in Britain*, London 2006–07, no. 22

SELECTED LITERATURE

RWC 102
Venturi 1936, no. 837; Cooper 1954 (2), no. 309; Neumeyer 1958, p. 55; W. V. Andersen, 'Watercolor in Cézanne's artistic process', *Art International*, 25 May 1963, p. 25

the space. A similar ambiguity characterises the space created in the lower right corner of Hortense Fiquet's portrait, executed about the same time (cat. 11), where the chair seat, rails, and back are interlocked with the background. As in that portrait, the broadly applied diagonal hatchings in *A Shed* – for the most part, continuous, unbroken zigzag strokes applied without lifting the pencil from the paper – unite the picture and draw the single forms together but do not try to model them or accurately capture shade. The clear legibility of the motif is thus relinquished in favour of a firm tectonic structure on the two-dimensional plane. This approach seems intentional; according to Maurice Denis, who visited the artist in 1906, Cézanne claimed: "I wanted to make of Impressionism something solid and enduring like the art in museums."[6]

The image is predominantly formed by the pencil drawing while the colour amplifies and accentuates the design. The colour does, however, play a vital part in balancing the composition; the patches of translucent greys on the right function as a vertical framing device that links up with the darker greys on the left, putting the wall in relief. Most striking is the daringly bright viridian green horizontal strip in the foreground, into which are interwoven strokes of yellow ochre and cobalt blue, subtly corresponding to the same hues on the building as well as the nests of colour in the canopy of leaves. Thus the arrangement of colour has been carefully balanced, while the predominant use of monochrome serves to convey the sense of a simple building organically integrated into its natural surroundings. SB

NOTES

1 This possibility was mentioned in *Impressionism for England*, London 1994, no. 71, and *Cézanne in Britain*, London 2006–07, no. 22.
2 Neumeyer 1958, no. 67.
3 Rewald 1983, no. 102.
4 *Mantegna to Cézanne*, London 1983, no. 98.
5 *Impressionism for England*, London 1994, no. 71.
6 First published in an article in *L'Occident*, September 1907, here quoted from Doran 2001, p. 169.

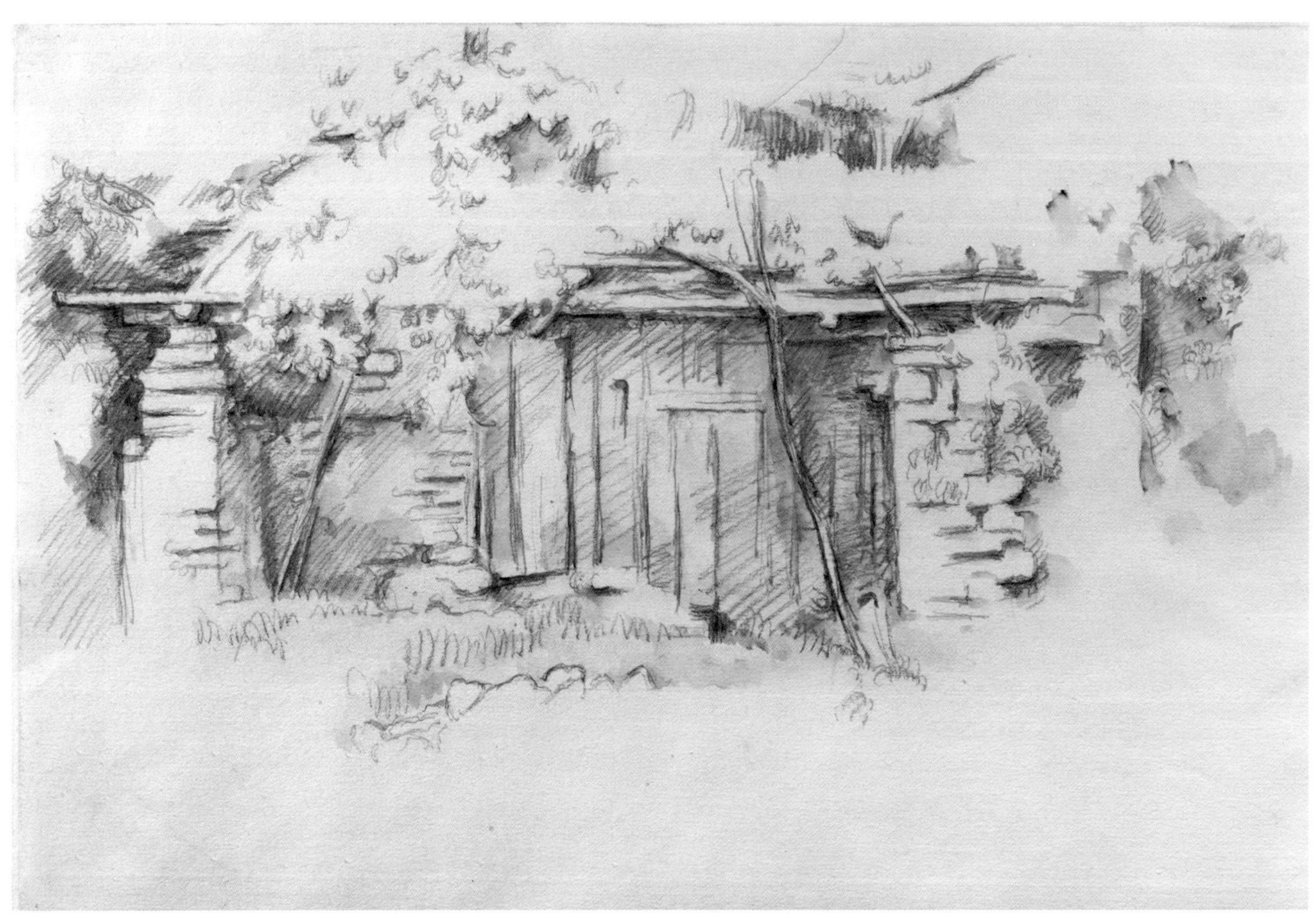

FIG. 64
Digital infrared reflectogram of cat. 12

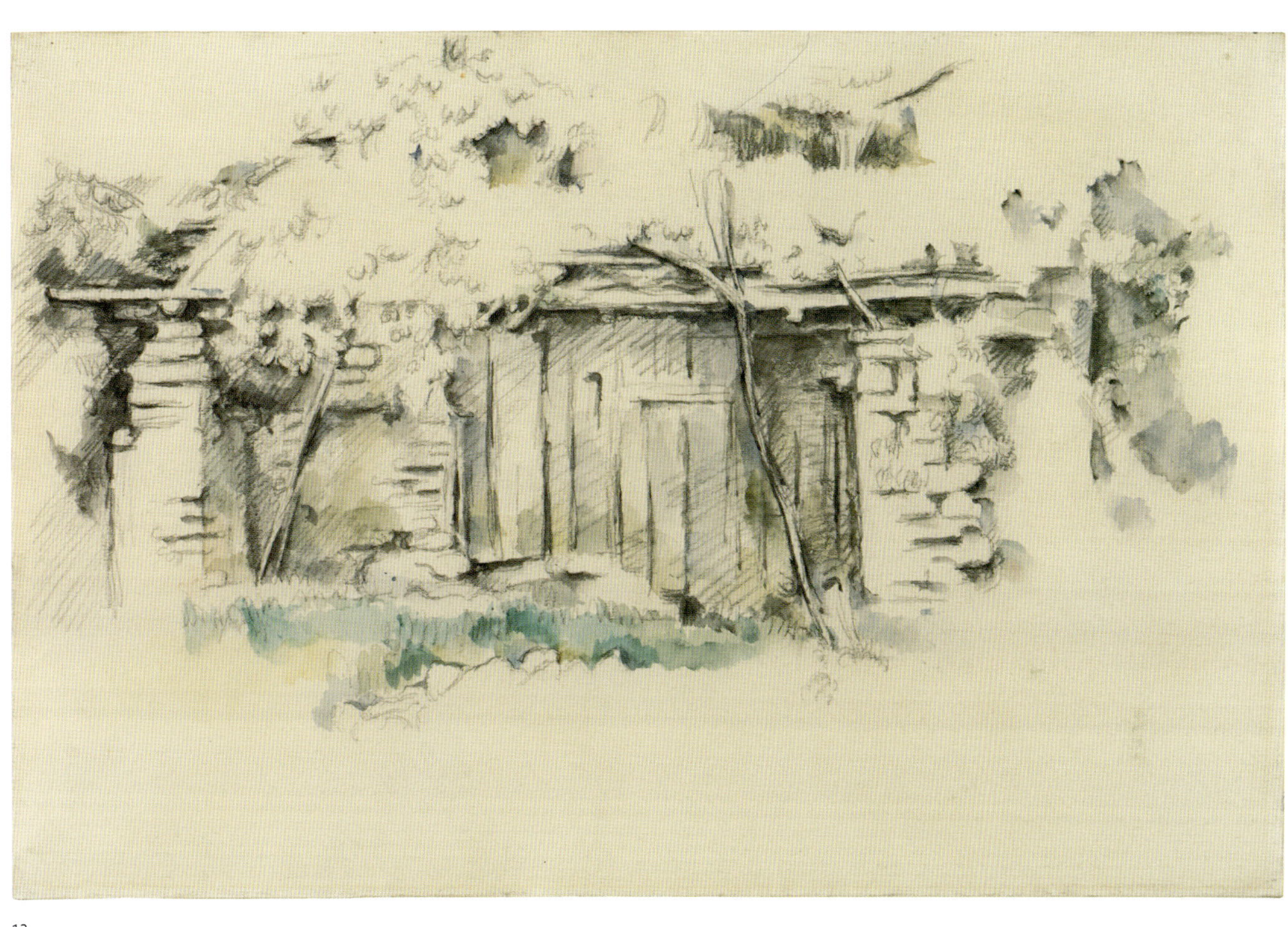

12

Graphite on pale cream wove paper
314 × 473 (upper)/477 (lower) mm
The Courtauld Gallery, London (Samuel Courtauld Trust)
D.1981.XX.4
Accessioned in 1981 from an unknown source

Pencil studies of individual trees are relatively rare in Cézanne's drawn oeuvre, as the artist preferred to study the landscape and its vegetation in watercolour, working outdoors. This large drawing stands out for its balanced composition in which a clear structure is combined with rhythmic movement, as vividly curved and entwined branches rise and fall from a slim but firm trunk that supply bends backwards. Framing the composition at the left, it functions as its pliant spine. A clearly indicated line in the centre marks the horizontal axis of the composition, which concentrates on the middle of the sheet; broad strips of paper on the left and right were left untouched and frame the motif generously. The focus on the centre becomes all the more clear since the branches end abruptly on the right as if cut off. The short diagonal hatchings in the otherwise empty zone below the foliage are critical to the delicate balance of the composition: though not enclosed within contours, these hatchings indicate the vertical axis of the drawing and correspond in length and placement to the diagonal striations that shade the trunk. Despite this pictorial correspondence, these marks do not seem to represent a second trunk but refer to a shadow or a form in the landscape, seen and registered but not described further.

A similar ambiguity characterises the central horizontal line, which has been interpreted as possibly representing the top of a wall.[1] Short crisp curved marks at either side of this line suggest volume and argue against the line indicating the horizon. The form registered by this line was, however, not necessarily located in the foreground but might have been a more distant landscape formation. Through the graphic structure, the pictorial planes are tightly interlocked which is typical of Cézanne's work in the 1880s.

Rather than aiming at a detailed mimetic surface description of bark and leaves, Cézanne visually analysed the relationship of the tree's various parts – trunk, main strong boughs, branches, twigs, and leaves – in order to create a harmonious composition that is both equivalent and parallel to nature. His realisation is based on close observation – a laborious process that relates to his cautious drawing technique. Initially, light pencil strokes established the tree's form. Next, these lines were overwritten with curved strokes and marks; shapes were accentuated and set in relief, spaces were excavated, until a complex structure of relationships evolved. Although using a linear vocabulary, Cézanne thus abandoned the continuous unbroken contour that clearly delineates forms and separates them from one another in an abstract manner. In this respect his denial of the existence of line is comprehensible, as he put it: "Line and modelling do not exist. Drawing is the relationship of contrasts or, simply, the rapport between two tones, white and black."[2] SB

TECHNICAL NOTE

Stains, particularly at the left; pinholes at upper and lower right corners, and above and below centre at the left edge; small repaired tears at left and lower edges; a faint line in blue crayon, probably in a later hand, forms a vertical rectangle at the top right corner, numbered in graphite, top right, *1*, and inscribed once in blue crayon, once in pencil, lower right, *au 1/3*; the sheet unevenly torn, apparently along a fold at the top; fold at the upper right

WATERMARK

Blindstamped . . . NONAY A (reversed, picture side)

PROVENANCE

Margarete Oppenheim, Berlin (?) (see *Sammlung Frau Margarete Oppenheim*, Julius Böhler, Munich, 18–20 May 1936, no. 1231, not reproduced; but the identification remains tentative as this drawing measured 475 × 305 mm, indicating a vertical format); Kenneth Clark, London

SELECTED EXHIBITION

Impressionist, Post-Impressionist and Related Drawings, London 1988, no. 6

SELECTED LITERATURE

CD 911
Venturi 1936, I, p. 348 ('Oeuvres inédites'; not reproduced)

NOTES

1 *Impressionist, Post-Impressionist and Related Drawings*, London 1988, no. 6.
2 Léo Larguier in *Le Dimanche avec Paul Cézanne*, 1901–02; see Doran 2001, p. 17. See also Chappuis 1973, pp. 12–13.

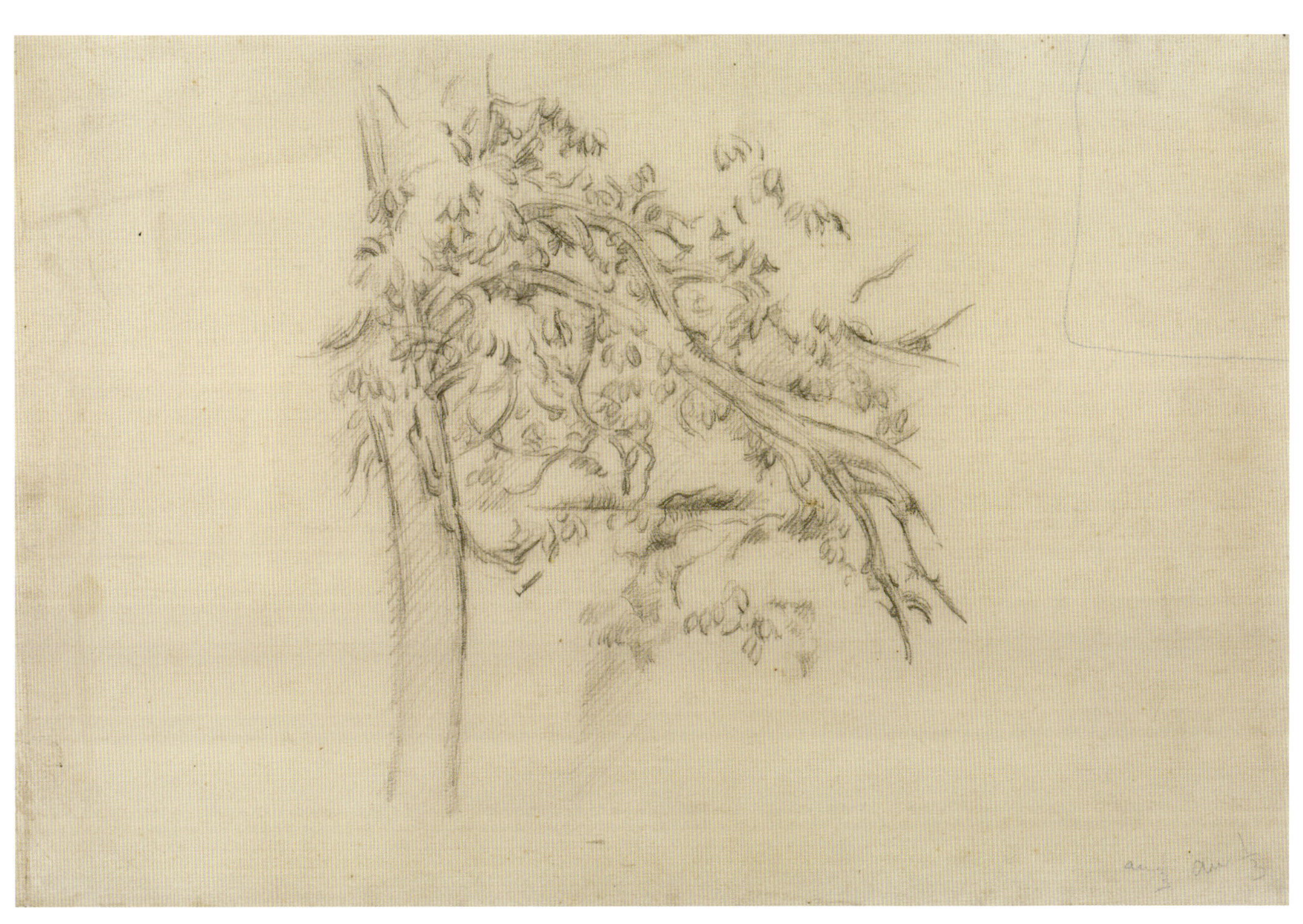

 La Montagne Sainte-Victoire, *c*.1885–87

The Montagne Sainte-Victoire

Graphite and watercolour on off-white laid paper
327 (left) / 320 (right) × 505 mm
The Courtauld Gallery, London (Samuel Courtauld Trust)
D.1932.SC.110
Courtauld Gift 1932

Cézanne continued to depict Montagne Sainte-Victoire from the late 1870s until the end of his life. When executing this watercolour he chose a position about one kilometre southwest of the Jas de Bouffan, one of his preferred vantage points.[1] Oil paintings in The Courtauld Gallery (cat. 4) and the Barnes Foundation (RP 767), among others, show the motif from the same direction, as do a pencil drawing (CD 895) and several watercolours (RWC 241; fig. 49; RWC 280–284) from about 1885–87, a date that has been widely accepted for the Courtauld watercolour.[2]

The distance to the mountain varies in every view, as does the artist's choice of such landmarks as trees and buildings that structure the compositions. In this respect the Courtauld watercolour is especially subtle and restrained. Cézanne refrained from clearly identifying houses and trees and placed only two cone-shaped forms – probably indicating trees – and a cube, presumably a building, at the centre to anchor the composition. Horizontal bands define the foreground and perhaps suggest hedges or the boundaries of fields. The strip of blue on the right, an abstract patch of colour when seen in isolation, may refer to the viaduct recorded in the Courtauld (cat. 4) and Barnes paintings.

From the chosen vantage point the mountain rises along the middle axis, resulting in a balanced, calm composition. Being only sparsely described by light pencil lines – first sketched in freely with continuous sweeps cautiously shaping the highest slope and subsequently by a few more persistent broken curves at the outlines (fig. 65) – the mountain is largely deprived of substance. Its main slope is scarcely modelled with hatching; untouched paper dominates the centre, and the modulated watercolour is mainly limited to the left side. There, shades of cobalt blue are sparsely applied, broadening the contours and shading the sides of the mountain. While the blue colour pushes the motif further into the distance, a stroke of yellow at the top left adds light and links the mountain to the foothills in the middle ground as well as to the foreground, where the

---

TECHNICAL NOTE

Acid burns of an old mount on all borders, paper discoloured and watercolour faded; stained at the left and right edges; tears repaired on the left and right; verso: numbered in blue crayon 158; the sheet unevenly torn at the bottom and left edges

WATERMARK

VIDALON

PROVENANCE

Paul Cézanne *fils*, Paris; Bernheim-Jeune, Paris (bought from the artist's son, 12 February 1907); Gottlieb Friedrich Reber, Lausanne; Percy Moore Turner, London; Samuel Courtauld, London (bought in 1924)

SELECTED EXHIBITIONS

Watercolors by Cézanne, New York 1911, no. 8; *Paintings and Drawings*, London 1925, no. 4; *French Art*, London 1932, no. 989; *Samuel Courtauld Memorial Exhibition*, London 1948, no. 85; *Landscape in French Art*, London 1949–50, no. 554; *Drawings and Engravings*, London 1959–60, no. 13; *Paul Cézanne*, Vienna 1961, no. 65; *Exposition Cézanne, Tableaux-Aquarelles-Dessins*, Pavillon de Vendôme, Aix-en-Provence, 1961, no. 27; *Watercolour and Pencil Drawings by Cézanne*, Newcastle and London 1973, no. 55; *Mantegna to Cézanne*, London 1983, no. 100; C. Lloyd and R. Thomson (ed.), *Impressionist Drawings from British Public and Private Collections*, Ashmolean Museum, Oxford, City Art Gallery, Manchester, and Burrell Collection, Glasgow, 1986, no. 9; *Impressionist, Post-Impressionist and Related Drawings*, London 1988, no. 7; *Cézanne and Poussin*, Edinburgh 1990, no. 52; *Impressionism for England*, London 1994, no. 72; *The Prismatic Palette. Four Centuries of Watercolors*, The J. Paul Getty Museum, Los Angeles, 2005

SELECTED LITERATURE

RWC 279
The New York Times, 12 March 1911, Section V, p. 15; Sitwell 1925, p. 65; Venturi 1936, no. 1023; Novotny 1938, p. 201, no. 68; Loran 1943, p. 101; J.M. Carpenter, 'Cézanne and Tradition', *Art Bulletin*, vol. 33, 1951, pp. 182, 183, 186; Cooper 1954 (2), no. 100; L. Dittmann, 'Zur Kunst Cézannes', *Festschrift für Kurt Badt*, Berlin, 1961, p. 205; V. De Mazia: 'Expression', *The Barnes Foundation Journal of the Art Department*, vol. 5, no. 2, 1974, pp. 19–20; L. Gowing, 'The Logic of Organized Sensations', in London and Houston 1977, p. 58

colour also appears. These areas are modelled more
intensely with linear diagonal pencil strokes as well as
with a variety of green, greyish blue, yellow, and orange
shades and, consequently, gain more weight. Cézanne
was certainly aware of the visual effects of colour; as he
wrote in his first letter to Emile Bernard (15 April 1904):
"Now, we men experience nature more in terms of depth
than surface; hence the necessity to introduce into our
vibrations of light, represented by reds and yellows, a
sufficient quantity of blue tones, to give a sense of the
atmosphere".[3]

Through the artist's manipulation, not only does
colour organise the space, but the repetition of hues also
helps to interlock the different surface planes, while the
warm white of the paper is instrumental in unifying the
whole. The scarcity of applied colour and the large areas
of uncovered paper pose the question as to whether this
watercolour is finished. As Cézanne usually indicated
the major landmarks – even if briefly – in pencil, it is
clear that in this watercolour he aimed at a rather open

composition from the start. In its present, final, state
it conveys a strong sense of serenity which makes the
watercolour a successful and in this sense finished
work. This atmosphere reminded a reviewer of the
first exhibition of Cézanne's watercolours in New York,
organised by Alfred Stieglitz in 1911, of Japanese landscapes. He compared *La Montagne Sainte-Victoire* to Mount
Fuji and likened it to the work of the greatest Chinese
and Japanese artists, in that it was executed "almost in
monochrome and with an extreme economy of treatment, on the ground". He went on to quote a Japanese
critic: "The provision of too many sensible attributes in
a painting is apt to hinder the play of the imagination
on the part of its beholders . . . . In its ultimate analysis
painting is, aesthetically speaking, but a product of
the imagination."[4] SB

NOTES

1 Loran 1943, p. 101 and Ratcliffe in *Watercolour
   and Pencil Drawings by Cézanne*, Newcastle and
   London, 1973, p. 162 published photographs
   of the motif.
2 For a useful comparison of all versions see de
   Mazia 1974, n. *, pp. 18–25. The present dating
   of the Courtauld watercolour goes back to
   Ratcliffe's suggestion made in *Watercolour
   and Pencil Drawings by Cézanne*, Newcastle and
   London 1973, which was accepted in Rewald
   1983.
3 See Letter B1.
4 *The New York Times*, 12 March 1911, Section V,
   p. 15.

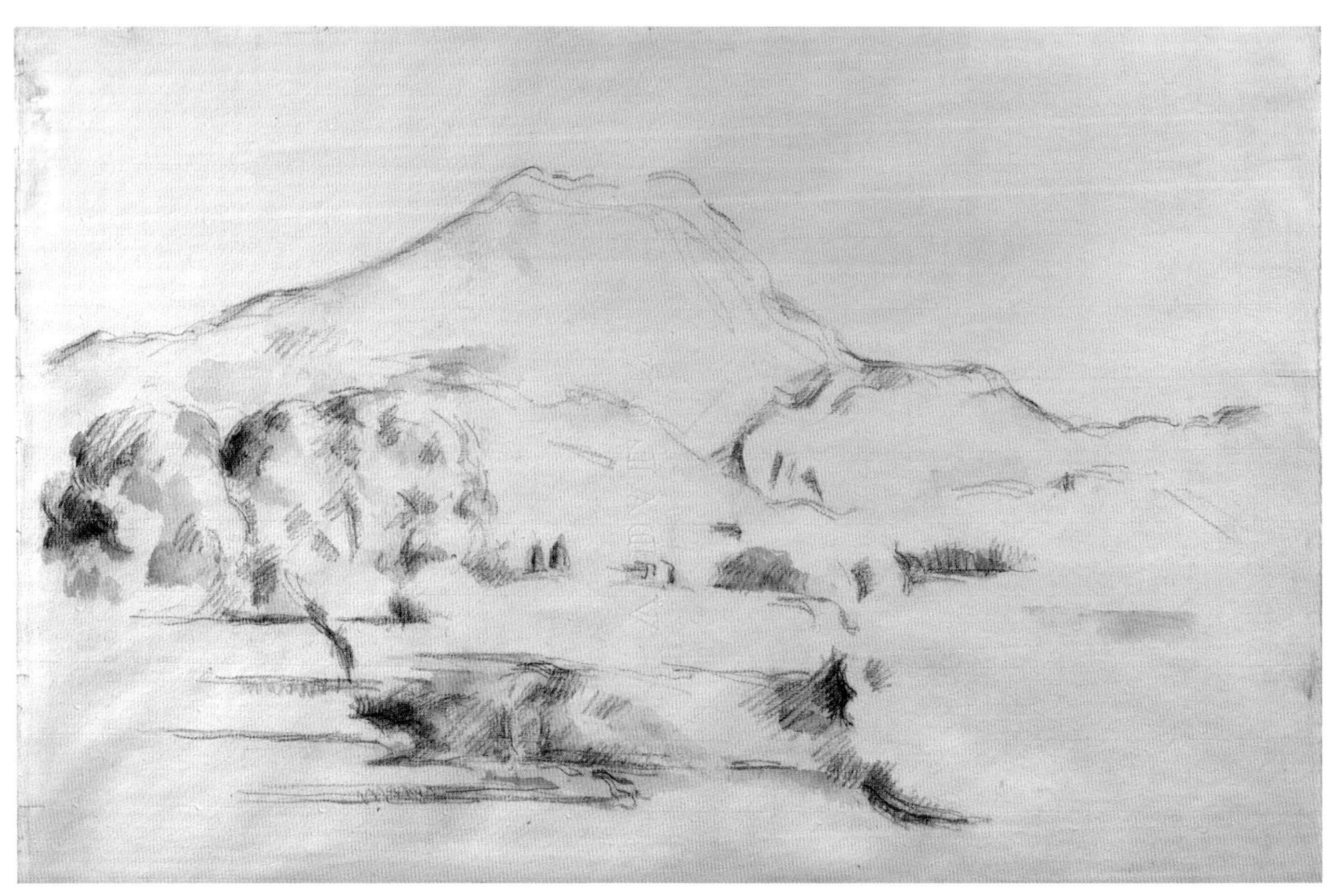

FIG. 65
Digital infrared reflectogram of cat. 14
Copyright © The National Gallery, London.
All rights reserved

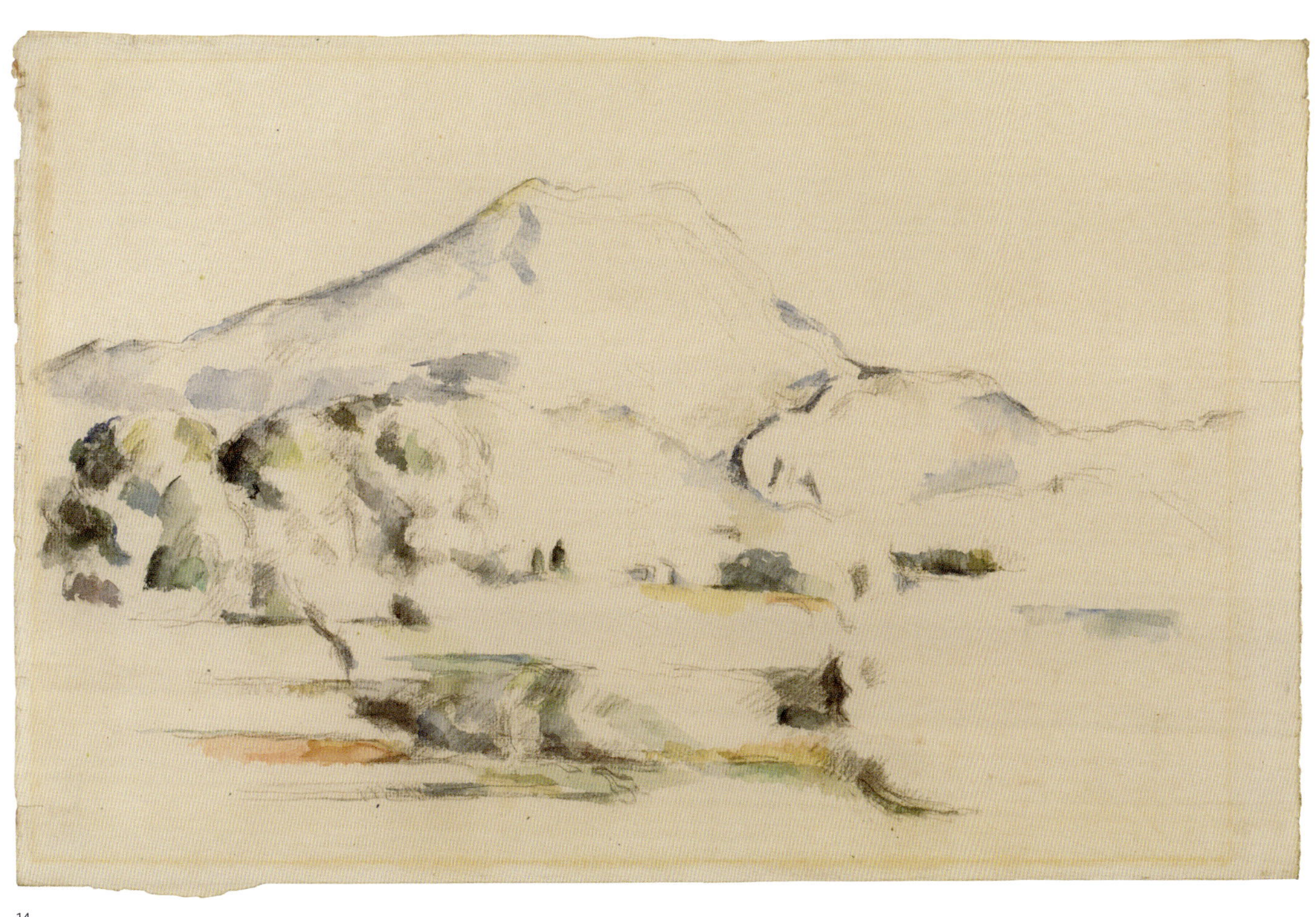

14

 Fauteuil, c. 1885–90

Armchair

Graphite, watercolour and gouache on pale cream laid paper
323 (left) / 316 (right) × 343 (upper) / 337 (lower) mm
The Courtauld Gallery, London (Samuel Courtauld Trust)
D.1978.PG.238
Princes Gate Bequest 1978

This complex watercolour, executed in the late 1880s, when Cézanne had full command of the technique, has rightly been characterised as a "portrait" of an armchair.[1] Standing on a typical Provençal floor covered with octagonal reddish tiles known as *tomettes d'Apt*[2] and set in front of a panelled wall with a pale wainscotting, the upholstered piece of furniture, viewed frontally, dominates the composition, occupying the full height of the large sheet of paper.[3] A thick and somewhat haphazardly folded textile, seemingly a Provençal quilt known as a *boutis,* rests on the seat. The blanket overlaps the armrest on the right and fills the space between the seat and the armrest on the left; it clearly does not belong to the chair but was perhaps temporarily left there, adding a narrative element to the composition. The chair itself shows traces of age and use – the wood displaying various shades of reddish brown as is typical of aged polished furniture and the stitching that trims the upholstered seat being torn in the centre and dangling down.

These elements suggest that the chair – which Cézanne portrayed as a familiar, rather than a neutral item – has been regularly used and allude to its history and context. Since the artist depicted the same chair in a pencil drawing, concentrating on the detail of a cushion leaning against the armrest (CD 960),[4] it seems likely that the watercolour was executed at the Jas de Bouffan, the family estate that Cézanne inherited when his father died in 1886.[5] The wainscotting, delineated in pencil without the addition of watercolour for shading, also

suggests the family home. Like the light *boutis*, the white paper alone conveys the colour of the panelling, which seems to be a pale wood. Similar wainscotting appears in the room in *Girl at the Piano* (*The Overture to Tannhäuser*), a painting of about 1869–70 (RP 149; fig. 66), certainly executed at the Jas de Bouffan. The ornamental frieze above the wainscotting in the watercolour, however, does not correspond exactly with the pattern of large leaves depicted in the painting, which likewise does not show the tiles. Instead, a striped carpet lies on the floor, possibly covering the tiles. Either the armchair was standing in another room at the Jas de Bouffan or Cézanne deliberately changed the pattern into a more densely composed cluster of swirls reminiscent of foliage.

In any case, the frieze in the watercolour corresponds with the generous floral upholstery on the chair, which helps unite the setting – otherwise dominated by geometric forms and straight lines (the octagonal tiles and the squares of the wainscotting) – and the piece of furniture. Compositionally, this interrelationship is tightly knit on the picture plane. The straight parts of the chair's wooden frame – for example, the seat rail – are deliberately aligned with the verticals and horizontals of the wall panelling while the more decorative curved carvings as well as the fluid outline of the blanket, with its freely sketched stripes, connect with the floral décor. In the same vein, the colour scheme of reds in the tiles and the frieze – containing red lake and vermilion – is echoed in the wooden frame, helping to root the chair

---

TECHNICAL NOTE

Slight acid burns from an old mount to the chair's left and right; small pin holes at the upper edge, short pencil marks on all four borders (probably in a later hand); the sheet unevenly torn, top, to a horizontal fold, all other sides unevenly trimmed

WATERMARK

AGM (in monogram)

PROVENANCE

Ambroise Vollard, Paris; Simon Meller; Count Antoine Seilern, London (bought in 1937)

SELECTED EXHIBITIONS

Princes Gate Collection, London 1981, no. 132; *Mantegna to Cézanne*, London 1983, no. 97; *Impressionist, Post-Impressionist and related drawings*, London 1988, no. 8; *Cézanne in Britain*, London 2006–7, p. 13, no. 24

SELECTED LITERATURE

RWC 191
Venturi 1936, no. 851; F. Novotny, *Paul Cézanne*, Vienna, Paris and New York, 1937, p. 101; Seilern 1961, p. 104, no. 238

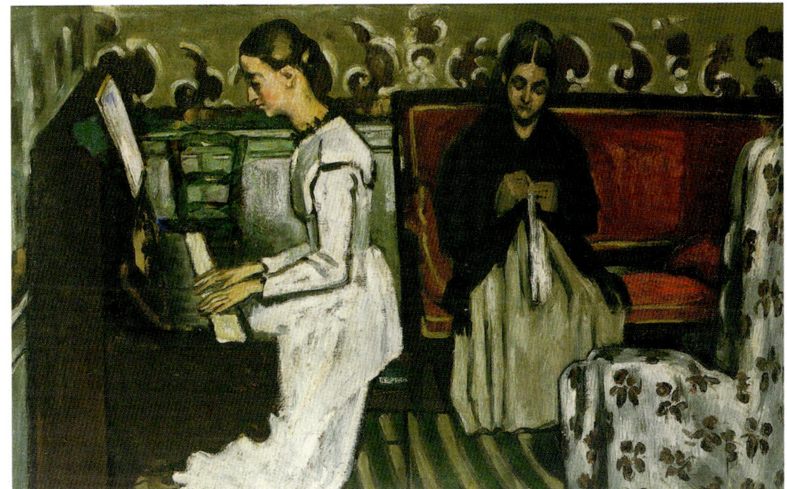

firmly on the ground,[6] and the cool blues and greens of the upholstery recur in the greyish purple of the lowest board of the wainscotting. The careful consideration that went into composing the picture becomes particularly evident when examining the working process with infrared reflectography (fig. 67). It shows that Cézanne first sketched the tiles with faint pencil lines; then, after adding the colour, he outlined them more vigorously in slightly different positions using their pattern to organise the space between the legs of the chair by lining up the different elements as explained above. At the same time, the free and loose handling of the pencil and the multiplying of the contours help to connect the individual forms as they are not separated by rigid lines.

Considering the deliberate construction of the watercolour, the repetition of the chair's right front leg seems unusual. William Bradford noted several *pentimenti*, such as the chairback being initially positioned further to the left and being conceived on a smaller scale.[7] These changes were carried out during the first step of the creative process, while working exclusively with the pencil. The detached chair leg, however, is a finished pictorial element and thus part of the final composition. It is seen only slightly from the left, while the chair's frame is "shown at a pronouncedly oblique angle",[8] a viewpoint that conflicts with the depiction of the left half of the chair, which is seen frontally. The motif of the detached leg thus seems to correct a depiction that, in academic terms, is inaccurate. With regard to the thoughtful balancing of the composition on the picture plane, this calling attention to the error in applying basic rules of linear perspective and its subsequent correction by the master himself may be read as a deliberate – and ironic – denunciation of academic principles. A similar attitude is evident in a remark Cézanne made when the artists R.P. Rivière and Jacques Félix Schnerb visited him in January 1905: "I am a primitive, I have a lazy eye. I applied twice to the École des Beaux-Arts, but I can't pull a composition together. A head interests me, I make it too large."[9] S B

NOTES

1 See Rewald 1983, no. 191, p. 130 citing Chappuis; *Cézanne in Britain*, London 2006–07, no. 24.
2 See *ibid*., p. 13.
3 The sheet seems to have been severely trimmed on the right resulting in a change of the *mise-en-page*. For a comparison to other formats see *Classic Cézanne*, Sydney 1998–99, p. 59.
4 The drawing was sold at Christie's, New York, 10 May 1994, Important Impressionist and Modern Paintings, lot 1.
5 Rewald 1983, p. 130.
6 The greyish-brown colour to the left of the chairback and on the left corner of the blanket is due to a discoloration of lead white. Originally the tone must have been light.
7 *Impressionist, Post-Impressionist and Related Drawings*, London 1988, no. 8, p. 6.
8 *Ibid*.
9 They published their account in 1907 in *La Grande Revue*, 25 December 1907, pp. 811–17; see Doran 2001, p. 86. For the French original see Doran 1978, p. 87, quoted in John House's essay (p. 43, note 33), where an alternative translation is used. See also Smith 2007, p. 95.

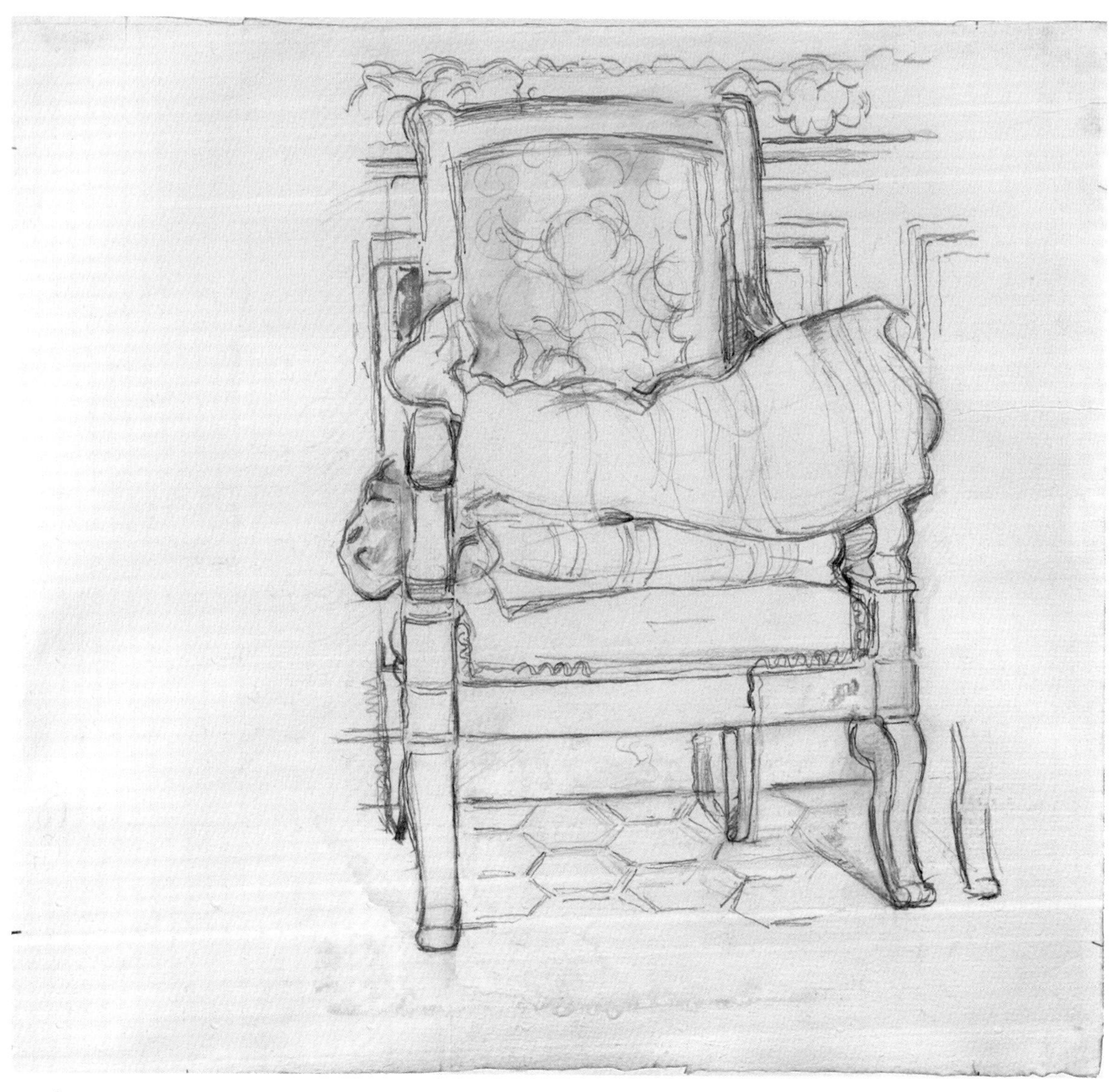

FIG. 67
Digital infrared reflectogram of cat. 15
© The National Gallery, London
All rights reserved

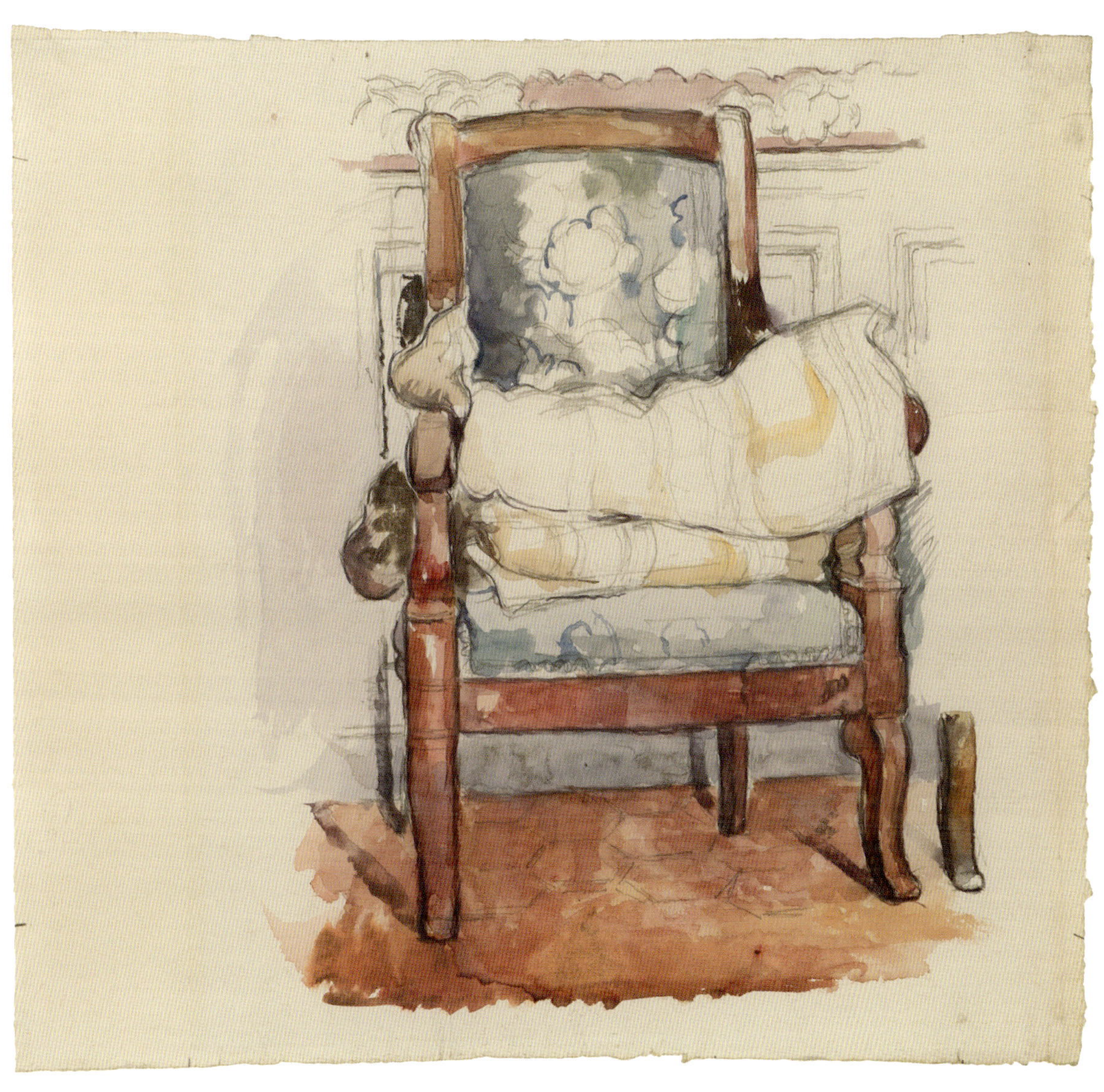

15

16 **Route forestière avec une statue**, *c*. 1895–1900

Statue under Trees

Graphite and watercolour on white wove paper
480 × 312 mm
The Courtauld Gallery, London (Samuel Courtauld Trust)
D.1978.PG.240
Princes Gate Bequest 1978

This freshly preserved watercolour is the most informal of all Cézanne's works on paper in The Courtauld Gallery. Traces of the artist's working process that were not integrated into the final composition are clearly visible: midway on the right edge of the sheet are stains of diluted purple, where he seems to have wiped off his brush rather than having deliberately placed a patch of colour. The lively appearance is also due to the unforced relationship between the initial drawing, which may be seen in many areas, and the subsequent colour composition. The pencil sketch – fully visible through infrared reflectography (fig. 69) – was done freehand. It maps out the composition in only the most general terms and seems to have been revised later, when the painter applied washes of colour. In addition, large areas of the picture have been left undefined. Thus, the reading of the composition and the identification of the motif remain somewhat unclear.

The initial pencil drawing shows a central, free-standing figure on a pedestal surrounded by sinuous lines and loops indicating the foliage of a grove of trees and bound together by mostly unrelated loose patches of zigzags that summarily indicate shadow. Generous curved lines in the foreground indicate a path leading to the statue, and several distinct tapered lines surmount the circular design. As horizontals and verticals are limited to the plinth in the pencil drawing, these tapered lines seem to indicate a powerful tree trunk.[1] This identification, however, is problematic because in the painted state the most densely coloured immediate surroundings of the statue – dominated by superimposed touches of purples and blues – suggest architecture. Indeed, the straight horizontals and verticals made during the final stage of the working process, when Cézanne redefined the amorphous colour pattern with strictly linear strokes drawn with the tip of the brush, mostly in dark blue watercolour, block out a building with a clearly indicated base.[2] The tapered verticals might thus relate to a tower or spire behind the sculpture. Presumably the setting is a park rather than a forest, however the sculpture and the location have not been identified.[3] The motif appears in another, smaller watercolour (RWC 462), but this does not help with the identification, as it shows only the statue's plinth surrounded by landscape elements similar to the ones seen in the foreground of the Courtauld sheet.

The form of the sculpture was evidently of no concern to Cézanne. He left it largely undefined, as he fragmented the contours in order to integrate the statue rhythmically into the surroundings and refrained from modelling the figure. The setting is described by a vivid matrix of touches of translucent colour washes stratified in several layers where shadowy dark areas are suggested. These are mainly placed at the centre of the sheet while the

TECHNICAL NOTE

Numerous pinholes at each corner; verso: numbered in a later hand in pencil *III 31*; the sheet unevenly torn bottom and right

BLINDSTAMPED

. . .OLFIER SAINT MARCEL LES ANNONAY

PROVENANCE

Ambroise Vollard, Paris; Kenneth Clark, London; Count Antoine Seilern, London (bought in 1941)

SELECTED EXHIBITIONS

Princes Gate Collection, London 1981, no. 157; *Mantegna to Cézanne*, London 1983, no. 101; *Impressionist, Post-Impressionist and Related Drawings*, London 1988, no. 9

SELECTED LITERATURE

RWC 490
Rewald 1937, fig. 47; Seilern 1961, p. 106, no. 240

layering tends to loosen up toward the borders. These
lighter areas are pushed visually closer to the viewer.
The various hues of purple, blue, and green are evenly
distributed on the picture plane, and the light colour of
the paper penetrates the composition as a whole, serving
to break up the carpet of unevenly shaped patches of
colour. This stresses the two-dimensionality of the picture
and helps to control the impression of spatial depth. At
the same time the white ground is an overall source of
luminosity that binds the composition together. Of
particular importance is the touch of vermilion in the
foreground that anchors the scene. Integrated into a
stroke of chrome yellow, it is visually linked to the few
yellow patches in the foreground, centre and upper parts
of the picture that indicate a plane close to the viewer.

The intense, carefully balanced yet unforced colour
composition, which abandons clear contours and borders
and is fully integrated into the paper ground, is typical
of Cézanne's late watercolour technique. When first
publishing the sheet in the catalogue of the French
drawings of the Princes Gate Collection in 1961, Count
Antoine Seilern thus suggested a date of about 1895 to
1900 – a period slightly narrowed down by Rewald (1983),
who dated the work to about 1898–1900. As Cézanne did
not date any of his watercolours and as clear benchmarks
are missing, a dating to 1895 to 1900 on stylistic grounds
seems sensible. SB

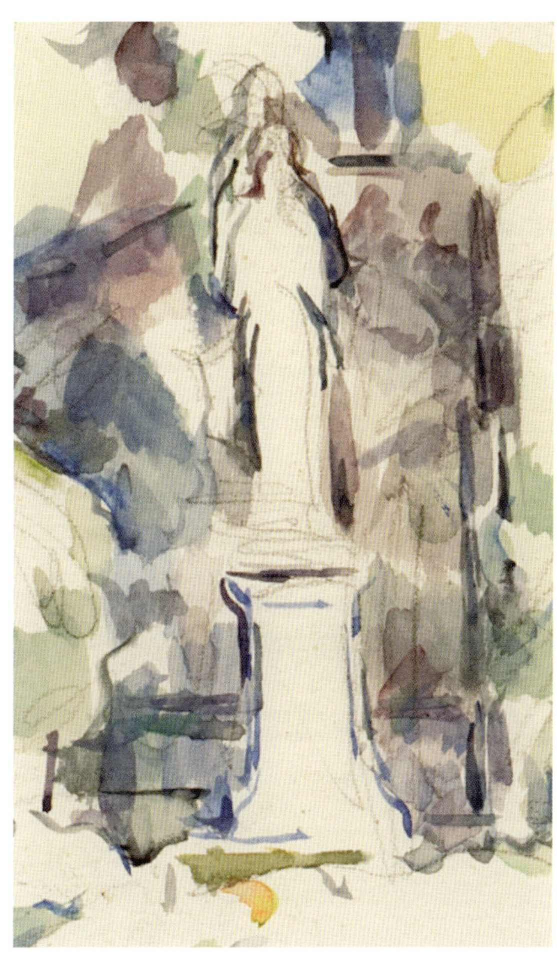

FIG. 68
Detail of cat. 16

NOTES

1 See *Impressionist, Post-Impressionist and Related
   Drawings*, London 1988, no. 9 with a very
   precise description of the composition.
2 For an interpretation of these lines in relation
   to colour see Elisabeth Reissner's essay in
   this catalogue.
3 Rewald (1983) suggested a statue of the
   Virgin Mary or of a saint.

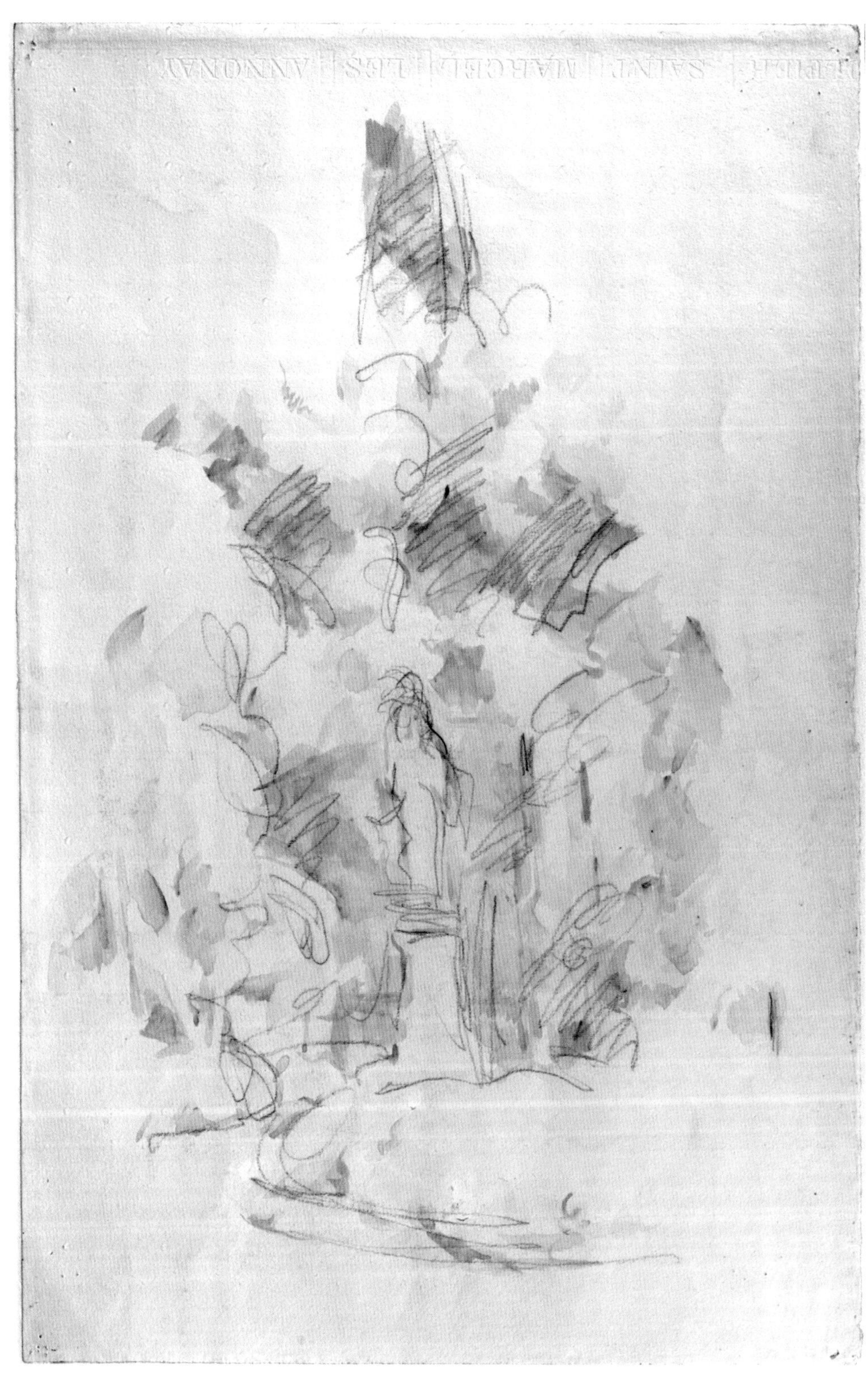

FIG. 69
Digital infrared reflectogram of cat. 16
© The National Gallery, London
All rights reserved

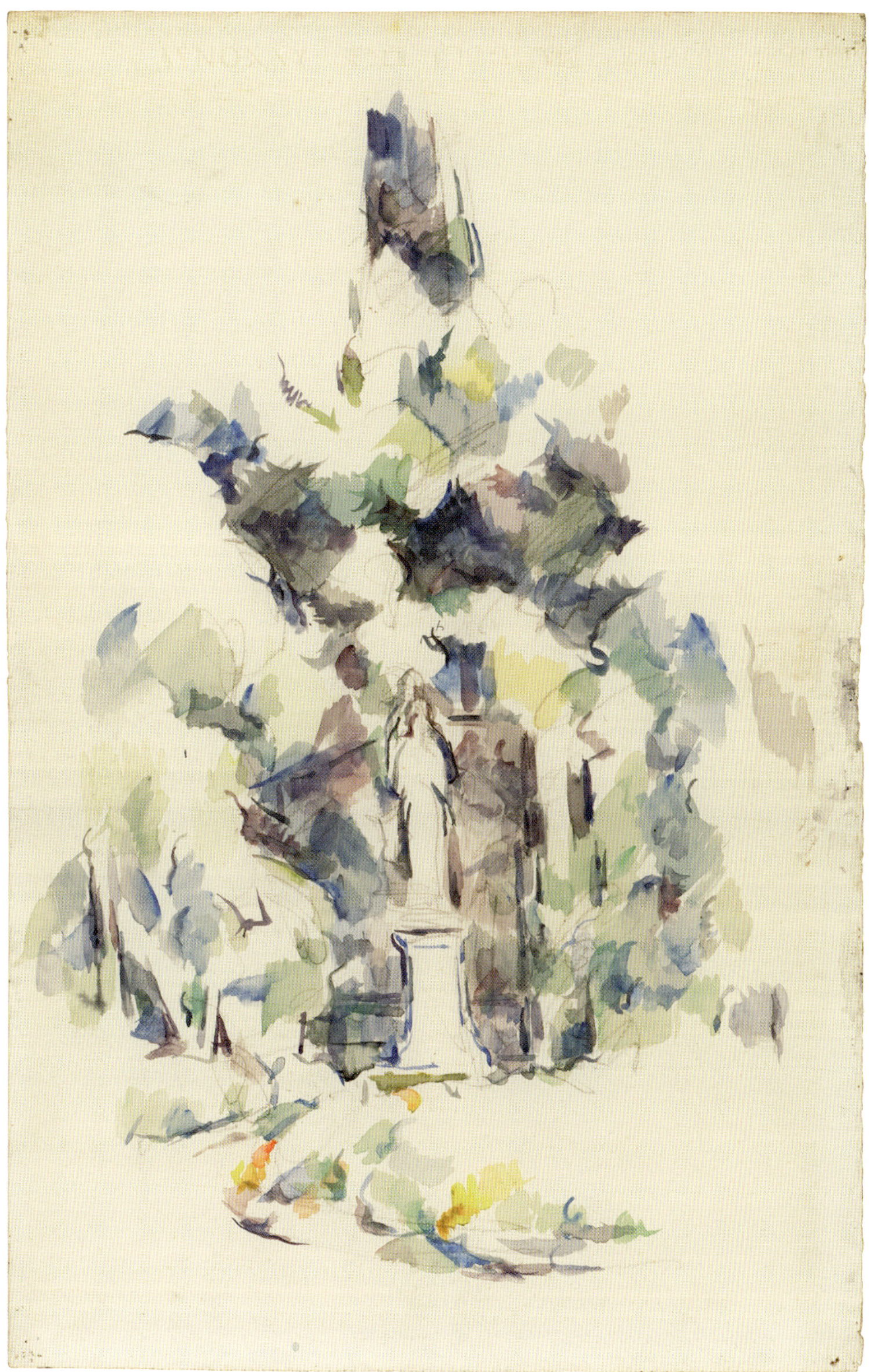

17 **Pommes, bouteille, dossier de chaise**, *c.* 1904–06

Apples, Bottle and Chairback

Graphite and watercolour on white wove paper
457 (left) / 462 (right) × 604 mm
The Courtauld Gallery, London (Samuel Courtauld Trust)
D.1948.SC.111
Courtauld Bequest 1948

The rich harmony and lush, deeply saturated primary colours of this vibrant yet solidly balanced composition evoke an unusual splendour and claim a place for this large elaborate watercolour among Cézanne's ultimate masterpieces in this medium. Unanimously dated to the last years of his career, the work is reminiscent of Venetian Renaissance painting, which Cézanne understood to embody a profound vision and its comprehensive realisation in painting,[1] not only colouristically but also in terms of the treatment of the subject. Despite its simplicity, the arrangement of a glass, a bottle and a plate laden with fruit on a table with a chair close by alludes to a festive dining scene,[2] and is comparable in spirit to Veronese's richly set tables in the monumental *Marriage at Cana*, which Cézanne praised when studying it at the Louvre with Joachim Gasquet.[3] Cézanne, however, did not aim simply to imitate an Old Master but to re-create nature in his work.[4]

As is typical of his still lifes, he chose basic objects and conceived the composition parallel to the picture plane, with the predominant motifs – the plate of apples and the chair – placed in the centre, thus achieving a serene balance, also characteristic of Renaissance painting. Yet in this watercolour, unlike the others at the Courtauld, Cézanne did not arrange the objects symmetrically. The tall wine bottle and flute glass – precisely aligned – on the left create a framing device that is absent on the right side. There, instead, an undefined square above the table – possibly wallpaper or an opening into another room – functions as a counterbalance, as it echoes the indigo colour of the bottle. The composition opens further where the apples seem to tumble off the table – the piece of fruit cut off at the edge of the picture stresses this openness. While the left side provides a relatively clear sense of the relationship of distinguishable objects in space, the right abandons the mimetic requirements of spatial definition. The apples overlap the rear edge of the table and are piled up in a manner impossible in real space, as if floating above the tabletop. This ambiguity presents a particular challenge to the viewer's perception

since the objects are depicted at approximately life size.
Judging from the balance on the picture plane, the
arrangement is, however, satisfactory, reinforced as it is
by the distribution of colour. The intense red that dominates the table and the chair recurs in the apples as well
as in the background on the right, and hues of cobalt and
indigo blue are suffused throughout. Thus all the colours
are interwoven to create a complex relationship. The
omnipresent paper support represents the space; it
integrates not only the various forms but also the planes,
indicating both "the culminating point . . . closest to our
eye"[5] and the most distant points – as they are represented by the convex apples, where the area in reserve is
read as a highlight, and by the wall behind the chair,
where the paper is understood as flat background.

As recorded in Gasquet's *Conversations with Cézanne,* the
artist admired the gradual build-up of Veronese's canvas,
based on a grisaille underpainting over which translucent glazes and painted layers modulate the final image,
in which "all the tones blend into one another, all the

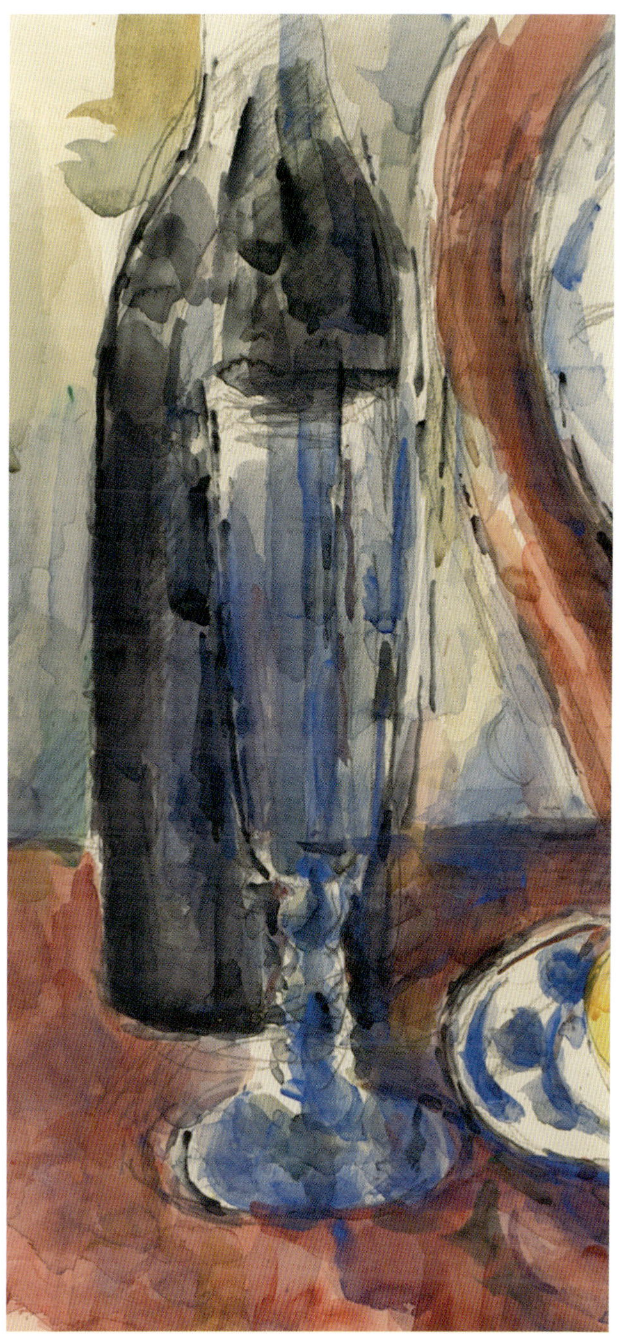

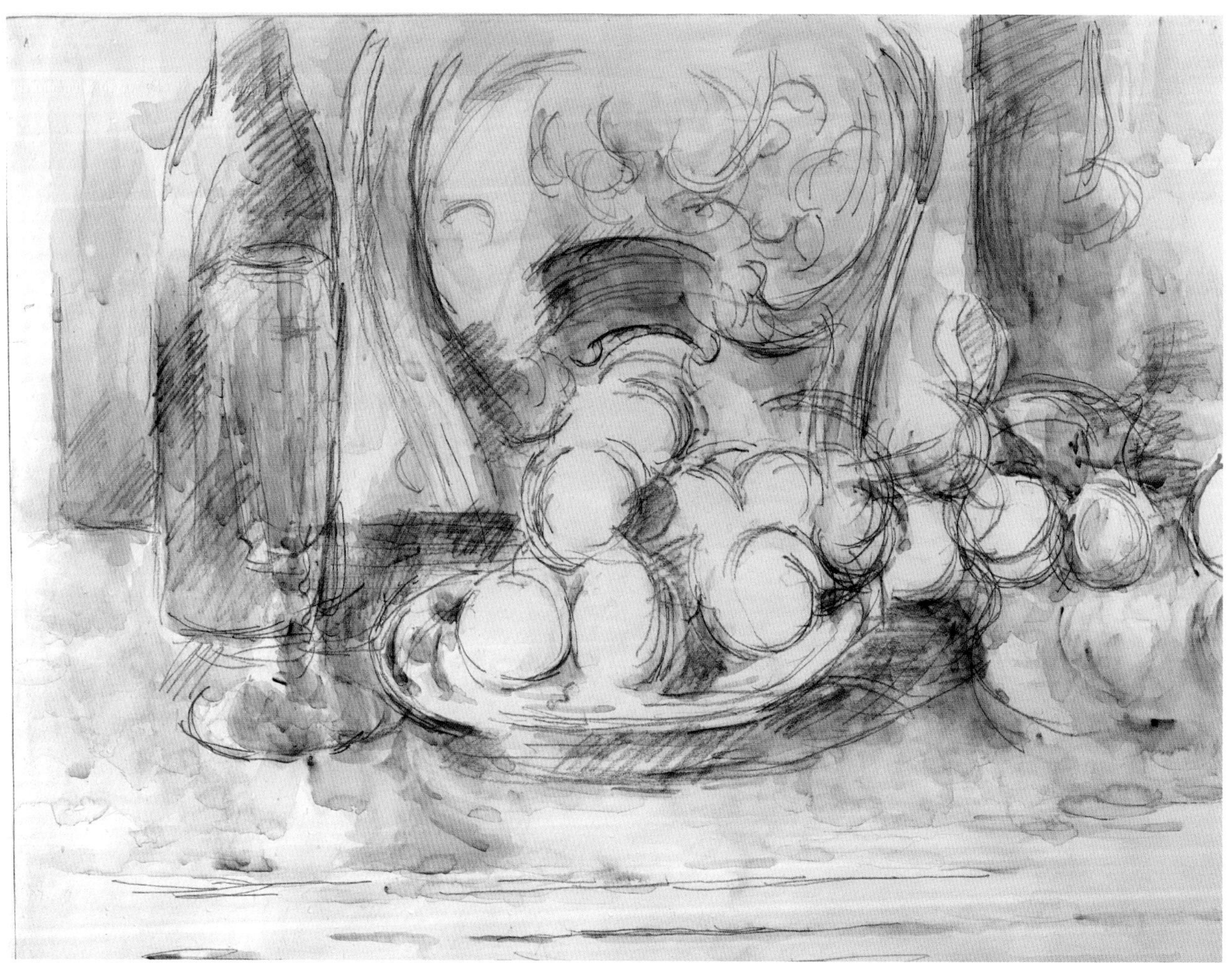

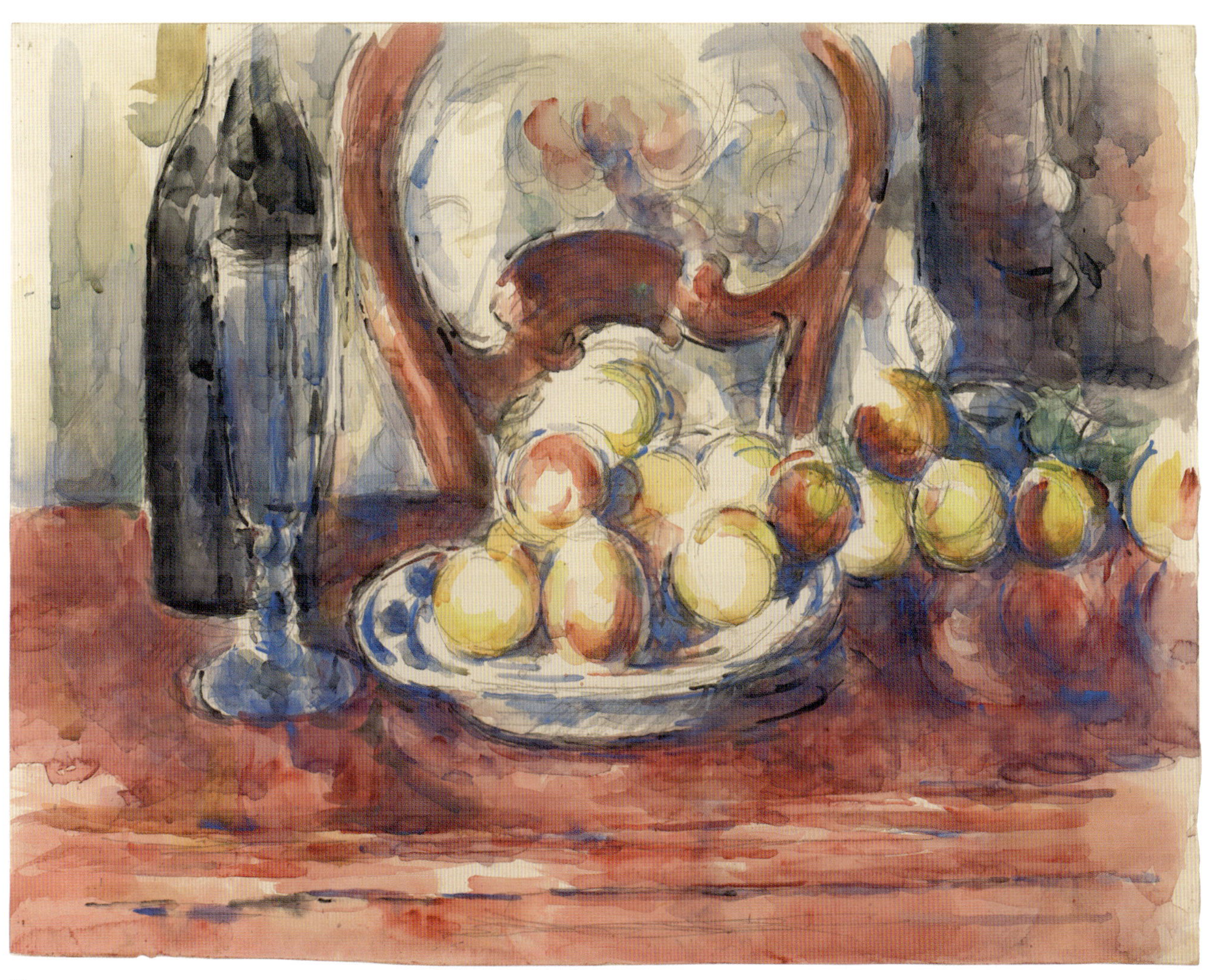

17

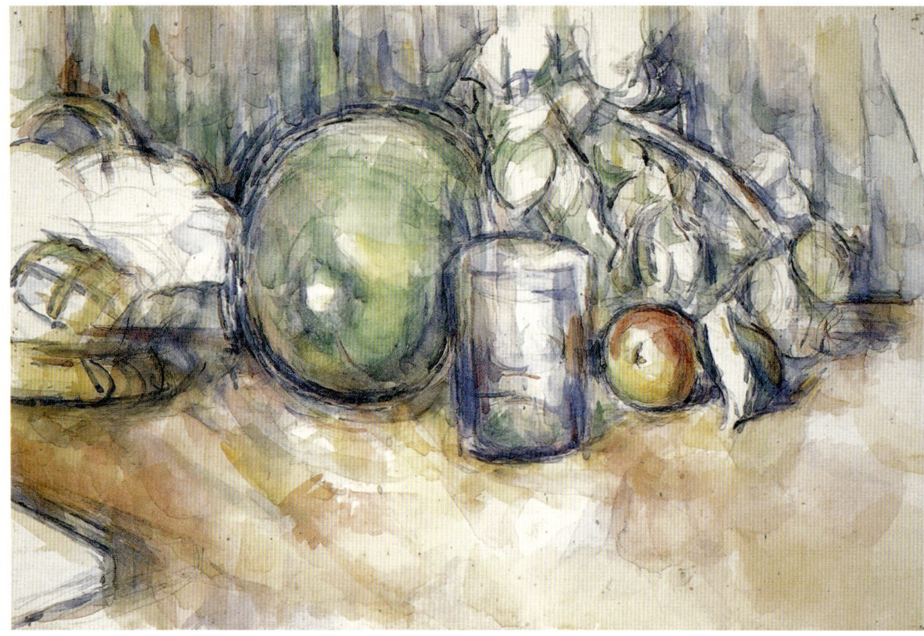

volumes interlock. There is continuity."[6] This coherence, at which Cézanne aimed, is achieved in this still life through an interplay of line and colour on the paper. This is, for the most part, harmonious but allows the two elements to stand in some parts independently, as is evident in a comparison between the underdrawing (fig. 71) and the final painting. The digital infrared reflectogram shows how the composition was mapped out: Cézanne defined the principal forms of the still life with loose pencil lines, typically avoiding precise contours so as not to flatten the space. Vigorously placed clumps of hatching only roughly mark volume and shadow and do not necessarily correspond precisely to the forms they shade, such as at the back of the chair, where they crudely overlap the contours. While the left half of the picture was resolved from the beginning of the creative process, the right proved to be more challenging, as the multitude of changes attests. Cézanne experimented with the placement of the apples and also

indicated two larger rounded forms, possibly melons. Such a combination of fruit can be found, for instance, in *Still Life with Green Melon* (RWC 610; fig. 72),[7] executed at about the same time. Other interlocked arcs are not easily recognizable as objects. It seems clear that the upper right, where broadly applied hatching indicates a deep space, was conceived as an opening into an adjacent room comparable to the one in *The Dessert* (RWC 569; fig. 73).[8] Furthermore, the infrared reflectogram clearly shows that the decorative organic forms loosely described in the irregular oval of the chairback initially were more concretely conceived as blossoms and leaves that overlap the crosspiece at the spot where the wood seems to be diaphanous in the finished watercolour. Thus the foliage, possibly describing the pattern of a cloth or a screen covering the back wall, was transformed into a purely decorative form.

Writing to Emile Bernard on 23 October 1905, Cézanne declared that his "unique goal, which leads, at moments

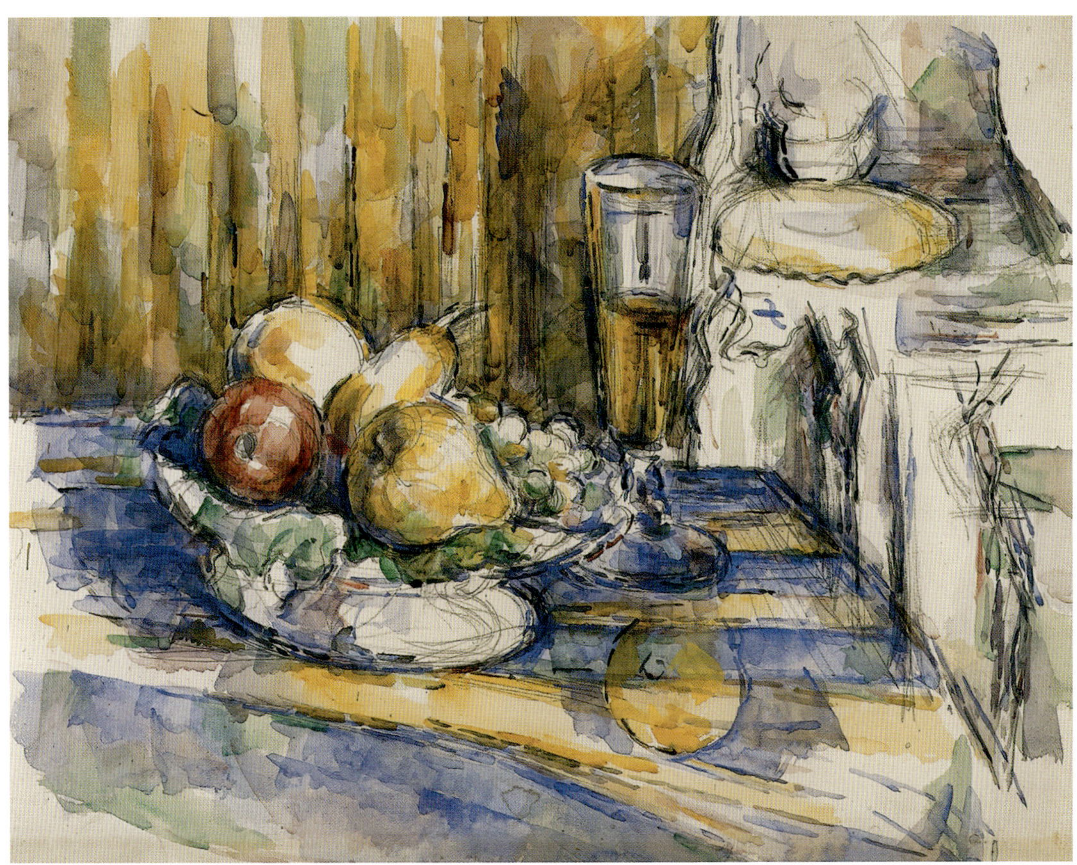

of physical fatigue, to a sort of intellectual exhaustion" was the pursuit of "the realisation of that part of nature which, falling before our eyes, gives us the picture. So, the principle to develop – whatever our temperament or power in the presence of nature – is to give the image of what we see."[9] For Cézanne, the challenge was not the slavish reproduction of objects but rather the exploration of their relationships – both spatial and colouristic – and, finally, the development of a harmonious composition that presented a painted universe parallel to that of nature. SB

NOTES

1 See the so-called 'opinions' of Cézanne recorded by Emile Bernard, 1904: "We must learn to read nature and represent our sensations by way of an aesthetic that is both personal and traditional. The strongest among us will be he who sees most profoundly and who represents most fully like the Venetian masters" (translation from Doran 2001, p. 38). And in a letter to Charles Camoin, 3 February 1902: "… *faites d'après les grands maîtres decoratifs, Véronèse et Rubens, des études, mais comme vous feriez d'àprès nature – ce que je n'ai su faire qu'incomplètement*" (*Correspondance* 1978, pp. 280–81): "… make studies of the great decorative masters, Veronese and Rubens, but as though you were working from nature – which I myself never quite succeeded in managing" (see Rewald 1984, p. 278). On Christmas 1898 Maurice Denis noted in his diary that Edouard Vuillard had told him about Cézanne's highest admiration of Veronese and that both artists treated in fact the same subjects: "*Vuillard me rapporte que Cézanne parle avec la plus vive admiration de Véronèse, qu'il semble préférer à tout. Vuillard remarque qu'il a en effet les mêmes sujets que Véronèse: rapports, entente des arrangements*": see Denis 1957, p. 149. For Cézanne's interest in the Old Masters see also Berthold 1958 and Smith 1996, pp. 25–35.

2 See *Cézanne in the Studio*, Los Angeles 2004, p. 38.

3 See Doran 2001, pp. 132–34.

4 See Letter B2: "The Louvre is a good book to consult, but it should only be an intermediary. The real, prodigious study to undertake is the diversity of nature's appearance".

5 See Letter B5.

6 Doran 2001, p. 134.

7 The watercolour was last sold at Sotheby's, New York, 8 May 2007, lot 8.

8 See *Cézanne in the Studio*, Los Angeles 2004, p. 39, pl. 8.

9 See Letter B8.

18 **Guillaumin au Pendu**, 1873

Guillaumin with the Hanged Man

Etching with surface tone, in sepia, on Japan paper; sheet 262 × 206 mm; image 157 × 121 mm; only state
From the deluxe edition (100 copies) of *Histoire des Peintres Impressionistes*, issued by Théodore Duret,
published by H. Floury, Paris, 1906
The Courtauld Gallery, London (Samuel Courtauld Trust)
G.2008.XX.1
Acquired in 2008

Cézanne was a reluctant printmaker, producing only five etchings and three lithographs in his entire career, his attempts due to the encouragement of friends and to his dealer's demands rather than to any particular interest in printmaking itself. In 1872 he moved with his family to Auvers-sur-Oise, some twenty miles north-west of Paris, attracted by the artistic community which was forming around Camille Pissarro and Paul Ferdinand Gachet, a doctor and amateur artist working under the pseudonym of Paul van Ryssel. Among Cézanne's neighbours was his friend Armand Guillaumin, whom, like Pissarro, he had first met at the Atelier Suisse.[1]

A keen etcher and owner of a printing press, Gachet persuaded the group to experiment with printmaking. Cézanne's etchings were executed in the summer and autumn of 1873. His first and largest etching, *Barges on the Seine at Bercy*, was copied after Guillaumin's oil of the same name,[2] painted in September of that year, and owned by Gachet, while *Landscape at Auvers*[3] was based on one of his own paintings which he later gave to Pissarro (RP 196; private collection). The other three were *Garden at Bicêtre*,[4] *Head of a Girl* (cat. 19) and the present subject, the last two studied from life. Cézanne's etchings printed on Gachet's press are rare, as he pulled only a few trial proofs. The Courtauld's etching of Guillaumin is from the first published issue, one of a hundred sepia impressions on Japan paper that Théodore Duret had bound into the deluxe edition of *Histoire des*

Peintres Impressionistes (Paris 1906) under the title *Portrait of Guillaumin*.[5]

Armand Guillaumin (1841–1927), a Paris civil servant working for the Highways Department, devoted his spare time to painting. In this informal portrait, Cézanne depicts his friend casually sitting on the ground, with arms crossed over his raised knee, a jaunty hat and neck scarf giving him a bohemian air. The sketchy handling, disproportionate limbs and absence of feet suggest that the image was rapidly drawn from life, possibly directly on the plate. Unlike his other etchings, which are densely worked and more heavily textured through biting, this print has the feel of a sketch. The shimmering line and abundance of white space create a sense of sunlight and movement. Within flowing outlines, applied as if with a pen or pencil, the artist dashes off a series of short diagonal strokes and small, dark areas of tone that give the figure solidity and spatial depth. Small pitted marks on the paper are the outcome of hasty and insufficiently careful biting of the plate – a defect that bothered neither Cézanne nor his teacher.[6]

Gachet supposedly encouraged the three artists to adopt an emblematic signature. Cézanne chose the image of a hanged man, possibly an in-joke with his friends, relating to the ambitious oil painting he was working on at the time, known as *The House of the Hanged Man* (RP 202).[8] The device appears only on his etching of Guillaumin, hence its title. JS

PROVENANCE

Marcel Lecomte; Bernard Lecomte

SELECTED LITERATURE
Venturi 1936, no. 1159; Gachet 1952; Andersen 1970, pp. 13, 205; Cherpin 1972, no. 2, p. 64; Leymarie and Melot 1972, no. 2

NOTES

1 See D. Cooper, 'The Painters of Auvers-sur-Oise', *Burlington Magazine*, vol. 97, 1955, pp. 100–10.
2 *Péniches sur la Seine à Bercy*, Musée d'Orsay, Paris, Gachet Collection.
3 Venturi 1936, no. 1161; Cherpin 1972, no. 5.
4 Cherpin 1972, no. 3.
5 Two plates, one sepia on Japan paper and one black on laid paper, were inserted together between pp. 172 and 173. Around 1500 copies of the book were printed, only the first 100 of which (the *exemplaire de tête* or deluxe edition)

contained the sepia impression. I am grateful to Bernard Lecomte and William Weston for their information.
6 Cherpin 1972, p. 26.
7 Impressions of the print with no surface tone are considered to be restrikes made after Cézanne's death.
8 Exhibited at the first Impressionist exhibition in 1874. I am grateful to John House for this suggestion.

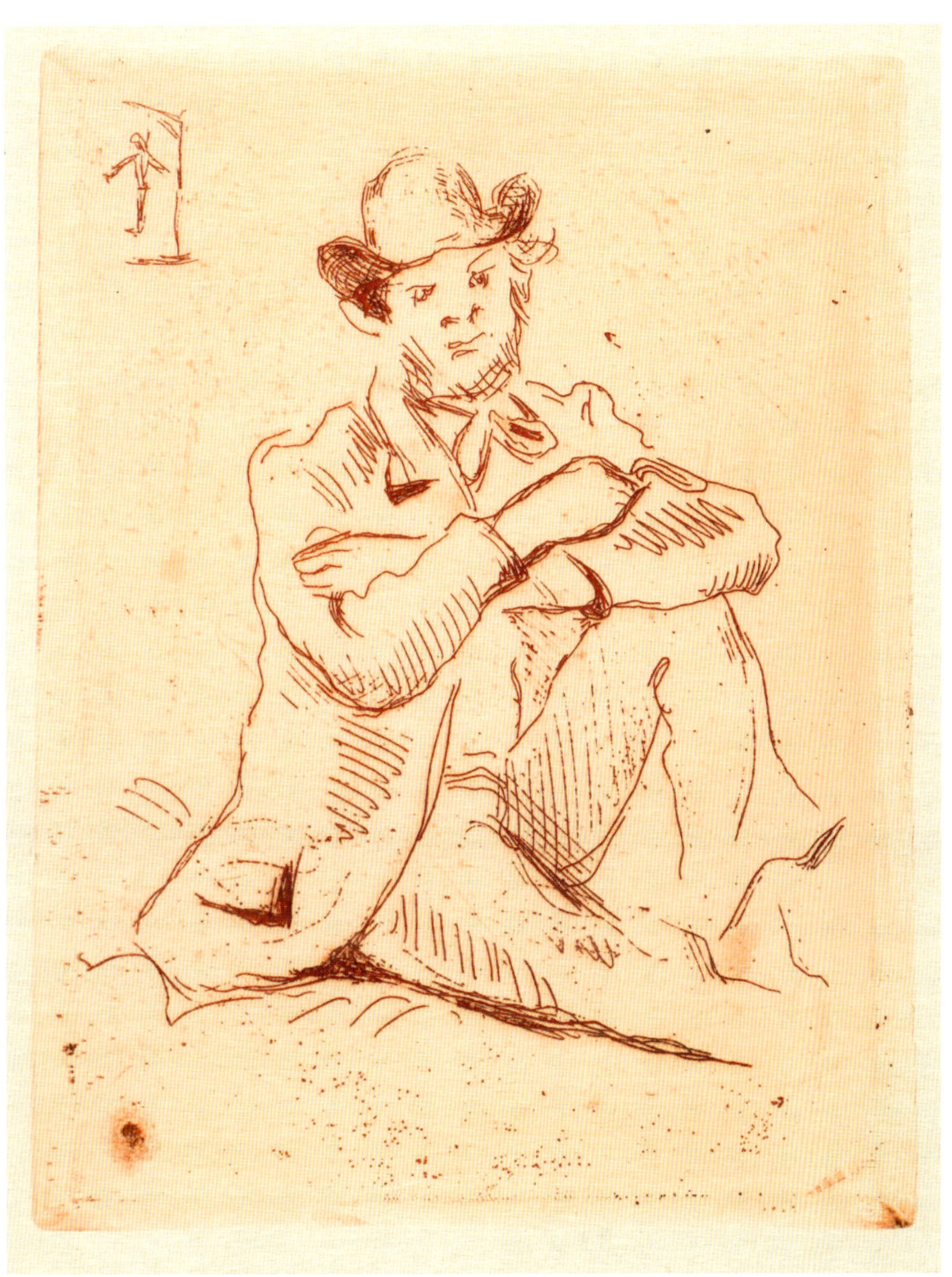

19 **Tête de Jeune Fille**, 1873

Head of a Girl

Original etching with surface tone, and roulette work, in black-brown ink
on Japan paper; sheet 323 × 249 mm; plate 122 × 97 mm; 3rd state of three, with bevel as issued
Signed and dated in the plate lower right
Frontispiece from the first published edition of *Cézanne*, issued by Ambroise Vollard in 1914 in
1,000 numbered copies
no. 16 of 150 impressions on Japan paper manufactured by Shizuoka
The Courtauld Institute of Art Book Library, Special Collections

This powerful image of a girl's face, one of a group of five etchings made by Cézanne in 1873 (see cat. 18), was chosen by Ambroise Vollard as the frontispiece to his 1914 monograph on the artist. Chappuis considers that it relates to a pencil drawing, *Peasant Girl wearing a Fichu*, of *c*. 1873 (CD 273; Philadelphia Museum of Art).[1] Andersen's suggestion,[2] that the model for the etching was the girl who posed for Guillaumin's pastel *Head of a Girl* (formerly Collection Durand-Ruel, New York)[3] seems more plausible, however, as the facial features show strong similarities, notably the dark, staring pupils, arched eyebrows and the distinctive curvature of the nose and lips.

Proofs of *Head of a Girl* printed by Cézanne on Dr Gachet's press are extremely rare. According to a note inscribed on a first state, probably in Gachet's hand, only six proofs were pulled from this plate.[4] The second state shows extensive reworking with a roulette to the left of the girl's head and shoulder, whilst in the third and final state, that used in Vollard's book, the edges of the plate have been bevelled for publication, slightly reducing its size and shortening the signature in the process.

Lack of expertise and the mediocre quality of Cézanne's materials largely account for the somewhat crude appearance of *Head of a Girl*, his most elaborate etching. The copper is pitted with acid spots and the biting is so deep in places that the eyes appear like two black marbles in a sea of tangled lines, while the marks around the head and collar form a dense network that is positively rough to touch. A small patch of light beside the girl's right eye brightens her otherwise darkened face, which looms out from a paler, two-toned background. Merlot describes Cézanne's etchings as characterised by the "extraordinary violence" with which he attacked the plate, experimenting with a technique in which he had never been trained.[5] Cézanne's improvised, almost brutal style contrasts with his less vigorous pencil drawing at this time. The parallel hatchings are more reminiscent of the ink drawings of the 1860s.[6] Whether intentional or not, his robust etching style and technique conjure up a new and original vision.

According to Gachet, a drawing attributed to Cézanne and dated to *c*. 1873, known as *La Morsure*, shows the artist biting a plate under his watchful eye.[7] Although its authorship has been questioned, Anne Distel believes the subject convincingly represents the two friends.[8] The drawing is thus of particular importance as evidence both of Gachet's teaching and of Cézanne's rudimentary working practice. JS

PROVENANCE

E. Weyhe, New York; Samuel Courtauld, London (bought in 1924)

SELECTED LITERATURE

Venturi 1936, no. 1160; Johnson 1944, no. 33; Gachet 1952; Andersen 1970, pp. 10, 12, 13, 234; Cherpin 1972, pp. 66–67, no. 4; Leymarie and Melot 1972, no. 4; Melot 1996, p. 105

NOTES

1 Reff 1975, p. 490, and Clark 1974, pp.79–90 have argued for a later date. See *Cézanne*, Paris, London and Philadelphia 1995–96, cat. 33, p. 144.
2 Andersen 1970, no. 256, p. 234. See also pp. 10, 12 and 13.
3 Andersen 1970, no. 257, p. 234.
4 According to Cherpin 1972, p. 66, the annotation was found on a proof sold at the Hotel Drouot in 1960.
5 Melot 1996, p. 105.
6 Andersen 1979, p. 13.
7 CD 292; Musée du Louvre, Département des Arts graphiques, Gachet Bequest (1951); see Gachet 1952 and also Cherpin 1972, p. 67.
8 See Distel 1999. Camille Pissarro and Armand Guillaumin have also been proposed as authors. I am grateful to Marie-Pierre Salé for her comments on this drawing.

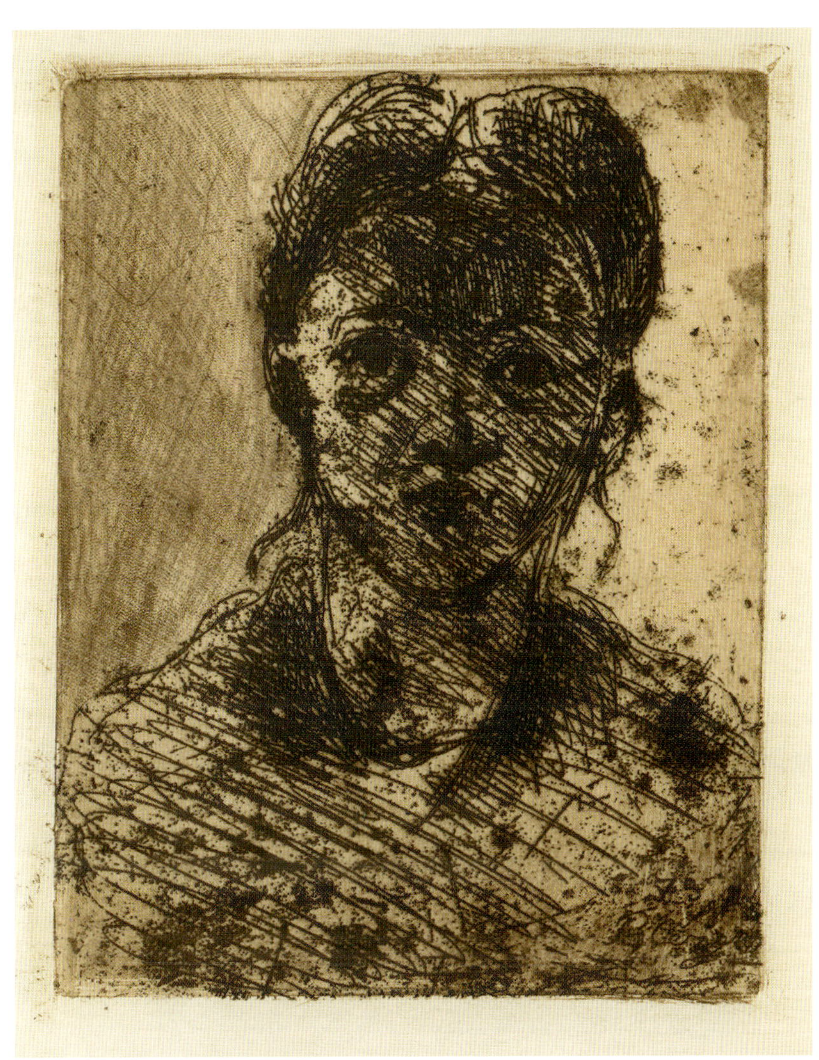

Self-portrait

Lithograph, printed in black ink, on cream laid paper
sheet 489 × 362 mm; plate 330 × 280 mm; only state
From the 2nd edition, 1920 (of at least 100 impressions printed in black)
The Courtauld Gallery, London (Samuel Courtauld Trust)
G.1935.SC.180
Courtauld Gift 1935

Throughout his career Cézanne maintained a fascination for his self-image. He produced around sixty portraits of himself in various media, including about twenty-four drawings, most of them frontal views of his head, his penetrating eyes looking out toward the viewer. From the swarthy black-bearded youth to the intensively reflective old man, as seen in this print, Cézanne explored his identity with a certain amount of restraint, scrutinising himself more intensely in his final years. Generally he refrained from portraying himself as an artist until well into the 1880s. Here, as in his painting *Self-portrait with Palette* (RP 670; fig. 74) of around 1888–90, he depicts himself in front of the easel in a conventional pose employed by many artists in the *fin de siècle*.[1] With his goatee beard and distinctive cocked right eyebrow, his facial features resemble more closely those in the final *Self-portrait in a Beret*, painted around 1898–1900 (RP 834; Museum of Fine Arts, Boston). The type of hat that he wears possibly alludes to the Provençal peasantry with whom he identified.[2]

After his few attempts at etching in 1873 (see cat. 18, 19), Cézanne took no further interest in printmaking until almost twenty-five years later, when he produced three lithographs, two on the theme of Bathers.[3] The impetus behind his lithographic production was the close relationship with his dealer, Ambroise Vollard,

who, as Druick suggests, was determined to make a *peintre-graveur* of him, as well as to promote a greater appreciation of the artist as a figure painter and portraitist.[4] On his part, Cézanne may well have wanted to repay Vollard for giving him his first one-man show in 1895, and was evidently willing to comply with the dealer's insistent requests for lithographs. When Vollard commissioned this self-portrait it is likely that he intended it to be included in his third *Album des Peintres-Graveurs*. Owing to the commercial failure of the first two issues of 1896 and 1897, however, the idea of a further series was abandoned in 1898. Vollard subsequently commissioned the master printer Auguste Clot (1858–1936) to print two editions, in 1914 and 1920 respectively, each of at least a hundred impressions, the first in grey ink and the second, to which the Courtauld print belongs, in black ink.

As indicated by the grain on the image of *Self-portrait*, Cézanne did not draw it directly on the stone but on lithographic transfer paper, which was then worked on to the stone by Clot. Cherpin noted the existence of an impression heightened by the artist with watercolour in the collection of Vollard, who had described it in his monograph of 1914 as a "watercolour maquette for a colour lithograph".[5] His remarks imply that the original intention was to use the black image, seen here, as a

---

PROVENANCE

Published by A. Vollard, Paris; E. Weyhe, New York; Samuel Courtauld, London (bought in 1925)

SELECTED EXHIBITIONS

Samuel Courtauld Memorial Exhibition, London 1948, no. 122; *Watercolour and Pencil Drawings by Cézanne*, Newcastle and London 1973, no. 86, pp. 168–69

SELECTED LITERATURE

Venturi 1936, no. 1158; Johnson 1944, no. 31; Cherpin 1972, no. 8, pp. 60 and 69 Leymarie-Merlot 1972, no. 7; Druick 1977, no. 2, pp. 123–28, 130–36; Platzmen 2001, p. 205

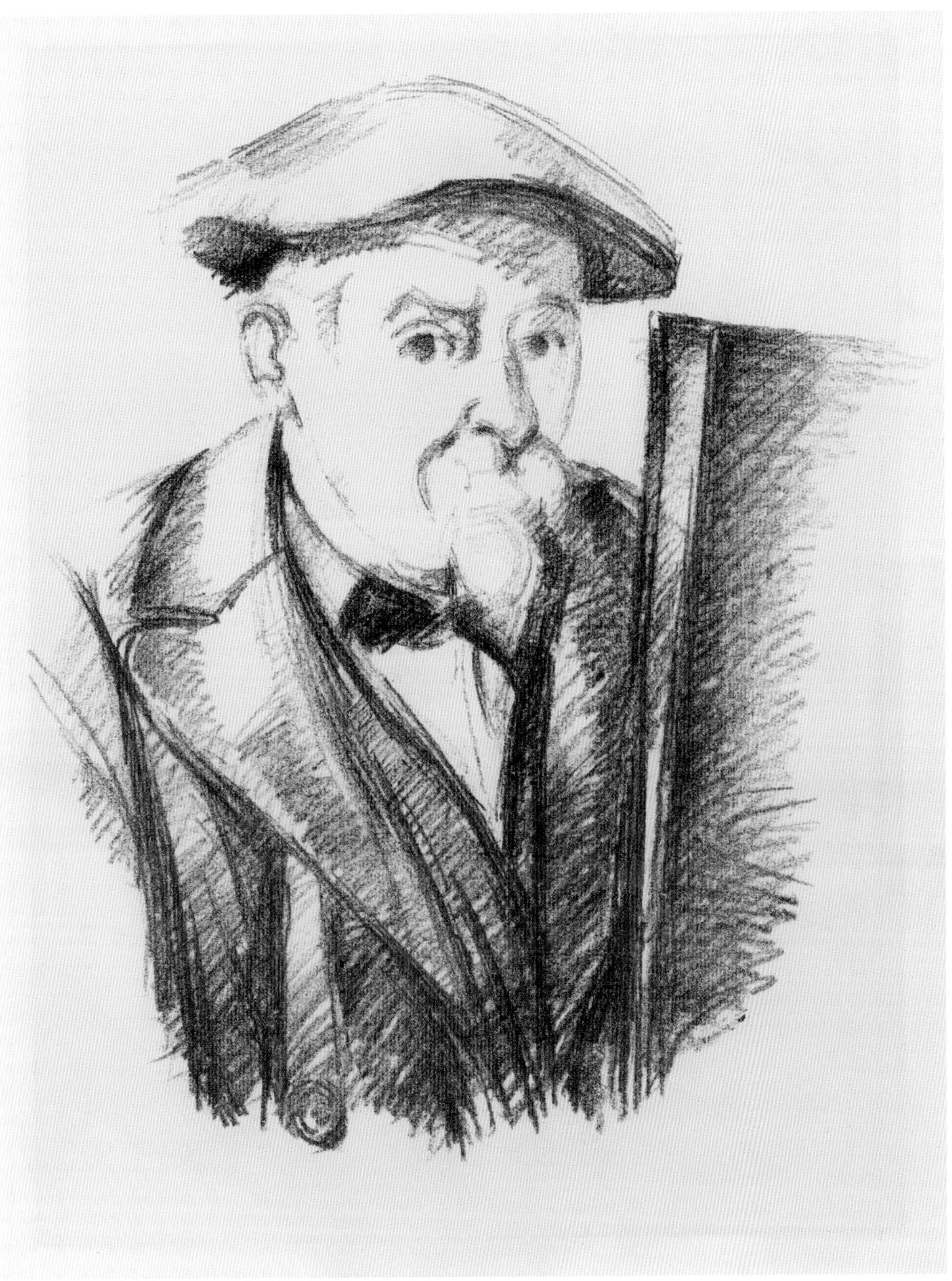

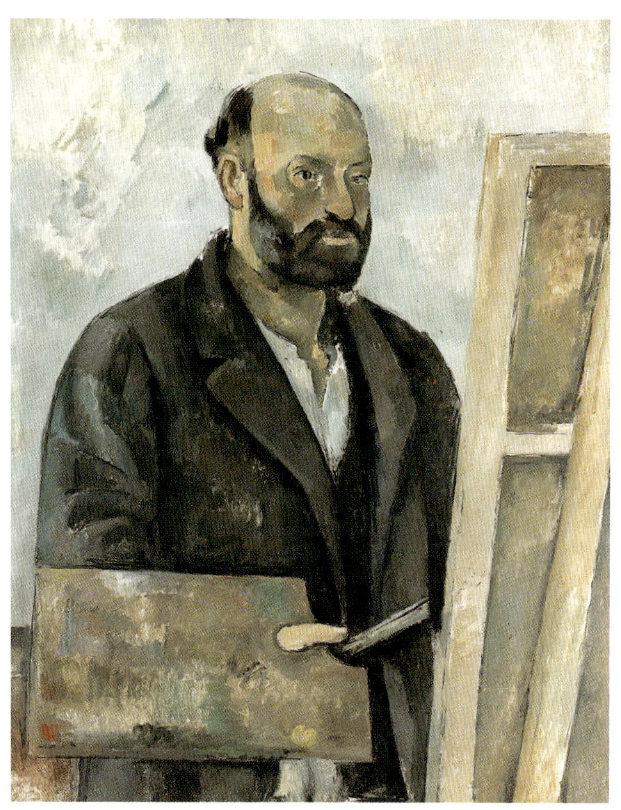

keystone to be printed over colour. Yet no colour lithographs of the self-portrait are known, and a comparison with the loose manner in which the black stones of the Bather subjects are worked shows the Courtauld image to be too finished and shaded to have been used in this way.[6] The lithograph is clearly conceived in terms of black and white and is complete in its monochromatic state. The use of shading and the strongly defined structure is typical of Cézanne's drawing style of the 1890s, the undelineated mouth characteristic of the self-portrait drawings of the period.[7] His usually vibrant line is somewhat diminished, however, possibly through the need to produce a 'finished' work for publication.

Throughout his life Cézanne was plagued by a sense of isolation and loneliness, exacerbated in his later years by a morbid fear of death. Whether he drew his face from a photograph or from a mirror, in this, his final print, he looks away from his easel, staring wistfully at both himself and the imaginary viewer – an outward yet self-reflecting gaze. JS

NOTES

1 See Platzmen 2001, p. 178.
2 *Ibid.*, p. 189.
3 *Small Bathers*, Venturi 1936, no. 1156, and *Large Bathers*, Venturi 1936, no. 1157.
4 Druick 1977, pp. 123, 130.
5 Cherpin 1972, no. 8, p. 69. The work was reproduced in Vollard 1914, p. 90, and described as *Portrait of Cézanne* (ibid. p. 179). Its present location is unknown.
6 For the procedure with the Bather maquettes, see Druick 1977, pp. 126–31.
7 *Ibid.*, p. 136, note 86; see CD 1125.

Cézanne's Letters to Emile Bernard

Transcribed and translated by

JOHN HOUSE

Since their first publication in 1907, Cézanne's nine letters to the younger painter Emile Bernard have been recognised as offering perhaps the single most coherent account of his views on art. Throughout, the letters set out to counter Bernard's penchant for abstract theorising, and to justify Cézanne's own insistence that art should be based on the scrupulous study of nature. Rainer Maria Rilke, on reading the letters when they were first published, saw them as virtually unintelligible, and as evidence of Cézanne's loathing of verbal expression. Indeed, their language is at times terse and even convoluted. However, taken together with letters to other correspondents and interviews from Cézanne's last years, they show that he himself was keen to articulate his aims in words, and to present a cogent and searching view of his artistic project, even while insisting that precept could never replace practice.

The letters have been newly transcribed from the manuscripts in the collection of The Courtauld Gallery for the present volume. The occasional oddities of Cézanne's spelling have been retained. At times his punctuation, paragraph breaks, capital letters and accents are ambiguous, and the most plausible reading is given here. At most points, these new versions agree with the texts as transcribed by Douglas Cooper and published in *Impressionnistes de la Collection Courtauld de Londres* (Musée de l'Orangerie, Paris, 1955) and in *Conversations avec Cézanne*, edited by Michael Doran (Paris, 1978).

In translating these letters, I have erred on the side of literal translation rather than fluent idiomatic English, seeking to preserve as far as possible the nuances of Cézanne's writing, both his vocabulary and his at times convoluted phrasing. The letters have been translated in their entirety three times before, by Marguerite Kay (*Paul Cézanne, Letters*, ed. John Rewald, Oxford, 1941), by Seymour Hacker (*Paul Cézanne, Letters*, ed. John Rewald, New York, 1984), and by Julie Lawrence Cochran (*Conversations with Cézanne*, ed. Michael Doran, Berkeley and London, 2001). In addition, passages from them have been translated in various other publications. At certain points I have adopted phrases from each of these previous versions that seemed to me to convey Cézanne's pattern of thinking particularly clearly.

NOTE

The letters are written on both sides of a folding sheet. The first and last (front and back) pages are here illustrated on the left-hand page, the middle pages on the right.

A number of key terms in Cézanne's letters to Bernard need brief explanation. The nuances of Cézanne's thinking are inseparable from the technical vocabulary that he used, much of which has no straightforward English equivalent.

For further discussion of these and other terms, see Michael Doran's preface and notes in *Conversations avec Cézanne* (Paris, 1978); they appear in English, together with a valuable introduction by Richard Shiff, in *Conversations with Cézanne* (Berkeley and London, 2001); unfortunately, the English translations in this volume, by Julie Lawrence Cochran, are not consistently reliable.

Sensation/sentir this term was fundamental to the aesthetic of the Impressionists, characterising the individual's sensory experiences which were, by definition, unique to that individual. The English word 'sensation' does not carry the same associations; it is here pedantically translated 'sensory experience' (letters B2, B3, B4, B6).

Sensations colorantes Cézanne seems to be making a subtle point by using this term rather than the more obvious *sensations colorées*, perhaps to suggest the active role of the *sensation* in generating the experience of colour (letters B5, B6, B8).

Réalisation/réaliser this term is the fundamental counterpoint to the *sensation* in Cézanne's aesthetic, characterising the process of recreating, or realising, the *sensations* in paint on canvas (letters B4, B8, B9). In some letters (letter B9, and see above, p. 34–35), he seems to establish a significant disjunction between learning to see, to understand the *sensations*, and the material processes (*procédés*) that led to *réalisation*.

Concret, concrète used as a contrast to the *abstractions* of *litterateurs* and those who put theory before practice (letter B2); also the seemingly incorrect verb *concréter* is used (letter B3) as a rough equivalent to *réaliser*, emphasising the physical outcome, in the form of drawing and colour, of the painter's expression of his *sensations*.

Abstractions used in three rather different ways, to characterise the ideas of *litterateurs*, in contrast to the 'concrete' product of the painter (letter B3), to describe analysis of visual experience in terms of the contrast between black and white, rather than in terms of *sensations colorantes* (letter B6), and to characterise his own inability adequately to 'realise' delicate

sensations colorantes in paint (letter B8); the last of these can perhaps also be read as a way of describing the actual marks on the canvas at the points where 'realisation' was not achieved.

Tempérament used to characterise the distinctiveness of the individual artist's personality (letters B5, B7, B8), and may be 'large' or 'small' (letter B8); this usage picks up on the famous definition by Cézanne's friend Emile Zola in 1866 of a work of art as 'a corner of creation seen through a temperament' ('un coin de la création vu à travers un tempérament').

Enveloppe this term, frequently used by Claude Monet, described the unifying effects of the atmosphere on a scene, generally viewed in terms of colour (letter B7).

Reflet coloured reflections were a primary means by which the artists of the Impressionist group established relationships between the diverse objects in their scenes; in letter B7, Cézanne is stating that the overall play of reflections across an entire scene constitutes the *enveloppe*.

Effet this term was regularly used to describe the overall effect of a scene, as modified by light and atmosphere; where he uses it in his parenthesis to letter B5, Cézanne seems to be contrasting his primary topic, the study of three-dimensional solids, with the ways in which light and atmosphere modified and complicated the representation of solids.

Etude/étudier this is used throughout the correspondence to describe the close visual study of nature that was the essential basis of Cézanne's aesthetic; the noun *étude* is also used for the resulting painting, a standard usage in nineteenth-century writings on art to describe either a preparatory study or a rapid sketch.

Optique the noun *l'optique* (letter B8) seems to be used to characterise the sum of the artist's optical experience, developed through study of nature, rather than any abstract concept or science of optics.

La belle nature this phrase (letter B7), rather than the simple *nature* used elsewhere throughout the correspondence, picks up on a usage that specified that the particular configuration of natural forms gave aesthetic pleasure.

Aix-en-Provence, 15 avril 1904

Cher Monsieur Bernard,

Quand vous recevrez celle-ci vous aurez très-probablement reçu une lettre venant de Belgique, je crois et à vous addressée rue Boulegon. – Je suis heureux du témoignage de Bonne Sympathie d'art que vous voulez bien m'adresser par le fait de votre lettre. –

Permettez-moi de vous répéter ce que je vous disais ici. Traiter la nature par le cylindre, la sphère, le cone, le tout mis en perspective, soit que chaque côté d'un objet, d'un plan, se dirige vers un point central. – Les lignes parallèles à l'horizon donnent l'étendue, soit une section de la nature ou si vous aimez mieux du Spectacle que le Pater omnipotens, [oeterne Deus,]* étale devant nos yeux. Les lignes perpendiculaires à cet horizon donnent la profondeur. – or la nature pour nous-hommes est plus en profondeur qu'en surface, d'où la nécessité d'introduire dans nos vibrations de lumière, représentées par les rouges et les jaunes, une somme suffisante de Bleutés, pour faire sentir l'air. – Permettez-moi de vous dire, que j'ai revu votre étude faite du rez-de-chaussé de l'atelier elle est bonne, vous n'avez je crois qu'à poursuivre dans cette voie. – Vous avez la intelligence de ce qu'il faut faire, et vous arriverez vite à tourner le dos aux Gauguins et Gogs.

Veuillez remercier Madame Bernard, du bon souvenir qu'elle a bien voulu garder du signataire de cette lettre, un bon baiser de père Goriot aux enfants, Tous mes Respects à votre bonne famille.

[]* phrase added above text

Aix-en-Provence, 15 April 1904

Dear Monsieur Bernard,

When you receive this, you will very probably have received a letter coming from Belgium, I think, and addressed to you at Rue Boulegon. I am happy at the testimony of artistic sympathy that you are kind enough to send me by the fact that you wrote to me.

Allow me to repeat what I told you here: to treat nature in terms of the cylinder, the sphere and the cone, everything placed in perspective, so that each side of an object, of a plane, leads to a central point. Lines parallel to the horizon give breadth, be it a section of nature, or, if you prefer, of the spectacle that Pater Omnipotens [Oeterne Deus]* spreads before our eyes. Lines perpendicular to this horizon give depth. Now, we men experience nature more in terms of depth than surface; hence the necessity to introduce into our vibrations of light, represented by reds and yellows, a sufficient quantity of blue tones, to give a sense of the atmosphere.

Let me tell you that I have looked again at the study that you made of/from the ground floor of the studio; it is good. You need only pursue this path, I think; you understand what you need to do, and you will soon be able to turn your back on the Gauguins and Van Goghs.

Please thank Madame Bernard for the kind memory that she has retained of the undersigned, a kiss from Père Goriot for the children, and all my respects to your good family.

[]* phrase added above text

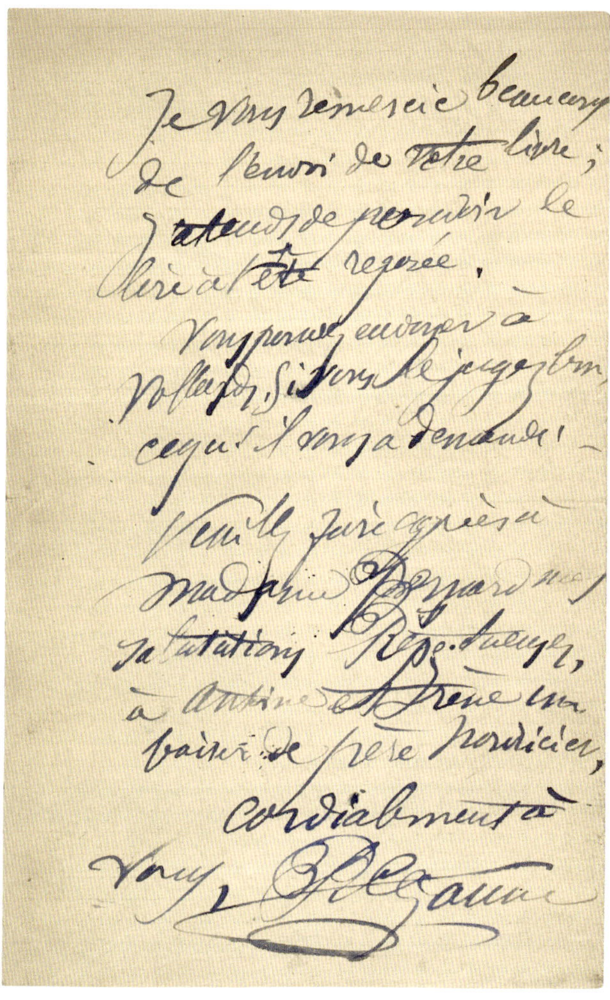

Aix, 12 mai 1904

Mon cher Bernard,

Mon assiduité au travail et mon âge avancé vous expliqueront assez le retard que j'ai apporté à vous répondre.

Vous m'entretenez d'ailleurs de choses si variées dans votre dernière lettre, toutes cependant se rattachant à l'art, que je ne puis la suivre dans tout son développement.

Je vous l'ai dit déjà le talent de Redon me plait beaucoup et je suis de cœur avec lui pour sentir et admirer Delacroix. Je ne sais si ma précaire santé, me permettra de réaliser jamais mon rêve de faire son apothéose.

Je procède très-lentement. La nature s'offrant à moi très-complexe, et les progrès à faire sont incessants.

Il faut bien voir son modèle et sentir très-juste; et encore s'exprimer avec distinction et force. –

Le goût est le meilleur juge. Il est rare. L'art ne s'adresse qu'à un nombre excessivement restreint d'individus.

L'artiste doit dédaigner l'opinion qui ne repose pas sur l'observation intelligente du caractère. Il doit redouter l'esprit littérateur, qui fait si souvent le peintre s'écarter de sa vraie voie, l'étude concrète de la nature, pour se perdre trop longtemps dans des spéculations intangibles, –

Le Louvre est un bon livre à consulter, mais ce ne doit être encore qu'un intermédiaire. L'étude réelle et prodigieuse à entreprendre c'est la diversité du tableau de la nature.

Je vous remercie beaucoup de l'envoi de votre livre; j'attends de pouvoir le lire à tête reposée.

Vous pouvez envoyer à Vollard, si vous le jugez bon, ce qu'il vous a demandé. –

Veuillez faire agréer à Madame Bernard mes salutations Respectueuses, à Antoine et Irène un baiser de père nourricier,

cordialement à vous, P. Cézanne

Aix, 12 May 1904

My dear Bernard,

My commitment to work and my advanced age will explain well enough my delay in replying to you.

Moreover, you write to me about such varied things in your most recent letter, though all of them relate to art, that I cannot follow it in all its arguments.

I have already told you that I much admire Redon's talent, and I quite agree with him in his feeling and admiration for Delacroix. I do not know if my precarious state of health will ever allow me to realise my dream of painting his apotheosis.

I proceed very slowly, since nature presents itself to me in very complex forms; and constant progress is necessary. One must see one's model clearly and experience it very accurately, and also express oneself with distinction and power.

Taste is the best judge. It is rare. Art addresses itself only to an excessively small number of people.

The artist should disdain opinions that are not based on the intelligent observation of character. He should be wary of the literary spirit, which so often diverts the painter from his true path, the concrete study of nature, to lose himself for too long in intangible speculations.

The Louvre is a good book to consult, but it should only be an intermediary. The real, prodigious study to undertake is the diversity of nature's appearance.

Thank you very much for sending me your book; I look forward to being able to read it in a restful frame of mind.

If you think it is a good idea, you may send Vollard what he has asked you for.

Please give Madame Bernard my respectful greetings, and a kiss for Antoine and Irène from their adoptive father.

Greetings to you.

P. Cézanne

Aix, 26 mai 1904

Mon cher Bernard,

J'approuve assez les idées que vous allez développer dans votre prochain article destiné à l'Occident. Mais j'en reviens toujours à ceci: Le peintre doit se consacrer entièrement à l'étude de la Nature, et tâcher de produire des tableaux, qui soient un enseignement. Les causeries sur l'art sont presque inutiles. Le travail, qui fait réaliser un progrès dans son propre métier est un dédommagement suffisant de ne pas être compris des imbéciles.

Le littérateur s'exprime avec des abstractions, tandis que le peintre concrète au moyen du dessin et de la couleur ses sensations, ses perceptions. – On n'est ni trop scrupuleux, ni trop sincère, ni trop soumis à la nature; mais on est plus ou moins maître de son modèle, et surtout de ses moyens d'expression. Pénétrer ce qu'on a devant soi, et persévérer à s'exprimer le plus logiquement possible.

Veuillez faire agréer mes Salutations Respectueuses à Madame Bernard, une bonne poignée de main à Vous et souvenir aux enfants.

Pictor P. Cézanne

Aix, 26 May 1904

My dear Bernard,

I am largely in agreement with the ideas that you are going to develop in your forthcoming article for *L'Occident*. But I always come back to this: the painter must dedicate himself totally to the study of nature, and seek to produce paintings that will be an education. Talking about art is virtually useless. The hard work that leads to progress in one's own craft is a sufficient compensation for not being understood by imbeciles.

The *litterateur* expresses himself in abstractions while the painter gives concrete expression to his sensory experiences, his perceptions, by means of drawing and colour. One cannot be too scrupulous, too sincere or too submissive to nature; but one is more or less master of one's model, and especially of one's means of expression. One should penetrate what one has in front of one, and make every effort to express oneself as logically as possible.

Please give my respectful greetings to Madame Bernard, and a good handshake for you, and remember me to the children.

Pictor P. Cézanne

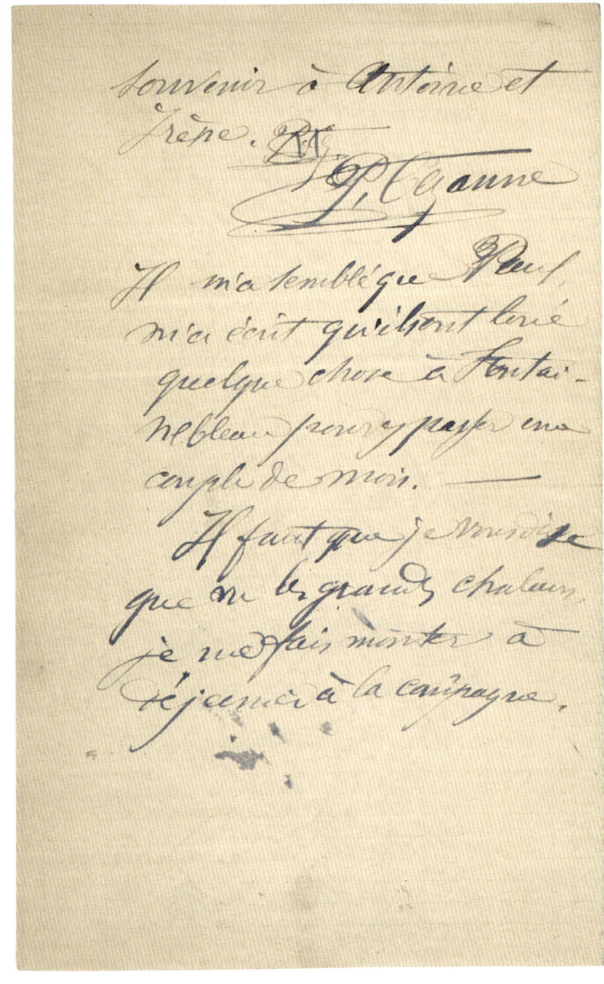

Aix, 27 juin 1904

Mon cher Bernard,
J'ai bien reçu votre honorée du., que j'ai laissée à
la campagne. si j'ai tardé à y répondre, c'est que je
me trouve sous le coup de troubles-cérébraux, qui
m'empêchent d'évoluer librement. Je demeure sous
le coup de sensations, et malgré mon âge vissé à
la peinture.

Le temps est beau, j'en profite pour travailler,
il faudrait faire dix bonnes, les vendre cher, puisque
les amateurs spéculent dessus. –

Hier est arrivée ici une lettre adressée à mon fils,
[que Mme Brémond a conjecturée être de vous,]* je la
lui est fait adresser rue Duperré, 16, Paris IX arrond. –

Il paraît que Vollard, il y a quelques jours a donné
une soirée dansante, où on a beaucoup boustifaillé. –
Toute la jeune école s'y trouvait paraît-il. Maurice
Denis, Vuillard etc. Paul et Joachim Gasquet s'y

sont rencontrés. – Je crois que le mieux est de
travailler beaucoup. Vous êtes jeune réalisez et
vendez. –

Vous vous rappelez le beau pastel de Chardin,
armé d'une paire de bésicles, une visière faisant
auvent. – C'est un roublard ce peintre. Avez-vous pas
remarqué, qu'en faisant chevaucher sur son nez un
léger plan transversal d'arête, les valeurs s'établissent
mieux à la vue. – Vérifiez ce fait, et vous me direz,
si je me trompe. –

Bien cordialement à vous, et veuillez faire agréer
mes Respects par Madame Bernard, et un bon
souvenir à Antoine et Irène.
P. Cézanne
Il m'a semblé que Paul m'a écrit qu'ils ont loué
quelque chose à Fontainebleau pour y passer une
couple de mois. –

Il faut que je vous dise que vu les grandes chaleurs,
je me fais monter à déjeuner à la campagne.

[]* phrase inserted in margin

Aix, 27 June 1904

My dear Bernard,

I have safely received your esteemed letter, which I have left in the country. If I have delayed replying to it, this is because I have been suffering from cerebral troubles, which stop me moving about freely. I remain in the grip of my sensory experiences, and, despite my age, committed to painting.

The weather is fine, I am taking advantage of it to work, I need to paint ten good studies and sell them at high prices, since the collectors are speculating on them.

A letter arrived here yesterday addressed to my son, [which Mme Brémond guessed is from you;]* I have had her forward it to him at 16 rue Duperré, Paris IX. It seems that Vollard hosted a dinner dance a few days ago, where everyone feasted well. The whole young school was there, it seems, Maurice Denis, Vuillard, etc. Paul and Joachim Gasquet met there. I think that the best thing is to work hard. You are young, you should realise and sell.

Do you remember the beautiful pastel of Chardin, wearing a pair of spectacles, with a visor shading his eyes. He is a crafty one, that painter. Have you noticed that by placing a little horizontal plane across the bridge of his nose he made the values work together better? Check this, and let me know if I am wrong.

With my cordial greetings, and pay my respects to Madame Bernard, and best regards to Antoine and Irène.

P. Cézanne

I think that Paul wrote to tell me that they have rented a place at Fontainebleau to spend a couple of months there.

I must tell you that because of the great heat I have myself taken up to the country for luncheon.

[]* phrase inserted in margin

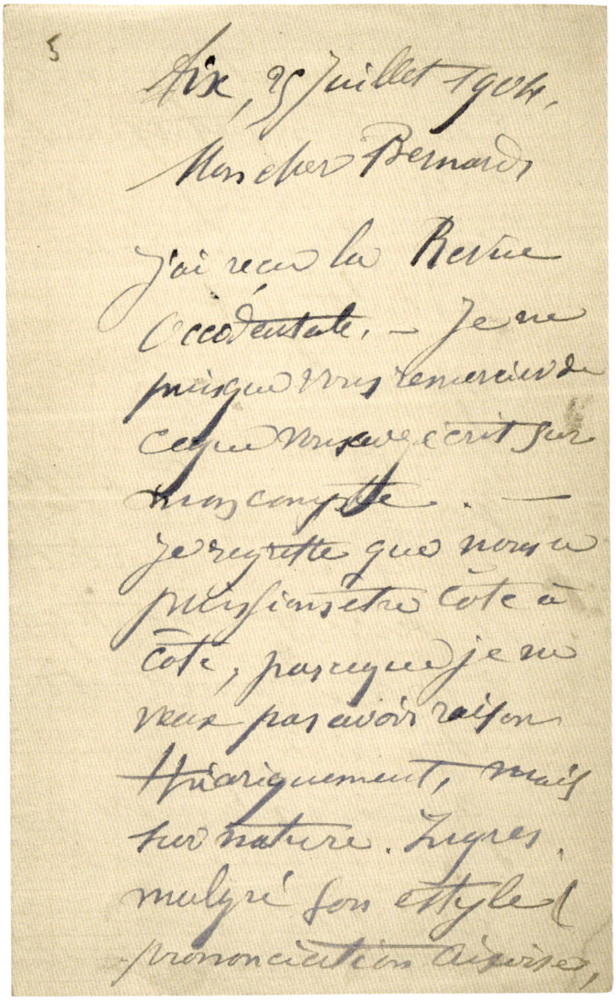

Aix, 25 juillet 1904

Mon cher Bernard,

J'ai reçu la *Revue Occidentale*. – Je ne puis que vous remercier de ce que vous avez écrit sur mon compte. –

Je regrette que nous ne puissions être côte à côte, parce que je ne veux pas avoir raison théoriquement, mais sur nature. Ingres, malgré son estyle (prononciation aixoise, et ses admirateurs, n'est qu'un très-petit peintre. Les plus grands, vous les connaissez mieux que moi, les Vénitiens et les Espagnols. – Pour les progrès à réaliser, il n'y a que la nature, et l'oeil s'éduque à son conctat. Il devient concentrique à force de regarder et de travailler. Je veux dire que dans une orange une pomme, une boule une tête, il y a un point culminant, et ce point est toujours, le plus rapproché de notre oeil, [malgré le terrible effet, lumière et ombre. – Sensations colorantes]* les bords des objets fuient vers un centre placé à notre horizon, avec un petit tempérament on peut être très-peintre. On peut faire des choses bien sans être très-harmoniste, ni coloriste. Il suffit d'avoir un sens d'art. – Et c'est sans doute l'horreur du bourgeois, ce sens là. – Donc les instituts, les pensions, les honneurs ne peuvent être faits que pour les crétins, les farceurs et les droles. Ne soyez pas critique d'art, faites de la peinture. C'est là le salut. – Je vous serre cordialement la main, votre vieux camarade,

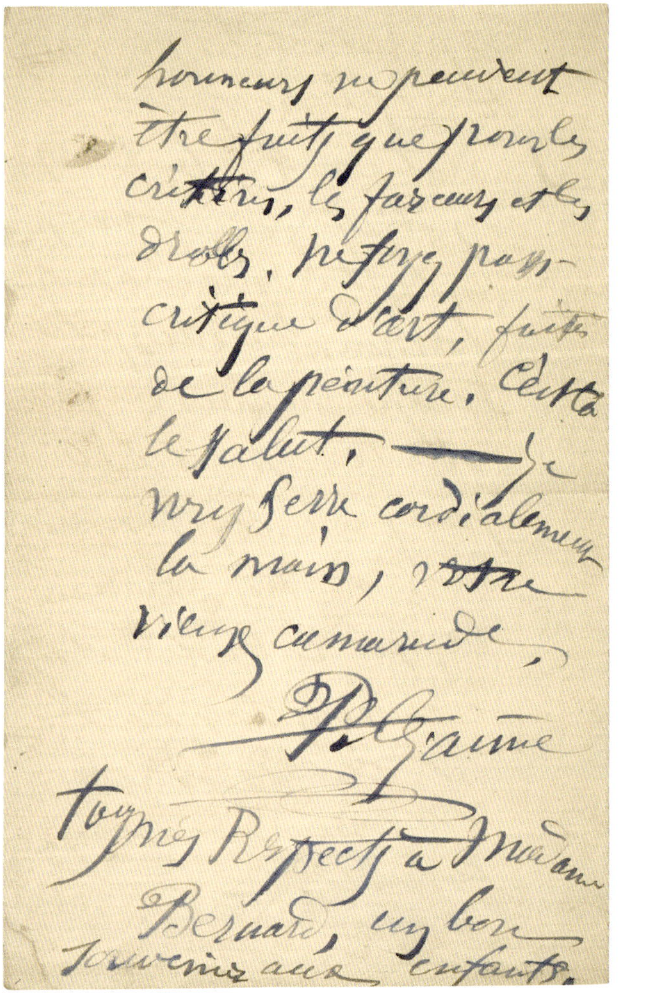

P. Cézanne

tous mes *Respects* à Madame Bernard, un bon souvenir aux enfants.

[]* phrases added in margin

Aix, 25 July 1904

My dear Bernard,

I have received the *Revue occidentale*. I can only thank you for what you have written about me.

I am sorry that we cannot spend time together, because I do not want to be correct in theoretical terms, but in front of nature. Ingres, despite his *estyle* (Aixois pronunciation) and his admirers, is only a very minor painter. The greatest, you know them better than I, the Venetians and the Spaniards.

In order to make progress, there is only nature, and the eye educates itself by contact with nature. It becomes concentric by looking and working. What I mean is that, in an orange, an apple, a ball, a head, there is a culminating point; and this point is always the closest to our eye; the edges of objects recede towards a centre placed on our eye level; [despite the terrible effect, light and shade, experiences of colour.]* with a little bit of temperament one can be very much a painter. One can do good things without being either a great harmonist or a great colourist. All one needs is an artistic sensibility. And this is doubtless what horrifies the bourgeois, that sensibility. Hence institutes, scholarships and honours can only be created for cretins, jokers and comics. Do not be an art critic, create paintings. There lies salvation.

I shake your hand cordially, your old comrade.

P. Cézanne

All my respects to Madame Bernard, and best regards to the children.

[]* phrases added in margin

Aix, 23 Xbre 1904

Mon cher Bernard,

J'ai reçu votre bonne lettre datée de Naples.
Je ne m'étendrai pas avec vous en des considérations
esthétiques. Oui j'approuve votre admiration pour le
plus vaillants des Vénitiens, nous célébrons Tintoret.
Votre besoin de trouver un point d'appui moral,
intellectuel dans des oeuvres qu'on ne surpassera
pas assurément, vous met sur le perpétuel qui vive,
sur la recherche incessante des moyens entreperçus
qui vous conduiront sûrement à sentir sur nature vos
moyens d'expression, et le jour où vous les tiendrez,
soyez convaincu, que vous retrouverez sans effort et
sur nature les moyens employés par les quatre ou cinq
grands de Venise, – Voici sans conteste possible – je
suis très-affirmatif, – une sensation optique se produit
dans notre organe visuel, qui nous fait classer par
lumière demi-ton ou quart de ton les plans représentés
par des sensations colorantes. [La lumière n'existe,
donc pas pour le peintre.]* Tant que forcément vous
allez du Noir au Blanc, La première de ces abstractions
étant comme un point d'appui autant pour l'œil que
pour le cerveau, nous pataugeons nous n'arrivons
pas à avoir notre maîtrise – à nous posséder. Pendant
cette période temps (Je me répète un peu forcément,
nous allons vers les admirables œuvres que nous ont
transmises[?] les âges, où nous trouvons un réconfort
un soutien, comme la fait la planche pour le baigneur.
– Tout ce que vous me dites dans votre lettre est bien
vrai. –

Je suis heureux d'apprrendre que Madame
Bernard, vous et les enfants allez bien. Ma femme
et mon fils sont à Paris en ce moment. Nous nous
retrouverons, j'espère bientôt. – Je souhaite répondre
autant que possible aux points principaux de votre
bonne lettre, et je vous prie de vouloir bien faire agréer
mes souvenirs respecueux à Madame Bernard, un

bon baiser à Antoine, à Irène, et vous mon cher
confrère, en vous souhaitant un bon an nouveau,
je vous serre cordialement la main
   P. Cézanne

[]* sentence inserted above main text
[?] reading uncertain

23 December 1904

My dear Bernard,

I have received your good letter from Naples. I won't elaborate with you about aesthetic questions. Yes, I endorse your admiration for the strongest of the Venetians; we celebrate Tintoretto. Your need to find a moral and intellectual reference point in works of art which will surely never be surpassed puts you constantly on the alert, incessantly searching for methods that you have glimpsed, which will surely lead you to experience your means of expression in front of nature; and rest assured that, the day that you find them, you will effortlessly rediscover in front of nature the methods that were used by the four or five great artists of Venice.

Incontestably – I am very positive about this – an optical experience takes place in our visual organ which makes us classify as highlight, half-tone and quarter tone the planes represented by coloured sensory experiences. [Thus light itself does not exist for the painter.]* As long as you pass inevitably from black to white, the first of these abstractions which is a reference point as much for the eye as for the brain, we flounder about, we cannot achieve mastery and self-possession. During this period (inevitably I am repeating myself) we look to the admirable works that the ages have passed down[?] to us, where we find a comfort and a support, like the plank for the bather. Everything that you say in your letter is quite true.

I am happy to learn that Madame Bernard, you and the children are all well. My wife and my son are in Paris at the moment. I hope that we will be together again soon.

I hope that I have responded as fully as possible to the principal points of your good letter, and I ask you to pass my respectful greetings to Madame Bernard, a good kiss to Antoine and Irène, and as for you, my dear colleague, I wish you a happy new year, with a cordial handshake.

P. Cézanne

[]* sentence inserted above main text
[?] reading uncertain

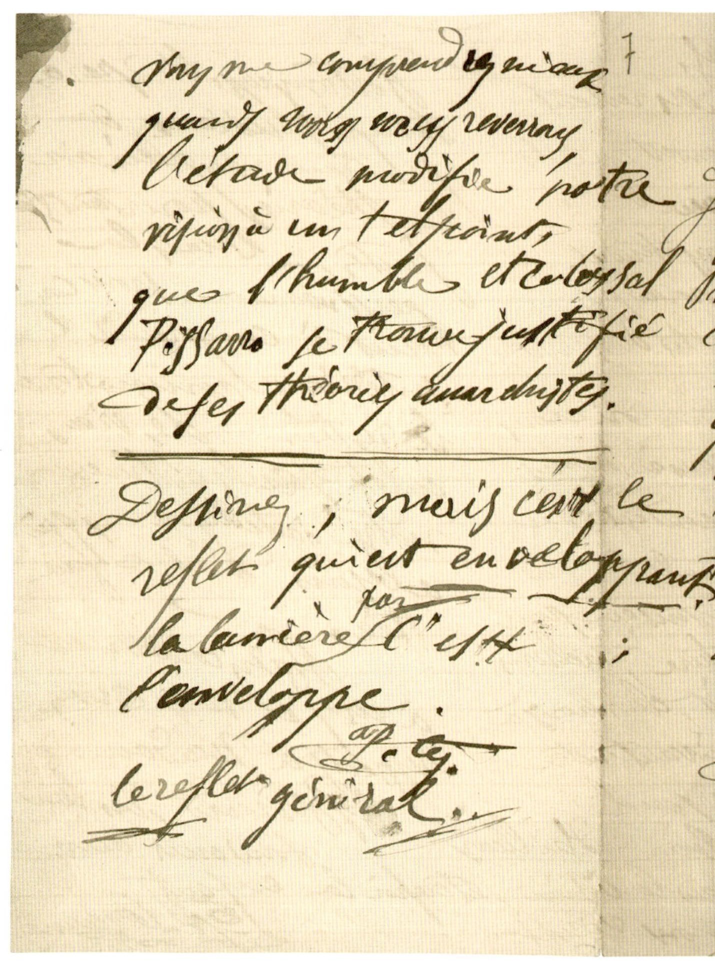

[1905] vendredi

Mon cher Bernard,

Je réponds succinctement à quelques uns des alinéas de votre dernière lettre. Comme vous me l'écrivez, je crois en effet avoir encore réalisé quelque progrès bien lents dans les dernières études que vous avez vues chez moi. Il est toutefois douleureux d'être obligé de constater que l'amélioration qui se produit dans la compréhension de la Nature au point de vue du tableau et du développement des moyens d'expression, soit accompagnés de l'âge et de l'affaiblissement du corps.

Si les Salons officiels restent si inférieurs, la raison est qu'ils ne mettent en oeuvre que des procédés plus ou moins étendus. Il vaudrait mieux apporter plus d'émotion personnelle, d'observation et de caractère.

Le Louvre est le livre où nous apprenons à lire. Nous ne devons cependant pas nous contenter de retenir les belles formules de nos illustres devanciers. Sortons en pour étudier la belle nature, tachons d'en dégager l'esprit, cherchons à nous exprimer suivant notre tempérament personel.

Le temps et la réflexion d'ailleurs modifient peu à peu la vision, et enfin la compréhension nous vient.

Il est impossible par ces temps pluvieux de pratiquer en plein air ces théories pourtant si justes. – Mais la persévérance nous conduit à comprendre les intérieurs comme tout le reste. – Les vieux culots seuls obstruent notre intelligence, qui a besoin d'être fouettée. –

Bien cordialement à vous et tous mes respects à Madame Bernard, un bon souvenir aux enfants.

P. Cézanne

Vous me comprendrez mieux quand nous nous reverrons, l'étude modifie notre vision à un tel point, que l'humble et colossal Pissarro se trouve justifié de ses théories anarchistes.

Dessinez, mais c'est le reflet qui est enveloppant. La lumière [par le reflet général]* c'est l'enveloppe. P. Cez.

[]* phrase added above and below the text

[1905] Friday

My dear Bernard,

I am replying briefly to some of the paragraphs of your last letter. As you write, I think that I have made some more very slow progress in the latest studies that you saw here. Yet it is distressing to have to say that this improvement in the comprehension of Nature, from the point of view of the painting and the development of means of expression, is accompanied by age and the weakening of my body.

If the official Salons remain so inferior, the reason is that they only employ more or less extensive procedures. It would be better to introduce more personal emotion, more observation and more character.

The Louvre is the book where we learn to read. But we must not be satisfied with holding on to the fine formulae of our illustrious predecessors. Let us leave the museum behind in order to study beautiful nature, let us try to capture its spirit, let us seek to express ourselves according to our personal temperament. Moreover, time and reflection gradually modify our vision, and at last understanding comes to us.

Though these theories are so sound, it is impossible in this rainy weather to put them into practice in the open air. But perseverance leads us to understand interiors like everything else. Only old habits obstruct our intelligence, which needs to be spurred into action.

With cordial wishes to you and all my respects to Madame Bernard, best regards to the children.

P. Cézanne

You will understand me better when we see each other; study modifies our vision to such an extent that the humble and colossal Pissarro is justified in his anarchist theories.

You should draw; but it is the reflection that creates the enveloping atmosphere; light, [through the overall play of reflections,]* is the enveloping atmosphere.

P. Cez.

[]* phrase added above and below the text

Aix, 23 8bre 1905

Mon cher Bernard,

Vos lettres me sont chères à un double point de vue, le premier purement égoïste puisque leur arrivée me tire de cette monotonie, qu'engendre la poursuite incessante du seul et unique but, ce qui amène dans les moments de fatigue physique une sorte d'épuisement intellectuel, et le second me permet de vous ressasser sans doute un peu trop l'obstination que je mets à poursuivre la réalisation de cette partie de la nature qui tombant sur nos yeux nous donne le tableau. Or la thèse à developper est – quelque soit notre tempéremment, ou forme[?] de puissance en présence de la nature, de donner l'image de ce que nous voyons, en oubliant tout ce qui a paru avant nous. Ce qui, je crois, doit permettre à l'artiste de donner toute sa personnalité, grande ou petite. – Or vieux, 70 ans environ, – les sensations colorantes, qui donnent la lumière sont [chez moi]* cause d'abstractions qui ne me permettent pas de couvrir ma toile, ni de poursuivre la délimitation des objets quand les points de conctat sont tenus, délicats, d'où il ressort que mon image ou tableau est incomplète. D'un autre côté les plans tombent les uns sur les autres, d'où est sorti le néo-impressionnisme qui circonscrit les contours d'un trait noir, défaut qu'il faut combattre à toute force. Or la nature consultée nous donne les moyens d'atteindre ce but. – Je me suis bien rappelé que vous étiez à Tonnerre, mais les difficultés [d'installation]** à m'installer m'ont fait [font]† me livrer entièrement à la disposition de ma famille, qui en use pour chercher ses commodités en m'oubliant un peu. –

C'est la vie, à mon âge, je devrais avoir plus d'expérience et en user pour le bien général.

Je vous dois la vérité en peinture et je vous la dirai.

Veuillez faire agréer tous mes respects par Madame Bernard, les enfants je dois les aimer St Vincent de Paule étant celui auquel je dois le plus me recommander.

Votre vieux,
Paul Cézanne
Bonne poignée de main et bon courage.
– L'optique se développant chez nous par l'étude. –
[nous apprend à voir.]‡

[?] reading uncertain
[]* *chez moi* inserted in margin; seems to belong here rather than after *m'installer* below
[]** *d'installation* erased
[]† *font* added on top of *fait*
[]‡ *nous apprend à voir* added in left margin

Aix, 23 October 1905

My dear Bernard,

Your letters are precious to me from two points of view, the first purely egotistical, since their arrival lifts me out of the monotony that is brought on by the incessant pursuit of my single and unique goal, which leads, at moments of physical fatigue, to a sort of intellectual exhaustion; and the second allows me to keep repeating to you, doubtless a little too much, the obstinacy with which I pursue the realisation of that part of nature which, falling before our eyes, gives us the picture. So, the principle to develop – whatever our temperament or power in the presence of nature – is to give the image of what we see, forgetting everything that has appeared before us. This, I think, would allow the artist to express his entire personality, be it large or small.

But being old, around seventy, the coloured sensory experiences that create light are the cause of abstractions that do not allow me to cover my canvas or to pursue the delimitation of objects when their points of contact are subtle and delicate; the result of this is that my image or picture is incomplete. The alternative is that the planes fall on top of each other, which resulted in [the] neo-impressionism which surrounds the contours with a black line, a defect that one must oppose with all one's strength. But if we consult nature we will find the means of achieving this goal.

I remembered that you were at Tonnerre but the difficulties of installing myself at home make me put myself entirely at the disposition of my family, who make use of this for their own convenience while forgetting me a little. That's life; at my age I should have more experience, and use it for the general good. I owe you the truth in painting, and I shall tell it to you.

Please give all my respects to Madame Bernard; I must love the children, since I should commend myself most of all to Saint Vincent de Paul.

Your old Paul Cézanne

With a good handshake and wishing you good luck.

Optical experience which develops in us through study [teaches us to see]‡.

[]‡ added in left margin

Aix, 21 septembre 1906

Mon cher Bernard,

Je me trouve en un tel état de troubles cérébraux, dans un trouble si grand, que j'ai craint à un moment que ma frêle raison y passât. Après les terribles chaleurs que nous venons de subir, une temperature plus clémente a ramené dans nos esprits un peu de calme, et ce n'était pas trop tot, maintenant il me semble que je vois mieux et que je pense plus juste dans l'orientation de mes études. Arriverai-je au but tant cherché, et si longtemps poursuivi. – Je le souhaite, mais tant qu'il n'est pas atteint, un vague état de malaise subsiste, qui ne pourra disparaître qu'après [avoir]* que j'aurai atteint le port, soit avoir réalisé quelque chose se développant mieux que par le passé, et par là-même devenant probant de théories, qui, elles sont toujours faciles, il n'y a que la preuve à faire de ce qu'on pense, qui – présente de sérieux obstacles. Je continue donc mes études, – mais je viens de relire votre lettre et je vois que je réponds toujours à côté. Vous voudrez bien m'en excuser, c'est je vous l'ai dit, cette constante préoccupation du but à atteindre qui en est la cause. –

J'étudie toujours sur nature, et il me semble que je fais de lents progrès. Je vous aurais voulu auprès de moi, car la solitude pèse toujours un peu. Mais je suis vieux, malade, et je me suis juré de mourir en peignant, plutot que de sombrer dans le gatisme avilissant, qui menace les vieillards, qui se laissent dominer par des passions abrutissantes pour leurs sens. – Si j'ai le plaisir de me retrouver un jour avec vous, nous pourrons mieux de vive voix nous expliquer. Vous m'excuserez de revenir sans cesse au même point, mais je crois au développement logique de ce que nous voyons [et ressentons]** par l'étude sur nature, quitte à me préocuper des procédés ensuite, Les procédés n'étant pour nous que de simples moyens pour arriver à faire sentir au public ce que nous ressentons nous-même et à nous faire agréer. Les grands que nous admirons ne doivent avoir fait que ça.

{Un bon souvenir de l'entêté macrobite qui vous serre cordialement la main.

P. Cézanne}

[]* avoir erased
[]** added above main text
{as published in previous editions of the letters; MS missing}

Aix, 21 September 1906

My dear Bernard,

I am in such a state of mental disturbance, a disturbance that is so great that at some moments I fear that I am losing my feeble reason. After the terrible heat that we have recently been experiencing, a more clement temperature has brought a little calm to our spirits, and none too soon; now I think that I am seeing better and am thinking more clearly about the direction of my studies. Shall I reach the goal that I have sought so hard and pursued for so long? I hope so, but, as long as I have not reached it, a vague state of disquiet remains, which can only disappear after I have reached my goal, that is to say when I have realised something that develops better than in the past, and thus lends conviction to theories which, themselves, are always easy; it is only having to prove what one thinks that presents serious obstacles. So I am continuing my studies.

I have just reread your letter and see that my whole reply is off the point. Please excuse me; as I have said, the reason for this is this constant preoccupation with the goal to be attained. I constantly study from nature, and I think that I am making slow progress. I should have liked you to be beside me, since the solitude is always something of a burden. But I am old and sick, and I have sworn to die while painting, rather than sinking into the degrading senility that threatens old men who let themselves be dominated by passions that stupefy their senses. If I have the pleasure of being with you again one day, we can discuss things better face to face. Please excuse me for returning constantly to the same point; but I believe in the logical development of what we see [and experience]** through the study of nature, even if that means concerning myself with technical questions afterwards; for us, technical questions are merely the means of making the public experience what we ourselves experience, and of making us acceptable. This is what the greats whom we admire must have done.

Warm regards from the pig-headed macrobite (old man?) who cordially shakes your hand.

P. Cézanne

[]** added above main text

Selected Bibliography

100 Masterpieces from the Courtauld Collection, London 1987

D. Farr, *100 masterpieces from the Courtauld Collections. Bernardo Daddi to Ben Nicholson. European Paintings and Drawings from the 14th to the 20th Century*, London, 1987

ADRIANI 1983
G. Adriani, *Cézanne Watercolours*, New York, 1983

ANDERSEN 1970
W. Andersen, *Cézanne's Portrait Drawings*, Cambridge, Mass., and London, 1970

ATHANASSOGLOU-KALLMYER 2003
N.M. Athanassoglou-Kallmyer, *Cézanne and Provence: The Painter in His Culture*, Chicago, 2003

BADT 1956
K. Badt, *Die Kunst Cézannes*, Munich, 1956

BERNARD 1924 (1)
E. Bernard, 'Le Dessin de Cézanne', *L'Amour de l'Art*, January 1924, p. 37

BERNARD 1924 (2)
E. Bernard, 'Les Aquarelles de Cézanne', *L'Amour de l'Art*, February 1924, pp. 33-36

BERTHOLD 1958
G. Berthold, *Cézanne und die alten Meister*, Stuttgart, 1958

BOIS 1998
Y.-A. Bois, 'Cézanne: Words and Deeds', *October*, no. 84, Spring 1998, pp. 31-43

BRUCE-GARDNER 1987-88
R. Bruce-Gardner, G. Hedley and C. Villers, 'Impressions of Change', in *Impressionist and Post-Impressionist Masterpieces*, Cleveland *et alibi*, 1987-88, pp. 21-34

Burlington Magazine 2006
A. Dombrowski, K. Schubert, R. Shiff *et al.*, 'Paul Cézanne: A Special Issue', *The Burlington Magazine*, September 2006

CALLEN 2000
A. Callen, *The Art of Impressionism: Painting Technique and the Making of Modernity*, New Haven and London, 2000

CHAPPUIS 1973/ CD
A. Chappuis, *The Drawings of Paul Cézanne. A Catalogue Raisonné*, 2 vols., Greenwich, Conn., and London, 1973

CHERPIN 1972
J. Cherpin, *L'Œuvre gravé de Cézanne*, Marseilles, 1972

CLARK 1974
K. Clark, 'The Enigma of Cézanne', *Apollo*, vol. 100, 1974, pp. 78-81

CLARK 1999
T.J. Clark, 'Freud's Cézanne', in *Farewell to an Idea: Episodes from a History of Modernism*, New Haven and London, 1999, pp. 138-67

CLARK 2007
T.J. Clark, 'Phenomenality and Materiality in Cézanne', in J. Harris (ed.), *Value: Art: Politics: Criticism, Meaning and Interpretation after Postmodernism*, Liverpool, 2007, pp. 147-74

COOPER 1954 (1)
D. Cooper, 'Two Cézanne Exhibitions', *The Burlington Magazine*, Vol. 96, 1954, pp. 378-83

COOPER 1954 (2)
D. Cooper, *The Courtauld Collection. A Catalogue and Introduction*, London, 1954

Correspondance 1978
Paul Cézanne, *Correspondance*, ed. J. Rewald, Paris, 1978

DENIS 1924
M. Denis, 'Le Dessin de Cézanne', *L'Amour de l'Art*, February 1924, p. 37

DENIS 1957
M. Denis, *Journal, 1884-1904*, Paris, 1957

DISTEL 1999
A. Distel, *Cézanne to Van Gogh: The Collection of Dr Gachet*, New York, 1999

DOMBROWSKI 2006
A. Dombrowski, *Modernism and Extremism: The Early Work of Paul Cézanne (1865-1875)*, PhD dissertation, University of California, Berkeley, 2006

DORAN 1978
M. Doran (ed.), *Conversations avec Cézanne*, Paris, 1978

DORAN 2001
M. Doran (ed.), *Conversations with Cézanne*, Berkeley, Los Angeles and London, 2001

DORIVAL 1948
B. Dorival, *Cézanne*, Paris and New York, 1948

DORMOY 1929
M. Dormoy, 'La Collection Courtauld', *L'Amour de l'Art*, 1929, pp. 15-20, 48-52

DRUICK 1977
D. Druick, 'Cézanne's Lithographs', in *Cezanne. The Late Work*, exh. cat., New York and Houston 1977-78, pp. 119-37

FREUDENBERG 2001
I. Freudenberg, *Der Zweifler Cézanne*, Heidelberg, 2001

FRY 1927
R. Fry, *Cézanne. A Study of His Development*, London and New York, 1927

GACHET 1952
P. Gachet, *Cézanne à Auvers, Cézanne graveur*, Paris, 1952

GAGE 1993
J. Gage, *Colour and Culture, Practice and Meaning from Antiquity to Abstraction*, London, 1993

GARB 2007
T. Garb, *The Painted Face. Portraits of Women in France 1814-1914*, New Haven and London, 2007

GASQUET 1921/26
J. Gasquet, *Cézanne*, Paris, 1921 and 1926

GREEN 1999
C. Green, *Art Made Modern: Roger Fry's Vision of Art*, London 1999

Home House 1935
Catalogue of the Pictures and Other Works of Art at Home House, 20 Portman Square, London, London, 1935

HOUSE 2004
J. House, *Impressionism: Paint and Politics*, New Haven and London, 2004

JAMOT AND TURNER 1934
P. Jamot and P. Turner, *Collection de tableaux français, faite à Londres, 20 Portman Square, par Samuel et Elizabeth Courtauld*, London, 1934

JOHNSON 1944
U.E. Johnson, *Ambroise Vollard Editeur 1867-1939. An Appreciation and Catalogue*, New York, 1944

KEAR 1998
J. Kear, *Cézanne and Genre: Readings in the Oeuvre of Paul Cézanne, c. 1859–1906*, PhD thesis, The Courtauld Institute of Art, London, 1998

KENDALL 1988
R. Kendall, (ed.), *Cézanne by Himself: Drawings, Paintings, Writings*, London, 1988

KITSCHEN 1995
F. Kitschen, *Cézanne Stilleben*, Ostfildern-Ruit, 1995

LARGUIER 1925
L. Larguier, *Le Dimanche avec Paul Cézanne*, Paris, 1925

LEYMARIE AND MELOT 1972
J. Leymarie and M. Melot, *The Graphic Works of the Impressionists. Manet, Pissarro, Renoir, Cézanne, Sisley*, London, 1972

LORAN 1943
E. Loran, *Cézanne's Composition. Analysis of His Form with Diagrams and Photographs of His Motifs*, Berkeley and Los Angeles, 1943

MACHOTKA 1996
P. Machotka, *Cézanne: Landscape into Art*, New Haven and London, 1996

MEIER-GRAEFE 1918
J. Meier-Graefe, *Cézanne und sein Kreis*, Munich, 1918

MELOT 1996
M. Melot, *The Impressionist Print*, New Haven and London, 1996

NEUMEYER 1958
A. Neumeyer, *Cézanne Drawings*, New York and London, 1958

NOVOTNY 1938
F. Novotny, *Cézanne und das Ende der wissenschaftlichen Perspektive*, Vienna, 1938

NOVOTNY 1950
F. Novotny, 'Cézanne als Zeichner', *Wiener Jahrbuch für Kunstgeschichte*, vol. 14, 1950, pp. 225–40

OSTHAUS 1920–21
K. E. Osthaus, 'Cézanne', *Das Feuer*, 1920–21, pp. 81–88

PLATZMEN 2001
S. Platzmen, *Cezanne. The Self Portraits*, London, 2001

RATCLIFFE 1961
R.W. Ratcliffe, *Cézanne's Working Methods and their Theoretical Background*, PhD thesis, The Courtauld Institute of Art, London, 1960

REFF 1962
T. Reff, 'Cézanne's Constructive Stroke', *Art Quarterly*, Autumn 1962, pp. 214–27

REFF 1975
T. Reff, 'Cézanne's Drawings', *The Burlington Magazine*, Vol. 97, 1975, pp. 489–91

REWALD 1937
J. Rewald (ed.), *Paul Cézanne. Correspondance*, Paris, 1937

REWALD 1948
J. Rewald, *Paul Cézanne*, New York, 1948

REWALD 1961
J. Rewald, *The History of Impressionism*, New York, 1961

REWALD 1983 / RWC
J. Rewald, *Paul Cézanne. The Watercolors. A Catalogue Raisonné*, Boston, 1983

REWALD 1984
J. Rewald (ed.), *Paul Cézanne. Letters*, New York, 1984

REWALD 1985
J. Rewald, *Studies in Impressionism*, ed. I. Gordon and F. Weitzenhoffer, New York, 1985

REWALD 1996/ RP
J. Rewald with W. Feilchenfeldt and J. Warman, *The Paintings of Paul Cézanne: A Catalogue Raisonné*, New York and London, 1996

RIVIÈRE 1923
G. Rivière, *Le Maître Paul Cézanne*, Paris, 1923

SCHAPIRO 1952
M. Schapiro, *Paul Cézanne*, New York, 1952

SCHAPIRO 1968
M. Schapiro, 'The Apples of Cézanne. An Essay on the Meaning of Still-life', *Art News Annual*, vol. 34, 1968, pp. 34–53

SCHAPIRO 1978
M. Schapiro, *Modern Art: 19th and 20th Centuries*, New York, 1978

SEILERN 1961
A. Seilern, *Paintings and Drawings of Continental Schools other than Flemish and Italian at 56 Princes Gate London sw7*, London, 1961

SHIFF 1984
R. Shiff, *Cézanne and the End of Impressionism*, Chicago, 1984

SHIFF 1998
R. Shiff, 'Cézanne's Blur, Approximating Cézanne', in R. Thomson (ed.), *Framing France: The Representation of Landscape in France, 1870–1914*, Manchester, 1998, pp. 59–80

SITWELL 1925
O. Sitwell, 'The Courtauld Collection', *Apollo*, August 1925, pp. 62–69

SMITH 1996
P. Smith, *Interpreting Cézanne*, London 1996

SMITH 2007
P. Smith, '"Real Primitives": Cézanne, Wittgenstein, and the Nature of Aesthetic Quality', in J. Harris (ed.), *Value, Art, Politics*, Liverpool 2007, pp. 93–122

STOKES 1978
A. Stokes, *The Critical Writings of Adrian Stokes, II, 1937–58*, London, 1978

VENTURI 1936
L. Venturi, *Cézanne. Son art, son œuvre*, 2 vols., Paris, 1936

VENTURI 1978
L. Venturi, *Cézanne*, Geneva, 1978

VOLLARD 1914
A. Vollard, *Paul Cézanne*, Paris, 1914

VOLLARD 1924
A. Vollard, trans. H.L. Van Doren, *Paul Cézanne: His Life and Art*, London, 1924

VOLLARD 1938
A. Vollard, *En écoutant Cézanne, Degas, Renoir*, Paris, 1938

WECHSLER 1975
J. Wechsler (ed.), *Cézanne in Perspective*, London, 1975

ZIESKE 2002
F. Zieske, 'Paul Cézanne's Watercolours: His Choice of Pigments and Papers', in *The Broad Spectrum: Studies in the Materials, Techniques and Conservations of Colour on Paper*, ed. Harriet K. Stratis and Britt Slavesen, London 2002, pp. 89–100

PAUL CÉZANNE, PARIS 1895
Paul Cézanne, Galerie Vollard, Paris, 1895
CÉZANNE AQUARELLE, BERLIN 1907
Cézanne Aquarelle, Paul Cassirer, Berlin 1907
LES AQUARELLES DE CÉZANNE, PARIS 1907
Les Aquarelles de Cézanne, Galerie Bernheim-Jeune,
Paris, 1907
WATERCOLORS BY CÉZANNE, NEW YORK 1911
Watercolors by Cézanne, Photo-Secession
Gallery, New York, 1911
SECOND POST-IMPRESSIONIST EXHIBITION,
LONDON 1912
Second Post-Impressionist Exhibition, Grafton Galleries,
London, 1912
PAINTINGS AND DRAWINGS, LONDON 1925
Paintings and Drawings by Paul Cézanne, Leicester
Galleries, London, 1925
FRENCH ART, LONDON 1932
Exhibition of French Art 1200–1900, Royal Academy
of Arts, London, 1932
PAUL CÉZANNE, EXHIBITION OF
WATERCOLOURS, LONDON, LEICESTER AND
SHEFFIELD 1946
K. Clark, *Paul Cézanne, Exhibition of Watercolours,*
Tate Gallery, London; Museum and Art Gallery,
Leicester; Graves Art Gallery, Sheffield (The Arts
Council of Great Britain), London, 1946
SAMUEL COURTAULD MEMORIAL EXHIBITION,
LONDON 1948
Samuel Courtauld Memorial Exhibition, Tate Gallery,
London, 1948
LANDSCAPE IN FRENCH ART, LONDON 1949–50
Landscape in French Art 1550–1900, Royal Academy
of Arts, London, 1949–50
CÉZANNE, EDINBURGH AND LONDON 1954
An Exhibition of Paintings by Cézanne, Royal Scottish
Academy, Edinburgh, and Tate Gallery,
London, 1954
DRAWINGS AND ENGRAVINGS, LONDON
1959–60
Drawings and Engravings from the Courtauld Collection,
Courtauld Institute Galleries, London, 1959
PAUL CÉZANNE, VIENNA 1961
F. Novotny, *Paul Cézanne 1839–1906,* Belvedere,
Vienna, 1961
WATERCOLOUR AND PENCIL DRAWINGS BY
CÉZANNE, NEWCASTLE AND LONDON 1973
L. Gowing, and R.W. Ratcliffe, *Watercolour
and Pencil Drawings by Cézanne,* Laing Art Gallery,
Newcastle, and Hayward Gallery, London, 1973
CÉZANNE. THE LATE WORK, NEW YORK
AND HOUSTON 1977–78
W. Rubin, *Cézanne. The Late Work,* The Museum of

Modern Art, New York, and The Museum of
Fine Arts, Houston, London 1977
CÉZANNE. LES DERNIÈRES ANNÉES, PARIS
1978
J. Rewald and A. Chappuis, *Cézanne. Les dernières
années (1895–1906),* Grand Palais, Paris, 1978
PRINCES GATE COLLECTION, LONDON 1981
H. Braham, *The Princes Gate Collection,* Courtauld
Galleries, London, 1981
PAUL CÉZANNE. AQUARELLE, 1866–1906,
TÜBINGEN AND ZURICH 1982
G. Adriani, *Paul Cézanne. Aquarelle, 1866–1906,*
Kunsthalle, Tübingen, and Kunsthaus,
Zurich, 1982
MANTEGNA TO CÉZANNE, LONDON 1983
W. Bradford and H. Braham, *Mantegna to
Cézanne: Master Drawings from the Courtauld.
A Fiftieth Anniversary Exhibition,* Courtauld Institute
Galleries, London, 1983
IMPRESSIONIST AND POST-IMPRESSIONIST
MASTERPIECES, CLEVELAND ET AL 1987–88
*Impressionist and Post-Impressionist Masterpieces:
The Courtauld Collection,* Cleveland Museum of Art,
Cleveland; Metropolitan Museum of Art, New
York; Kimbell Art Museum, Fort Worth; Art
Institute of Chicago; Nelson Atkins Museum of
Art, Kansas City, 1987
IMPRESSIONIST, POST-IMPRESSIONIST AND
RELATED DRAWINGS, LONDON 1988
W. Bradford, *Impressionist, Post-Impressionist and
Related Drawings from the Courtauld Collections,*
Courtauld Institute Galleries, London, 1988
CÉZANNE AND POUSSIN, EDINBURGH 1990
D. Coutagne *et al.*, *Sainte-Victoire Cézanne 1990,*
Musée Granet, Aix-en-Provence 1990
R. Verdi, *Cézanne and Poussin. The Classical Vision of
Landscape,* National Gallery of Scotland,
Edinburgh, 1990
CÉZANNE GEMÄLDE, TÜBINGEN 1993
G. Adriani, *Cézanne Gemälde,* Kunsthalle
Tübingen, 1993
IMPRESSIONISM FOR ENGLAND, LONDON 1994
J. House, W. Bradford *et al.*, *Impressionism for
England. Samuel Courtauld as Patron and Collector,*
Courtauld Institute Galleries, London, 1994
CÉZANNE, PARIS, LONDON AND
PHILADELPHIA 1995–96
F. Cachin, J. Rishel *et al.*, *Cézanne,* Galeries
nationales du Grand Palais, Paris; Tate Gallery,
London; Philadelphia Museum of Art, 1996
CÉZANNE, STOCKHOLM 1997–98
G. Cavalli Björkman, *Cézanne i blickpunkten,*
Nationalmuseum, Stockholm, 1997

CLASSIC CÉZANNE, SYDNEY 1998–99
T. Maloon, with essays by R. Shiff *et al.*,
Classic Cézanne, Art Gallery of New South Wales,
Sydney, 1998–99
1900: ART AT THE CROSSROADS, LONDON
2000
R. Rosenblum *et al.*, *1900: Art at the Crossroads,*
Royal Academy of Arts, London, 2000
CÉZANNE. FINISHED – UNFINISHED, VIENNA
AND ZURICH 2000
F. Baumann *et al.*, *Cézanne. Finished – Unfinished,*
Kunstforum, Vienna, and Kunsthaus, Zurich,
2000
VON LINIE UND FARBE, FRANKFURT
AM MAIN 2001–02
M. Stuffmann *et al.*, *Von Linie und Farbe: Französische
Zeichnungen des 19. Jahrhunderts aus der Graphischen
Sammlung im Städel und aus Frankfurter Privatbesitz,*
Städelsches Kunstinstitut, Frankfurt am Main,
2001
CÉZANNE IN THE STUDIO, LOS ANGELES 2004
C. Armstrong, *Cézanne in the Studio. Still Life
in Watercolors,* The J. Paul Getty Museum, Los
Angeles, 2004
CÉZANNE. AUFBRUCH IN DIE MODERNE,
ESSEN 2004–05
F. Baumann, W. Feilchenfeldt and H. Gassner
(ed.), *Cézanne. Aufbruch in die Moderne,* Museum
Folkwang, Essen, 2004–05
PIONEERING MODERN PAINTING, NEW YORK,
LOS ANGELES AND PARIS, 2005–06
J. Pissarro, *Pioneering Modern Painting: Cézanne and
Pissarro 1865–1885,* Museum of Modern Art, New
York; Los Angeles County Museum, Los Angeles;
Musée d'Orsay, Paris, 2005
CÉZANNE IN BRITAIN, LONDON 2005–06
A. Robbins *et al.*, *Cézanne in Britain,* National
Gallery, London, 2006
CÉZANNE IN PROVENCE, WASHINGTON AND
AIX-EN-PROVENCE 2006
P. Conisbee and D. Coutagne, *Cézanne in Provence,*
National Gallery of Art, Washington, D.C., and
Musée Granet, Aix-en-Provence, 2006
CÉZANNE TO PICASSO, NEW YORK ET AL,
2006–07
R. Rabinow, D. Druick and M. Assante di
Panzillo, *Cézanne to Picasso: Ambroise Vollard, Patron of
the Avant-Garde,* Metropolitan Museum of Art,
New York ex al., 2006–07